Intermediate Horizons

The History of Print and Digital Culture

James P. Danky and **Adam R. Nelson**
Series Editors

INTERMEDIATE HORIZONS

Book History and Digital Humanities

Edited by

Mark Vareschi and **Heather Wacha**

The University of Wisconsin Press

Publication of this book has been made possible, in part, through support from the Center for the History of Print and Digital Culture at the University of Wisconsin–Madison and the Anonymous Fund of the College of Letters and Science at the University of Wisconsin–Madison.

The University of Wisconsin Press
728 State Street, Suite 443
Madison, Wisconsin 53706
uwpress.wisc.edu

Gray's Inn House, 127 Clerkenwell Road
London EC1R 5DB, United Kingdom
eurospanbookstore.com

Copyright © 2022
The Board of Regents of the University of Wisconsin System
All rights reserved. Except in the case of brief quotations embedded in critical articles and reviews, no part of this publication may be reproduced, stored in a retrieval system, transmitted in any format or by any means—digital, electronic, mechanical, photocopying, recording, or otherwise—or conveyed via the Internet or a website without written permission of the University of Wisconsin Press. Rights inquiries should be directed to rights@uwpress.wisc.edu.

Printed in the United States of America

This book may be available in a digital edition.

Library of Congress Cataloging-in-Publication Data
Names: Vareschi, Mark, editor. | Wacha, Heather Gaile, editor.
Title: Intermediate horizons : book history and digital humanities / edited by Mark Vareschi and Heather Wacha.
Other titles: History of print and digital culture.
Description: Madison, Wisconsin : The University of Wisconsin Press, [2022] | Series: The history of print and digital culture | "The essays for this volume have been drawn from papers given at the biennial conference hosted by the Center for the History of Print and Digital Culture at the University of Wisconsin–Madison in 2017."—Introduction. | Includes bibliographical references and index.
Identifiers: LCCN 2021046865 | ISBN 9780299338107 (hardcover)
Subjects: LCSH: Digital humanities. | Books—History.
Classification: LCC AZ195 .I58 2022 | DDC 001.30285—dc23/eng/20211207
LC record available at https://lccn.loc.gov/2021046865

Contents

List of Illustrations	vii
Foreword: Intermediate Horizons	ix
Matthew Kirschenbaum	
Introduction	3
Mark Vareschi and **Heather Wacha**	

Section I. Approach

Benjamin Franklin's Postal Work	19
Christy L. Pottroff	
Linking Book History and the Digital Humanities via Museum Studies	41
Jayme Yahr	

Section II. Access

Material and Digital Traces in Patterns of Nature: Early Modern Botany Books and Seventeenth-Century Needlework	61
Mary Learner	
Opening the Book: The Utopian Dreams and Uncertain Future of Open Access Textbook Publishing	88
Joseph L. Locke and **Ben Wright**	

Books of Ours: What Libraries Can Learn about Social Media from
Books of Hours 109
    Alexandra Alvis

Section III. Assessment

Whose Books Are Online? Diversity, Equity, and Inclusion in Online
Text Collections 123
    Catherine A. Winters and **Clayton P. Michaud**

Electronic Versioning and Digital Editions 147
    Paul A. Broyles

Materialisms and the Cultural Turn in Digital Humanities 167
    Mattie Burkert

Contributors 185
Index 189

Illustrations

Figure 1. Benjamin Franklin, "Post-Office Leidger No. 1" 23
Figure 2. Benjamin Franklin, "Post Office Book, 1748, May 25" 25
Figure 3. Benjamin Franklin, "Incoming Philadelphia Mail, 1767–8" 28
Figure 4. Benjamin Franklin and Timothy Folger,
   Franklin-Folger Chart of the Gulf Stream 36
Figure 5. Crispijn de Passe, *Hortus Floridus: in quo rariorum & minus
   vulgarium Florum icones ad vivam veramque formam* (Arnhem, 1614) 70
Figure 6. Crispijn van de Passe, *Hortus Floridus in quo rariorum &
   minus vulgarium florum icones ad vivam veramq[ue] formam* (Arnhem, 1614) 71
Figure 7. Crispijn van de Passe, *A garden of flovvers* (Utrecht, 1615) 72
Figure 8. Crispijn van de Passe, *A garden of flovvers* (Arnhem, 1614) 73
Figure 9. Crispijn van de Passe, *A garden of flovvers* (Arnhem, 1614) 74
Figure 10. Simon van de Passe, *Animalium quadrupedum* (London, 1630) 75
Figure 11. Simon van de Passe, *Animalium quadrupedum* (London, [1628?]) 75
Figure 12. Tweet from @iwillleavenow 112
Figure 13. Tweet from @codicologist 113
Figure 14. Probability of appearing in a given repository as a function
   of demand 135

Foreword

Intermediate Horizons

Matthew Kirschenbaum

When I began attending my first Association for Computers and the Humanities (ACH/ALLC) meetings in the mid-1990s (these are the organizations that would first constitute the Alliance of Digital Humanities Organizations (ADHO) and co-sponsor what is now the annual Digital Humanities (DH) conference), the convergence between textual editing and digital tools was white hot. Focalized by a clash between well-intentioned standardization on the one hand and idiosyncratic approaches tied to the specifics of individual works and authors on the other, the debates around materiality and meaning that had raged in textual criticism in the preceding decade were injected with a new urgency. High-resolution JPEGs of manuscripts and printed book pages were projected at the front of the session rooms; sharp disagreements would ensue over elements and attributes and "overlapping hierarchies" as attendees sought to capture and formalize the material remains of cultural heritage in well-formed, computationally tractable tag sets. At stake was something very fundamental, or so we believed: the "entire" archive of literature, history, the arts, music, and more was being rekeyed, re-edited, and reimagined.

It was heady stuff to take in, especially for a wide-eyed early-career scholar like myself. Of course, it was also more than a bit naïve—my scare quotes around "entire" in the preceding paragraph being only one indication of why we might (must) now temper the import of the moment. Still, the energy was undeniable. For me, a student of Jerome McGann's theory of textuality, the pivot from my scholarly training to the minutiae of Text Encoding Initiative (TEI) and Standard General Markup Language (SGML) was as effortless as it was intoxicating. Suddenly the stakes of our arguments about the textual condition were plain: decisions about how to encode a manuscript or a book feature had direct, actionable implications for what was and wasn't visible or searchable or retrievable. Little wonder then that these were the sessions at the conference that were always overfull, held in rooms that always seemed too small.

But each year, on my way to and from the coffee, I would notice some other areas, down (it seemed) a dimly lit corridor. Peering in, one would see smaller crowds, though no less intense. Inexplicably for a digital humanities conference, they seemed to favor old-fashioned transparent overlays as visual aids. These were typically full of charts and graphs and . . . numbers. This was the linguistics and stylistics track of the conference, where individual texts were not objects of sustained critical and editorial attention and certainly not acknowledged as anything "material": they were data points in a corpus. And although the corpora were still relatively small (Google Books and other wide-scale digitization efforts did not yet exist), here you could find papers about the computational classification of Shakespeare's plays or papers purporting to tell us what computers could tell us about stylistic quirks in Jane Austen or *Jane Eyre*.

I was definitely not inspired. The work seemed like a grind, not to mention disconcertingly positivistic. I would hasten back to the bright, crowded spaces to take in another session on encoding Blake's illuminated canon or the Piers Plowman manuscripts. In retrospect, though, the presenters in those other rooms were practicing distant reading and computational literary criticism *avant la lettre*. These days, at the Digital Humanities conference, roles are reversed. The energy and excitement is with big data, text mining, topic modeling, macro analytics, and all manner of variations on Greg Crane's 2006 question, *What do you do with a million books?*[1] Although overlay projectors are scarce, graphs (and maps, and trees) abound. You can still find sessions on text encoding and editing, of course, augmented by 24-bit color images of ink blots and foxing; they just tend to be down dimly lit hallways, on the wrong end of the coffee service.

I tell this story because the conjoining of digital humanities with big data or quantitative approaches nowadays seems absolute. Certainly most popular press coverage of the digital humanities revolves around the work of those using computational tools to mine and scrape and visualize vast arrays of data to reveal large-scale patterns along a deep time axis. Research involving gender roles in the tens of thousands novels published over a span of centuries or the six (or seven) basic types of literary plots across an equally sizeable corpus tends to grab headlines, the scientific tools and methods bringing with them the sheen of scientific "discovery" that the public seems to crave.[2] Critics and skeptics of digital humanities, meanwhile, have similarly taken aim at the statistical and quantitative underpinnings of this work, questioning the practicality (and the politics) of a commitment to numeracy and abstraction in the increasingly precarious disciplinary spaces of the humanities—in short, whether numbers can tell us anything about "the inner literariness of literature," in the words of one commentator in the fray.[3] So severe has this quantitative turn been that a pioneer in electronic scholarly editing has gone so far as to suggest that it's time for textual scholars to throw "digital humanists" out of textual scholarship![4]

It would be a grievous mistake to position the essays in this volume as some nostalgic return to the moment of digital humanities that I described at the outset. By contrast, they seem to me to derive their energy and urgency precisely from renewing our attention to materiality amid what is now an unrelentingly data-driven society, a future whose harsh angles and asymmetrical edges were still smoothed by the slick covers of *WIRED* magazine twenty years ago. Christy L. Potroff, for example, reads Benjamin Franklin's postal ledgers as experiments in managing (and mining) large quantities of information. Catherine Winters and Clayton Michaud, in their chapter, expose the realities behind our fantasies of total archival access. At the same time, these essays once again center books, printing, publishing, and reading—indeed, all manner of material textual considerations, even unto the pinpricks of needlework in Mary Learner's chapter—as integral to a digital humanities research agenda. Not the distant horizons of millions of books or tens of thousands of novels, but *this* book, *this* printing, *this* edition, this *copy*—with its traces of *these* hands.

At the Madison, Wisconsin, conference where the essays that form these chapters originated, the confluence of book history and digital humanities was understood less as getting back to some (alternative) future than as continuing ground truth. For one thing, bibliography, textual criticism, and book history has always had its fair share of numeracy: whether collation formulae or the ledgers of early modern printing houses, paying close enough attention to the materiality of textual production often involves some counting. More fundamentally, though, book history and bibliography can be "disruptive" in some of the same ways it has been fashionable (and more lately, unfashionable) to claim of the digital humanities. The study of codex creation and distribution in earlier epochs invariably centers attention on our own economies and ecologies of publishing, as Joseph L. Locke and Ben Wright's study reminds us. Access to archives and collections, meanwhile, quickly involves us in questions about institutions and infrastructures and the politics and policies thereof. Book historians also often have need of specialized tools and facilities, whether it be a simple magnifying glass or a portable collator (a visualization device) or the even more elaborate equipment and accoutrements found in specialized conservation labs. Perhaps above all, the commitment to the individuality of texts—as embodied and instantiated in physical packages and carriers—has radical consequences for our understanding of the digital milieu, with its fractal halls of mirrors built on spectral promises of copies without originals. I have argued this in my own work; in this collection, Paul Broyles brings the sensibilities of the textual scholar to bear on the very platforms and formats that now support our digital representations of our digitized cultural heritage, denaturalizing and defamiliarizing the deep machinery of our online environments.

Digital humanities and book history (with textual studies and bibliography) thus offer what I would want to suggest are *intermediate horizons*. "Intermediate" both in the sense of a middle distance (far enough away for some perspective, close enough for regular and meaningful contact) and in the sense of *intermedial*, mutually constituting and informing the conditions under which each is practiced as a scholarly enterprise in the twenty-first-century academy.[5] This volume offers an up-close look at those horizons.

Notes

1. Greg Crane, "What Do You Do with a Million Books," *D-Lib Magazine* 12, no. 3 (March 2006), http://www.dlib.org/dlib/march06/crane/03crane.html.

2. I am thinking here of the press coverage of research conducted by Ted Underwood, David Bamman, and Sabrina Lee, and Matthew Jockers, respectively.

3. Ted Underwood, "It Looks Like You're Writing an Argument against Data in Literary Study," *The Stone and the Shell*, September 21, 2017, https://tedunderwood.com/2017/09/21/it-looks-like-youre-writing-an-argument-against-data-in-literary-study/.

4. Peter Robinson, "Why Digital Humanists Should Get Out of Textual Scholarship. And If They Don't, Why We Textual Scholars Should Throw Them Out," *Scholarly Digital Editions*, July 29, 2013, http://scholarlydigitaleditions.blogspot.com/2013/07/why-digital-humanists-should-get-out-of.html.

5. For an extended elaboration of that contention, see Matthew Kirschenbaum and Sarah Werner, "Digital Scholarship and Digital Studies: State of the Discipline," *Book History* 17 (2014): 406–58.

Intermediate Horizons

Introduction

Mark Vareschi and
Heather Wacha

Twenty-seven years ago, the Center for the History of Print Culture in America was founded at the University of Wisconsin–Madison. The current iteration of that organization, the Center for the History of Print and Digital Culture (CHPDC), continues to promote the interdisciplinary study of text, technology, and culture through this book series, as well as conferences, lectures, and more. As noted by Jonathan Senchyne and Brigitte Fielder in the CHPDC's most recent publication—*Against a Sharp White Background*—the early founders of the CHPDC supported research in book history and print culture "that looked beyond New England and the fetishization of rare or early imprints, and instead foregrounded, in Wayne Wiegand's words, the 'agency and practice' of diverse actors who created and used print 'from below.'"[1] This volume carries forward these ideals in a collection of essays that examine how book history and digital humanities practices are integrated through approach, access, and assessment.

* * *

The title for the volume comes from Matthew Kirschenbaum's insightful foreword that provides both the historical and contemporary context in which these essays appear. As Kirschenbaum writes, digital humanities and book history offer each other "'intermediate horizons.' Intermediate in both the sense of a middle distance (far enough away for some perspective, close enough for regular and meaningful contact) and in the sense of intermedial, mutually constituting and informing the conditions under which each is practiced as a scholarly enterprise in the twenty-first-century academy." Intermediate, here, describes the particular insight each field and its assorted methods affords on the other. Further, intermediate identifies the configuration of these fields within the institutional setting. We learn something(s) unique about book history when we draw upon the tools, methods, and institutional position of the digital humanities and, as Kirschenbaum has himself demonstrated throughout his scholarship, we learn something unique about the digital humanities when we draw on the tools, methods, and institutional position of book history.

We further expand upon these senses of the intermediate and approach the framing of this volume through the notion of intermediation which, as Ted Striphas explains, "describe[s] the complex relations that media share in determinate historical conjunctures." In his discussion of intermediation, Striphas offers two key proposals: "Media shouldn't be isolated analytically from one another" and "the relationships among media are socially produced and historically contingent rather than given and necessary."[2] The argument of this book and the conference from which it originated is grounded in this sense of intermediation: when book history and digital humanities methods and objects are brought alongside each other, we are invited not simply to see the differences in research approaches but to attend to the distinct, though connected, logics inherent in both the media of the methods and objects under study.[3]

N. Katherine Hayles has further theorized intermediation to argue that recursivity is inherent within the concept "in the co-production and coevolution of multiple causalities."[4] She writes, "Complex feedback loops connect humans and machines, old technologies and new, language and code, analog processes and digital fragmentations." This recursivity challenges any linear account we might offer of a trajectory from analog to digital, from codex to database. Hayles offers an important reminder of the persistence and prolonged interactions among media forms, what some scholars have dubbed "residual media,"[5] and an invitation to work comparatively among media.[6]

This volume takes up such an invitation as it brings together book history and digital humanities with a range of essays that explore topics as diverse (yet connected) as manuscript ledgers, digital corpora, and open-access textbooks. It reveals intermediation at the center of book history and digital humanities from their earliest formations and asks what such a combination of fields produces. We argue that this emphasis on intermediation enables a reimagining of the past and future of both book history and the digital humanities, and thus returns us to a more representative and human study of the humanities. One line of critique of the digital humanities has often noted an emphasis on tools or making and a resistance to interpretation within the neoliberal structures of the contemporary research university.[7] While another, exemplified by Nan Da's "The Computational Case against Computational Literary Studies," focuses its critique on methods of computational methods of analysis but excludes "histories of media and early computational practices, the digitization of texts for open access, digital inscription and mediation."[8] This exclusion is not incidental as these DH projects most fully demonstrate the recursivity not only between "humans and machines" but between analog humanities methods and those that are digitally augmented. Even though these critiques proceed upon different lines, it is our hope that the selection of essays in the volume work to answer them by exemplifying not just an "innovative" march toward a more objective analysis of cultural artifacts but "alongside" or intermediate approaches that never lose sight of the interpretive questions they ask or the humanness of the humanities.[9]

* * *

The marshalling of intermediation as a structuring concept for this volume takes its cue from book history. Since Robert Darnton posed the question "What Is the History of Books?", communication has been at the center of accounts of the object of book history. Darnton's famous diagram of the "Communications Circuit" depicts the many hands involved in book production and their connection to the "Economic and Social Conjuncture."[10] Thomas R. Adams and Nicolas Barker offer a significant revision to Darnton's diagram in their 1993 "A New Model for the Study of the Book" by essentially turning his model inside out and enveloping "the communications circuit" within the whole socioeconomic conjuncture. While differing importantly in their visions of the production and circulation of books in relation to the sociohistorical milieu, both models share a sense of the recursivity inherent in the communication process as ideas, humans, and media forms interact over and over again.

By placing communication at the center of book history, Darnton's account invites a broader consideration of media forms beyond the book and mediation itself. In his account of the genesis of what he dubs "the media concept," John Guillory asserts that mediation, and thereby media, implies communication.[11] The converse is also true: the concept of communication implies mediation and thereby media. The necessary coupling of communication and media, which has been taken as given at least since Marshall McLuhan's *Understanding Media* (1964), explicitly informs D. F. McKenzie's expanded notion of textuality to include "verbal, visual, oral, and numeric data in the form of maps, prints, and music, of archives of recorded sound, of films, videos, and any computer-stored information, everything in fact from epigraphy to the latest forms of discography."[12] McKenzie expands the purview of bibliography to include "text as recorded forms, and the processes of their transmission, including their production and reception."[13] This expansion is significant for bibliography and the history of the book not only because it broadens the range of objects to which the scholar may attend but also because it invites comparative, "alongside," analyses of media forms; the expansion is further significant because it marks a sharp turn against the tradition in analytical bibliography to disregard anything beyond of the physical text and thus, as Roger Chartier states, its refusal "to consider that the manner in which a work is read, received, and interpreted."[14] McKenzie puts it even more sharply in his call for a "sociology of texts": "Bibliography has a massive authority with which to correct that tendency [toward anti-humanism in American criticism]. It can, in short, show the human presence in any recorded text."[15]

That bibliography would be methodologically disinterested in "the human presence" was far from a given in its pre-nineteenth-century formations. Although Philip Gaskell would draw on W. W. Greg's insistence that "the chief purpose of bibliography is to serve the production and distribution of accurate texts. . . . bibliography's overriding responsibility must be to determine the text in its most accurate form,"[16] earlier imaginings of the field of bibliography were far less clear in their focus on the material text. In tracing what he dubs the "three epochs of bibliography," Archer Taylor begins in antiquity and finds not lists of material texts but lists of authors followed in the next epoch by the subject of the work. It is only at the beginning of the nineteenth century that the form of bibliography asserted by Greg becomes recognizable, as Taylor writes: "About 1800 G. W. Panzer printed lists of early books, J. B. B. van Praet listed books printed on vellum, Ludwig Hain compiled the first definitive catalog of incunabula, and A. A. Renouard collected the titles of books printed by the Aldine, Estienne, and Giunti presses. The compilation of bibliographies treating books as physical objects and not as the work of a man or as a treatise on a subject has flourished ever since."[17] The flourishing of the book as "physical object" represents a historical shift in emphasis in the object of bibliography; it is a turning away from authors and content such that Greg's infamous claim that "what the bibliographer is concerned with is pieces of paper or parchment covered with certain written or printed signs. With these signs he is concerned merely as arbitrary marks; their meaning is no business of his" could be taken as a truism.[18]

Darnton and McKenzie's emphasis on communication and "the human presence" is both a radical break with the traditions in bibliography that preceded them and a return to earlier epochs in the history of the study of material texts. We draw upon this long history of bibliography and the history of the book because these histories are very much intertwined with the history of digital humanities in its present formation, and the trajectories of each field very much echo each other. Although a line of critique of the digital humanities has rightly sited one of the origins of DH in the New Bibliography with its attendant focus on authoritative texts and disregard for interpretation and even, perhaps, "the human presence," a longer historical trajectory suggests alternate ways that the field has and could be organized that has shaped book history and digital humanities alike.

* * *

The typical origin story of the digital humanities begins with Father Roberto Busa's 1946 machine-generated *Index Thomisticus*, a concordance to the works of St. Augustine.[19] This well-known story is but one site of origin for the digital humanities, and it is an origin story that has privileged certain forms of work in the field that emphasize quantitative methods like text mining. To return to Hayles's insight that intermediation disrupts linear temporalities and instead recursively connects "technologies old and new," we draw on scholars who have sought to imagine diverse origins of DH to include a swath of projects from the archival to the creative to inform our sense of the field. Rather than moving in a linear fashion from the punch cards of Busa's collaboration with IBM to topic modeling performed in R, a free programming language, we might imagine media art projects both within and without the academy alongside early, and indeed contemporary, archival efforts as sites of emergence for the digital humanities.[20]

A necessary consequence of this reimagining is that it ceases to be driven by technological advancements. Instead of the story of digital humanities being its origins in humanities computing and advancements in hardware and software technology as motivators of progress in the field, which, to borrow from McKenzie, has "obscured the role of human agents," we might put at the center a recursive interplay between humans, humanities questions, and technologies—both old and new—to understand that, in Amy Earhart's words, "digital humanities is, in many ways, a living term, ever evolving, ever shifting in response to particular pressures of scholarship, the academy, and the individual."[21]

The "ever evolving, ever shifting" nature of work in the digital humanities is most evident in collectives such as #transformDH, which, as Alexis Lothian describes, "has sought to center critical race and gender analysis within and in critique of DH."[22] In fact, #transformDH began at the annual meeting of American Studies Association in 2011 and is, in its own words: "an academic guerrilla movement seeking to (re)define capital-letter Digital Humanities as a force for transformative scholarship."[23]

In the 2016 edition of *Debates in the Digital Humanities*, collective members Moya Bailey, Anne Cong-Huyen, Alexis Lothian, and Amanda Phillips lay out the three claims they take to be "constitutive of #transformDH":

1. Questions of race, class, gender, sexuality, and disability should be central to digital humanities and digital media studies.
2. Feminist, queer, and antiracist activists, artists, and media makers outside of academia are doing work that contributes to digital studies in all its forms. This work productively destabilizes the norms and standards of institutionally recognized academic work.
3. We should shift the focus of digital humanities from technical processes to political ones, and always seek to understand the social, intellectual, economic, political, and personal impact of our digital practices as we develop them.[24]

Through these claims, #transformDH argue for a much-needed reorientation of work in the digital humanities in order to focus more broadly on the political and ideological. This is a marked departure from some earlier formations of DH that had tended to privilege the development of technical processes while, at times, losing sight of the very humanities they purported to explore. The echoes of earlier transformations in bibliography and book history, here, are obvious. As the New Bibliography with its emphasis solely on determining "the text in its most accurate form" gave way to contemporary forms of book history with their interest in social processes, digital humanities are similarly undergoing a transformation, both broadening in methodologies—already robust and diverse—and, more importantly, addressing directly questions of race, gender, sexuality, class, and disability.

This transformation is exemplified by the January 2020 volume of *PMLA*, the flagship journal for scholars of modern languages and literatures. The special topic "Varieties of Digital Humanities," edited by Alison Booth and Miriam Posner, makes clear we are, to borrow the language of Archer Taylor, in a new epoch of digital humanities. In their introduction to the volume, Booth and Posner "reassert a fact that [they] believe to be self-evident: that DH must concern itself deeply with race, gender, disability, economic and linguistic access, and other intersecting axes of power embedded in our materials and methods, as demanded by this troubled world at this moment."[25] Essays throughout the volume explore the kind of work that is possible when DH practitioners ask a different set of questions. Even so-called distant reading methods, which have struggled to deal meaningful with race and gender, are shown in essays by Lauren F. Klein and Richard Jean So and Edwin Roland to offer new and meaningful insights on race, gender, and labor when the scholar(s) ask the right set of questions of both the data and method.[26] These essays demonstrate what work in DH can look like; more powerfully, they suggest, to draw on Alan Liu's essay in the same volume, "Potentially new concepts of identity and diversity inhere in such DH space because the data lines (vectors) that become visible there do not behave like physical lines in analog space or color lines in society that either connect or divide, bridge, or wall off."[27]

Liu offers a hopeful vision for the field of digital humanities and, more importantly, the larger culture. It is a vision we share: this vision relies upon a recursivity between humans and technology that does not lead to a reification of cultural, racial, ability, and gender differences in binary code (and vice versa). Further, it is a vision that we wish to extend to work in book history, and indeed to any field that takes as its object the study of media forms. For while we may wish to hold a distinction between analog and digital media, intermediation reminds us that these media are always in relation to each other, always alongside and among. This "alongside and among" asks us for a reimagining of the origins of both book history and digital humanities and offers not only an important corrective but, crucially, a means of reimagining the interconnected futures and horizons of book history and digital humanities. *Intermediate Horizons* is but one attempt at these reimaginings.

* * *

The essays for this volume have been drawn from papers given at the biennial conference hosted by the Center for the History of Print and Digital Culture at the University of Wisconsin–Madison in 2017. The conference, titled "BH & DH: Book History and Digital Humanities," sought to make space for scholars practicing in multiple disciplines—among them, librarians, historians, scholars of literature, and digital humanists—in order to conceptualize and reconceptualize the intersections of book history and digital humanities. The diversity of paper topics encouraged audience members to cross temporal, spatial, and disciplinary boundaries, and in so doing brought together new ways of configuring—as noted at the beginning of this introduction—"the distinct, though connected, logics inherent in both the media of the methods and objects under study." As the essays in this volume speak predominantly to their respective themes, they also address and overlap with essays from other sections, reinforcing the inextricable affinity of these two fields.

Approach

In this section, Christy Potroff and Jayme Yahr embrace their primary source collections through comparative media approaches. In "Benjamin Franklin's Postal Work," Potroff uses a digital humanities approach to reflect on Benjamin Franklin's postal ledgers, describing them as "tools to index, analyze, retrieve, and understand complex phenomena in his life." As Matthew Kirschenbaum and Sarah Werner note, the "desire to catalog and to count and to sort means that book historians have been long involved in digital humanities, whether it has been called by that name or no."[28] In presenting Franklin's postal ledgers as an historic pre-digital database, Potroff argues that the postal inspector's *re*-organization of data "did more than bring the colonial mail out of the red. It empowered Franklin and [his colleague] Hunter to make data-driven adjustments to postal operations to improve the speed, frequency, and reliability of textual circulation." Potroff's approach leads her to reconsider the purpose and use of Franklin's ledgers as more than just account books, demonstrating that these pre-digital tools "illustrate the degree to which Franklin himself was economically invested in the colonial postal system."

If Potroff approaches her eighteenth-century sources through the affordances of digital technologies, Jayme Yahr in "Linking Book History and the Digital Humanities via Museum Studies" draws upon the nineteenth-century concept of the cabinet of curiosity and the field of museum studies to reconsider how meaning is made when entering a collection of digitized printed material. For Yahr, the digital collection itself becomes the object of inquiry, much like one might critique a collection of artifacts found in a cabinet of curiosity. Yahr's comparative approach focuses on two points of access in a museum exhibit—the intention of the cabinet of curiosity collector, and the meaning a visitor constructs for themselves when being exposed to the collection of artifacts. For the digital collection, the cabinet-of-curiosity collector becomes the digital curator, and the visitor becomes the user. Yahr's critique calls upon digital curators to become more conscious of their users' experience, posing such questions as "how much of the experience does the curator impose upon the user, and how much does the digital collection allow the user to 'make' meaning for themselves?" Digital curators can benefit from considering their collections of digitized sources as constructed environments, much as one does with cabinets of curiosity, therefore pushing against ideologies fixing on the neutrality and objectivity of these collections.[29]

Access

With the advent of the internet, digitization, and social media, book historians have enjoyed incomparable virtual access to both primary source material and secondary information relative to these sources. The essays in this section examine digital collections from two perspectives—their limitations and their potentiality—asking us to reexamine and reframe our understanding of what we imagine access to mean. In "Material and Digital Traces in Patterns of Nature: Early Modern Botany Books and Seventeenth-Century Needlework," Mary Learner focuses on what happens when books are digitized: what disappears and what becomes more apparent and accessible? While some may argue that the digitization of manuscripts and early printed sources has led to more restricted access policies, especially at brick-and-mortar institutions, digitization has allowed Learner to conduct a more concentrated, surface reading of her sources. By reading the surfaces of both herbals and florilegia, the former traditionally perceived as more erudite and the latter more popular, Learner shows how seventeenth-century women made small pricks around drawings of plants and flowers in both herbals *and* florilegia in order to trace patterns for their embroideries. These women made meaning by "seeing through sewing," and sewing through seeing. Learner's work calls upon "the mutual elucidations of book history and digital humanities" to reconsider "the canonical male archive of the history of science and to imagine the incorporation of women's 'counterarchives.'"

Presenting another type of digitized collection, that of textbooks, Joseph Locke and Ben Wright in "Opening the Book: The Utopian Dreams and Uncertain Future of Open Access Textbook Publishing" discuss the early iterations of the Open Access movement, in particular Open Educational Resources (OER). Despite OER's ideal of democratization, the academy still harbors institutionalized contradictions and inequalities in its curation of texts and textbooks. The authors seek to historicize and evaluate the production of OER textbooks, and thus "reveal how shifting means of production are refashioning academic publishing and the field of digital humanities." In presenting their own case study of an Open Educational Resource, *American Yawp*, Locke and Wright intentionally created a "large and diverse yet loosely coordinated group of experienced contributors to construct a coherent and accessible narrative from all the best of recent historical scholarship." The authors remind us that the open licensing of digital material must continue to be evaluated in the context of the power structures of academic publishing and, more broadly, of higher education.

In "Books of Ours: What Libraries Can Learn about Social Media from Books of Hours," Alexandra Alvis, a special collections librarian, reflects upon the uses and promise of social media, in particular Twitter, for engagement with old books and book history. Alvis embraces the social media potential of digitized images, framing her work around the place of archives and libraries in the communication circuit. Ever vigilant of the "perceived conflict between collections care and access," Alvis carves out an infrastructure for the circulation of digitized images, as well as their sources, where the materiality of objects such as Books of Hours weighs heavily as an access point. She advocates for posts that make collections not only accessible but which also curate and enhance them. While one may imagine that institutional Twitter accounts enjoy large followings, the personal accounts of librarians associated with the institutions can often garner the largest followings. The thoughtful communication between creator and audience "encourages the establishment of relationships and trust between institutions and individuals," and in doing so makes library and museum collections more accessible than ever before.

Assessment

In this section, authors evaluate open access sources, digital editions, digital recovery, and preservation, highlighting the recursive interplay between humans, humanities questions, and technologies in the digital humanities. By offering critique of and changes to current systems, these essays call for the need to be more vigilant of the socially constructed nature behind digital infrastructures, as well as the often hidden intellectual, physical, and emotional labor inherent in digital humanities work.

In "Whose Books Are Online? Diversity, Equity, and Inclusion in Online Text Collections," Catherine Winters and Clayton Michaud challenge the claims of online text repositories such as Google Books and Project Gutenberg, among others, which aim to "play a significant role in rectifying issues of exclusion" in the digital and to make available "free, easily accessible texts that cover a more diverse range of authors and experiences through liberation from the physical library." Both Winters and Michaud apply statistical regression analysis to parameterize the effect of race and gender on the supply of digitally available texts, focusing their study on a manageable dataset (i.e., the one hundred most-assigned authors for nineteenth-century American Literature comprehensive exam lists). Their findings provide evidence "that both race and gender do indeed have a significant effect on which texts are available in online digital repositories." Contrary to their goals, these repositories "continue to reinforce the same biases and expectations when it comes to traditionally underrepresented authors." This essay reminds us that as we may aim for certain idealized outcomes, we continue to neglect the institutional and cultural biases that preclude those outcomes. These biases have not been eradicated, and their persistence only reinforces the silences in the archives.

In "Electronic Versioning and Digital Editions," Paul Broyles challenges book historians to extend their interests in bibliographical analysis to the creation of digital editions today. While the fields of textual studies and textual digital humanities are closely aligned, "robust analytic frameworks for understanding the history of textual objects" have yet to be promoted and standardized. This may come as a surprise, especially given the amount of attention directed toward documenting the digital, but Broyles emphasizes that "versioning a resource is an action distinct from maintaining a revision history." After discussing the advantages and drawbacks of calendar and semantic versioning, Broyles presents a versioning model he developed for the Piers Plowman Electronic Archive (PPEA). He builds on Matthew Kirschenbaum's "set of terms for describing first-generation electronic objects," and proposes a model that distinguishes between "the intellectual identity" of an encoded document and that document's rendering. Recognizing that his practices provide a starting point, he concludes with a set of three principles to help guide future discussions.

Finally, in "Materialisms and the Cultural Turn in Digital Humanities," Mattie Burkert recaps the last decade of scholarship in the digital humanities and book history and aims to show "work in these arenas is increasingly convergent and mutually informative, as the digital humanities community works together toward a fuller picture of the social and political networks in which our materials exist." She concludes by calling attention to digital recovery and preservation as "important and under-valued activities that bring together both of these threads, making visible the links between our data, tools, infrastructures, and politics." Burkert explores the tensions between earlier modes of scholarship influenced by poststructuralist critiques of linguistic, social, and cultural effects of digital technology but that were less interested in the material works of the digital. In turn, this led to ahistorical generalizations about the novelty, ephemerality, and singularity of new media technologies. While, on the other hand, media archaeologists paid close attention to the material and deep histories of technologies but much less attention to the broader cultural implications of those technologies. Burkert proposes bringing together questions of technologies' materiality with their social, political, and cultural meanings and doing so by "taking infrastructure itself as a key object of inquiry." She argues that "the act of making a dataset's history visible helps to surface [the] labor" behind that data. Burkert joins other scholars in positioning media archaeological work as a uniquely important site for exploring issues of identity, marginalization, and social justice that have long concerned cultural critics and that are increasingly central to book history and digital humanities conversations today.

* * *

Horizons appear to mark a limit or boundary to a given body of knowledge. The boundedness suggested by horizons is, however, challenged by the term that proceeds it in our title, intermediate. As we have argued, intermediate—and its adjacent term "intermediation"—suggest the ways that boundaries and linearity are incorporated recursively into the very objects they seek to define. The essays in this volume exceed the bounds of a single field by drawing together the insights, methods, and objects of book history and the digital humanities. They imagine rich, diverse histories and futures for BH and DH that promise to transform humanities scholarship.

Notes

1. Jonathan Senchyne and Brigitte Fielder, introduction to *Against a Sharp White Background* (Madison: University of Wisconsin Press, 2019), 14.

2. See Ted Striphas, *The Late Age of Print: Everyday Book Culture from Consumerism to Control* (New York: Columbia University Press, 2011), 5.

3. For more discussion on the unique logics of media and remediation, see J. David Bolter and Richard A. Grusin, *Remediation: Understanding New Media* (Cambridge, MA: MIT Press, 1999).

4. Katherine Hayles, *My Mother Was a Computer: Digital Subjects and Literary Texts* (Chicago: University of Chicago Press, 2005), 31.

5. See Charles R. Acland, ed., *Residual Media* (Minneapolis: University of Minnesota Press, 2007).

6. See also N. Katherine Hayles and Jessica Pressman, "Introduction Making, Critique: A Media Framework," in *Comparative Textual Media: Transforming the Humanities in the*

Postprint Era, ed. Hayles and Pressman (Minneapolis: University of Minnesota Press, 2013), vii–xxxiii.

7. See, for example, Daniel Allington, Sarah Brouillette, and David Golumbia, "Neoliberal Tools (and Archives): A Political History of Digital Humanities," *Los Angeles Review of Books*, https://lareviewofbooks.org/article/neoliberal-tools-archives-political-history-digital-humanities/, accessed January 29, 2020.

8. Nan Z. Da, "The Computational Case against Computational Literary Studies," *Critical Inquiry* 45, no. 3 (2019): 601.

9. We draw on the notion returning the "human" to digital humanities from Elizabeth Losh, Jacqueline Wernimont, Laura Wexler, and Hong-An Wu, "Putting the Human Back into the Digital Humanities: Feminism, Generosity, and Mess," in *Debates in the Digital Humanities 2016*, ed. Matthew K. Gold and Lauren F. Klein (Minneapolis: University of Minnesota Press, 2016), 92–103.

10. Robert Darnton, "What Is the History of Books?," *Daedalus* 111, no. 3 (1982): 68.

11. John Guillory, "Genesis of the Media Concept," *Critical Inquiry* 36, no. 2 (January 1, 2010): 357.

12. Marshall McLuhan, *Understanding Media: The Extensions of Man* (New York: McGraw-Hill, 1964), 13.

13. D. F. McKenzie, *Bibliography and the Sociology of Texts* (Cambridge: Cambridge University Press, 1999), 12.

14. Roger Chartier, *The Order of Books: Readers, Authors, and Libraries in Europe between the Fourteenth and Eighteenth Centuries* (Stanford, CA: Stanford University Press, 1994), 24.

15. McKenzie, *Bibliography and the Sociology of Texts*, 29.

16. Quoted in Philip Gaskell, *A New Introduction to Bibliography* (New Castle, DE: Oak Knoll Press, 1995), 1.

17. Archer Taylor, "Three Epochs in Bibliographical History," *University of Pennsylvania Library Chronicle* 18 (1951–52): 49.

18. W. W. Greg, "Bibliography—an Apologia," *Library*, 4th series, 13 (1932): 121–22.

19. Thomas N. Winter, for example, locates 1951 as "the beginning of humanities computing"; see "Roberto Busa, S.J., and the Invention of the Machine-Generated Concordance," *Classical Bulletin* 75, no. 1 (1999): 4.

20. We are particularly influenced by the scholarship of Tara McPherson who has located digital media arts and design as one crucial early locus of work in the digital humanities. See, for example, Tara McPherson, "DH by Design: Alternative Origin Stories for the Digital Humanities," Washington State University (March 3, 2016), https://www.youtube.com/watch?v=S4VRAQLLjRg, accessed February 20, 2020.

21. Amy Earhart, *Traces of the Old, Uses of the New: The Emergence of Digital Literary Studies* (Ann Arbor: University of Michigan Press, 2015), 3.

22. Alexis Lothian, "From Transformative Works to #transformDH: Digital Humanities as (Critical) Fandom," *American Quarterly* 70, no. 3 (2018): 371.

23. "About #transformDH," *#TransformDH* (blog), June 2, 2015, https://transformdh.org/about-transformdh/.

24. Moya Bailey, Anne Cong Huyen, Alexis Lothian, and Amanda Phillips, "Reflections on a Movement: #transfromDH, Growing Up," in Gold and Klein, eds., *Debates in The Digital Humanities 2016*, 71.

25. Alison Booth and Miriam Posner, "The Materials at Hand," *PMLA* 135, no. 1 (2020): 10.

26. Lauren F. Klein, "Dimensions of Scale: Invisible Labor, Editorial Work, and the Future of Quantitative Literary Studies," *PMLA* 135, no. 1 (2020): 23–39, and Richard Jean So and Edwin Roland, "Race and Distant Reading," *PMLA* 135, no. 1 (2020): 59–73.

27. Alan Liu, "Toward a Diversity Stack: Digital Humanities and Diversity as a Technical Problem," *PMLA* 135, no. 1 (2020): 144.

28. Matthew Kirschenbaum and Sarah Werner, "Digital Scholarship and Digital Studies: The State of the Discipline," *Book History* 17 (2014): 410.

29. See Mattie Burkert's essay "Materialisms and the Cultural Turn in Digital Humanities" in this volume.

Approach

Section I

Benjamin Franklin's Postal Work

Christy L. Pottroff

Benjamin Franklin knew the power of a good book. As a child, he spent hours reading *Pilgrim's Progress* and essays by Defoe and Mather, evidence of a "bookish inclination" he credits with setting him on his career path as a printer.[1] Books "printed and sold by B. Franklin" (as well as newspapers, broadsides, and pamphlets), were a common sight in eighteenth-century Philadelphia.[2] In early Americanist scholarship, Franklin's books—those he read, wrote, and manufactured—are most often understood through his relationship to print.[3]

But Franklin knew that books had important forms and functions beyond print. He also used books as tools to index, analyze, retrieve, and understand complex phenomena in his life. Most famously, he organized his pursuit of moral perfection around "a little book" in which he tracked every mistake he made. When describing his plan in the *Autobiography*, he emphasizes the technology of his manuscript book with great detail:

> I made a little book, in which I allotted a page for each of the virtues. I rul'd each page with red ink, so as to have seven columns, one for each day of the week, marking each column with a letter for the day. I cross'd these columns with thirteen red lines, marking the beginning of each line with the first letter of one of the virtues, on which line, and in its proper column, I might mark, by a little black spot, every fault I found upon examination to have been committed respecting that virtue upon that day.[4]

This book was small, well-made, and tractable; he likely carried it in his jacket pocket for easy access to record and review his moral progress each day. It functioned as a portable information management system to process qualitative human activity through a quantitative matrix. Franklin's "little book" was, in other words, a database of his own design. In keeping with Stephen Ramsey's formulation of database, his book was used "to store information about a particular domain . . . and to allow one to ask questions about the state of that domain."[5] Albeit reductive and constructed, the book helped Franklin understand himself and his faults in a new way. It was both a record-keeping tool and a reminder to act in accordance with his own virtues.

This chapter recovers yet another book-based database designed and maintained by Franklin: his post office accounts. He used these books, like the moral account book, to record and process complex human phenomena into easily understood data to better understand a given domain. The post office books record information about the movement of every single piece of mail that passed through the British colonial post, and were crucial tools for Franklin's oversight of the system as Deputy Postmaster General. Though these manuscript accounts have received little scholarly attention, they have profound implications for understanding the circulation of texts in eighteenth-century North America—a robust field of inquiry in early American studies. Following the work of Benedict Anderson, scholars like Michael Warner, Meredith McGill, and Eric Slauter have elucidated the profound effects of textual circulation in this era, crediting the circulation of print with the formation of translocal modes of affiliation.[6] Circulation studies have yet to attend to the infrastructures of the early American postal system, which was a substantial engine of textual exchange. Franklin's postal account books, which track the movement of each piece of mail within the British colonial post over several decades, offer fertile terrain for testing and retesting the work of circulation studies. Franklin designed his book-based database to better understand how and where texts circulated and with what effects—and it can teach us those same lessons today.

Franklin's postal account books are not "literary" in any respect, and their formal features foreclose a strict literary critical approach. The first section of this study instead employs the practice of thin description advanced by Heather Love, a mode of reading with "exhaustive, fine-grained attention to phenomena," in an attempt to revive the form, content, and uses of Franklin's post office books.[7] In this way, I am indebted to the work of book historians like Ann Blair and Kristen Case who make legible the epistemologies of unusual books.[8] By foregrounding the particular, this approach provides a crucial frame for the study's second section, which argues that Franklin's data structures, while informative and robust for their account of colonial communication, are constructed expressions that must be understood as part of the much broader multimedia and multicultural information landscape from which they emerged.

Franklin's Post Office by the Book

The Philadelphia Post Office was a mess when Franklin took over in 1737.[9] His predecessor, Andrew Bradford (who also happened to be his printing rival), was fired for "some Negligence in rendering, & Inexactitude of his Accounts."[10] Indeed, Bradford's boss lamented that he had "not been able to obtain any Account from Mr. Bradford of the Philadelphia Office" for three full years in advance of his firing.[11] Not wanting to make the same mistake, Franklin took his postal accounts seriously, always making sure to manage affairs, as he put it, with "great clearness and punctuality."[12] In the eighteenth-century postal system, however, "clearness and punctuality" were not easy to come by. The colonial Post Office was, according to Joseph Adelman, a "rickety provincial scheme" that "was a drain on the Treasury" until Franklin's tenure, and postal historians agree that the colonial mail did little to abet the circulation of letters and newspapers within North America before the middle of the eighteenth century.[13] When Franklin took office, there was no standard for keeping track of individual letters or for managing money. Some postmasters kept a running total of letters that passed through their offices, but most simply sent their revenues and expenditures to the colonial postmaster general every six months. With such an improvisational accounting system, it is not surprising that the colonial postal system frequently lost and misdelivered letters and consistently spent more money than it made.

But Franklin was determined to keep his job at the Philadelphia Post Office, and he knew that, above all, well-ordered accounts were a requirement. Drawing on his experience running a successful print shop, he devised a new system for tracking letters and managing money. The creation of his accounting system was a multistage process; over the course of fifteen years, he designed and tested several different books, lists, and charts to track the circulation of mail before perfecting a system of ledgers that would shape mail delivery on the North American continent for half a century after its inception. Of these accounts, only Franklin's final and formalized information management system has been studied by modern scholars who hold it in high regard. For William Beatty Warner, this final plan earned Franklin the title of "enlightenment communications engineer," and Jacob Soll describes it as "one of the most innovative . . . of all time."[14] Despite these accolades, no study has yet evaluated the series of manuscript ledgers that led Franklin to design this crowning achievement of postal accounting. In this section, I highlight three of Franklin's postal account books from 1737 to 1767 to provide a record of his evolving modes of data organization for recording and facilitating the movement of mail.[15] Read over these decades, it is possible to see the influence of these postal ledgers on Franklin's politics and the evolving political landscape of British North America. One of the most significant changes in Franklin's accounting system is a shift in data organization from the accounts of individual postal patrons to those of a community. In this way, the move from individual to communal data structures in Franklin's books corresponds to the move toward intercolonial collaboration fundamental to the project of American Revolution at the end of the eighteenth century. Accordingly, these books and their data structures offer an important intervention in debates about the circulation of texts in the decades leading up to the American Revolution. While I am not disputing the justly influential analyses of national culture and formation that have emphasized the importance of print, these manuscript ledgers speak to the full range of textual forms that circulated alongside print in the middle decades of the eighteenth century. Doing so reveals the way in which Franklin's methods for organizing the movement of letters provided him with a model for the transformation of colonial subjects into national citizens.

Franklin's first accounting system from 1737 was designed to record the communications history of individual Philadelphians (fig. 1). In a marbled paper-covered octavo book labeled "Post Office Leidger No. 1," he logged every letter received at the Philadelphia Post Office. This first book was organized alphabetically by recipients' names, next to which Franklin would record postage debts in rows from left to right. The thumbprint index on the right made it easier to find individual accounts as he sorted the letters.

Every time a mailbag arrived, Franklin would draw out each piece of mail and enter the date it was delivered and the amount of postage owed under a heading for the recipient's name (before 1847, recipients almost exclusively paid postage). For example, John Kinsey received a single letter on October 13 at a cost of 1 shilling and 3 pence, another single letter on November 3 at the same cost, and some greater combination of letters on November 20 at 5 shillings and 10 pence (see first row of fig. 1). Frequent mail users like Kinsey would have many entries associated with their names, while sporadic users like Dr. Kearsley had very few recorded entries (see fig. 1). Yet, over time, the first book became difficult to read, as debts were crossed out when they were paid, and the lines begin to run into one another.

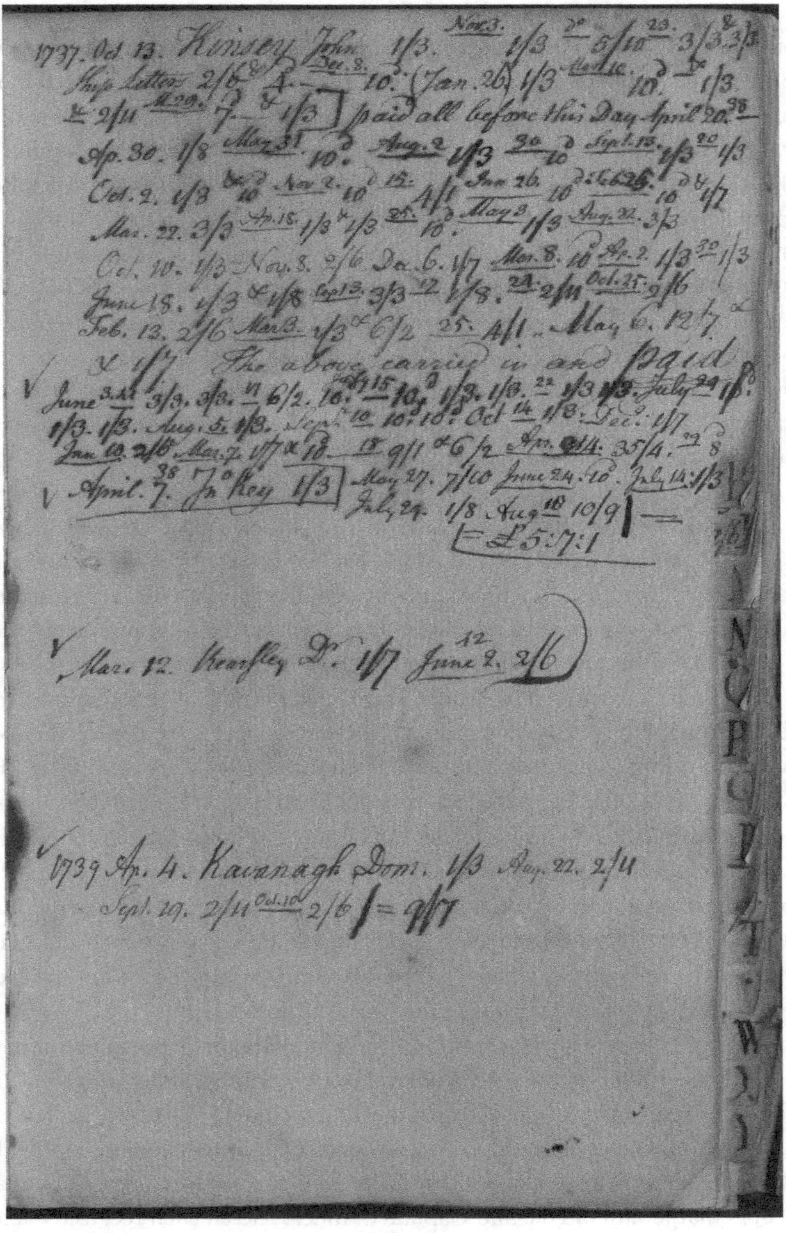

Figure 1. Benjamin Franklin, "Post-Office Leidger No. 1." (*Miscellaneous Benjamin Franklin Collections*, Mss. B.F.85.f6.11a, American Philosophical Society Library, Philadelphia, Pennsylvania)

Illegibility aside, Franklin soon discovered other inadequacies of this system. Although it prioritized individual debt collection, this book made totaling the accounts at the municipal level a difficult task—he or a clerk needed to flip through every page to calculate totals to report to the Deputy Postmaster General every six months. This book also helped Franklin manage the accounts of Philadelphians with speed and ease, but it made the rendering of Philadelphia's postal accounts a long and difficult task. Moreover, this system registers information only about incoming mail, preserving no record of materials leaving the Philadelphia office. This first system was designed for postal debt collection and around the individual postal user. The book allowed Franklin to observe the habits of individuals within Philadelphia but did not offer insight into communications patterns on a collective scale. Understanding these limits, Franklin adapted and fine-tuned his subsequent ledgers for greater ease in postage calculation and with new attention to both incoming and outgoing mail.

Franklin's third account book, implemented in 1748 and used until 1752, significantly departs from his first system.[16] This book was no longer organized as an alphabetized list of patron's debts. Rather, it was organized by the chronology of all mail movement in and out of Philadelphia, offering Franklin a more efficient way to retrieve and process information on a municipal scale (fig. 2). Entries for outgoing and incoming mail alternate (based on the date and time of their departure and arrival). Franklin kept track of different information for outgoing and incoming mail. Outgoing letters were recorded collectively according to the date and place from which they were sent (fig. 2). For example, on May 4, 1749, the notation "N.York 26.5.1.1" is Franklin's shorthand for the size and number of letters sent from Philadelphia. On that day, Philadelphians sent 26 single letters to New York City, along with 5 double letters, 1 triple letter, and 1 packet. The corresponding postage due is listed farther to the right in the row. On this day, Philadelphians carried out substantially more correspondence with New York and Boston (16 single letters and 1 packet) than with Rhode Island, Trenton, and [New] Brunswick.

Incoming letters, by contrast, are listed individually by recipient under a heading that preserves the date of arrival in Philadelphia along with the office of origin. For example, on May 10, the Philadelphia Post Office received a mailbag from Boston with thirty-two pieces of mail, which are listed individually by the name of recipient. Under the heading "From Boston 10th," Franklin records that Jonathan Pole and Captain Samuel Lincoln each received a letter weighing 7 pennyweights at the cost of 2 shillings and 4 pence. Pole paid for his letter, as denoted by the "x," while Captain Lincoln did not (and it is possible that he never received this letter at all). This book, narrower and taller than the

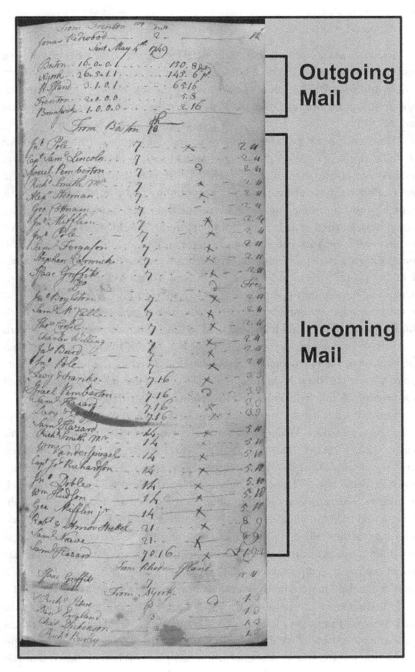

Figure 2. Benjamin Franklin, "Post Office Book, 1748, May 25." (*Miscellaneous Benjamin Franklin Collections*, Mss. B.F.85.f6.8, American Philosophical Society Library, Philadelphia, Pennsylvania)

previous one, makes totaling daily debits and credits to the Philadelphia office a much easier task. Franklin could quickly determine how much mail was being sent to and from Philadelphia.[17] Compared to the first book, this ledger prioritizes municipal communication patterns rather than those of individual postal patrons.

This book preserves a chronological account of communication in and out of Philadelphia between 1748 and 1752, and, as such, told Franklin a great deal not only about who used the mail but also which cities had the strongest postal ties to Philadelphia. Franklin almost certainly turned over the pages of this book to study communications trends in and out of Philadelphia. From it, he would have learned of the robust epistolary and economic ties between Philadelphia and New York City, strong ties between Philadelphia and Boston, and meager correspondence with other colonial towns; nearly 90 percent of Philadelphia's postal correspondence was with New York and Boston in those four years. The remaining 10 percent of mail to and from Philadelphia was limited to thirteen other colonial towns out of fifty-two available post offices. Even though postal users could have sent mail to any other office within the system for the cost of postage, they did not do so. During this five-year period, not a single piece of mail arriving at Philadelphia originated south of Yorktown, Virginia, or north of Boston. As these patterns suggest, textual circulation by mail was profoundly uneven and limited to certain established paths.

This book also preserves the accounts of Philadelphia's individual postal users and super users. While many different people received letters during this period—and most only received a letter or two in these five years—the top ten most frequent users account for nearly 21 percent of the letters received between 1748 and 1752.[18] These super users (John Mifflin, William Vanderspiegel, and others) were mostly merchants, illuminating a mercantile allegiance within the colonial mail (an allegiance that is sometimes overlooked in accounts that prioritize the ties between printers and postmasters). Taken together, this system maintains attention to the individual while also aggregating key information about municipal postal trends. This dataset would have taught Franklin a great deal about intercolonial communication and the circulation of the mail.

Franklin carried a version of this book-based accounting system with him when he was promoted to Joint Deputy Postmaster General (the highest postal appointment outside of Whitehall) in 1753. In fact, it was likely this accounting system that got him the promotion in the first place. When he heard that the standing Deputy Postmaster General of the North American colonies had fallen ill, Franklin wrote to London to request the position for himself. In his request, he enclosed "a Scheme long since form'd" that he hoped would improve the entire system.[19] His letter was also accompanied by a recommendation from a friend who was "persuaded that by Mr. Franklin's good Management, matters will be put upon a better footing, and that there will be a yearly some Ballance to be remitted to the General Post Office."[20] When the sitting Postmaster General died, Franklin was appointed to the position alongside William Hunter of Virginia.

One of their first acts as Joint Deputy Postmasters General was to standardize the accounting system throughout the colonies. After 1753, every local postmaster was required to keep track of mail in precisely the same way. To achieve this feat of bureaucratic standardization, Franklin and Hunter authored an accounting manual with documents titled *Instructions to Deputy Postmasters* and *Directions for Deputy Postmasters*, which, among other things, mandated a book-based accounting system heavily informed by Franklin's Philadelphia ledgers. Like his 1748 manuscript book, this intercolonial system tracks information about individual postal users as well as larger-scale municipal and intercolonial trends. In this new system, what had been the work of one book was now divided among four. One book was devoted to incoming mail, another to outgoing mail, a third to the debts of individual postal patrons (thereby refining the data of the first book). A fourth book was added to the system that aggregated totals drawn from these other four books, which would be sent to the Postmasters General every three months.[21]

These records standardize Franklin's scribal data structures into print form. Now, all local postmasters from Maine to the Carolinas would observe, record, and process mail as Franklin prescribed: through its communal rhythms while maintaining attention to the individual user. The example of "Letters received into the Post-Office at Philadelphia" illustrated in figure 3 bears similarities to Franklin's earlier accounts.

This book accounts for incoming mail packets arriving in Philadelphia (individual accounts were drawn out into a different book, which is now lost). On October 8, 1767, for example, the Philadelphia Post Office received packets of letters from Elizabethtown, [New] Brunswick, and Princetown, New Jersey (fig. 3). Information is entered into the postal ledger by the "time of receiving" in the first column (Oct. 8), and by destination in the second column (E Town, Brunswick, Princetown). The remainder of the columns record information about the cost of the letters in pennyweights (dwt. grs), and whether the letter was prepaid or not. On this date, for example, none of the mail was prepaid; the mail from Elizabethtown would cost the recipient 2.16 pennyweights (4 pence) while the mail from both Princetown and Brunswick was half the cost at 2 pence. There are other columns for tracking "Way" letters (letters taken by

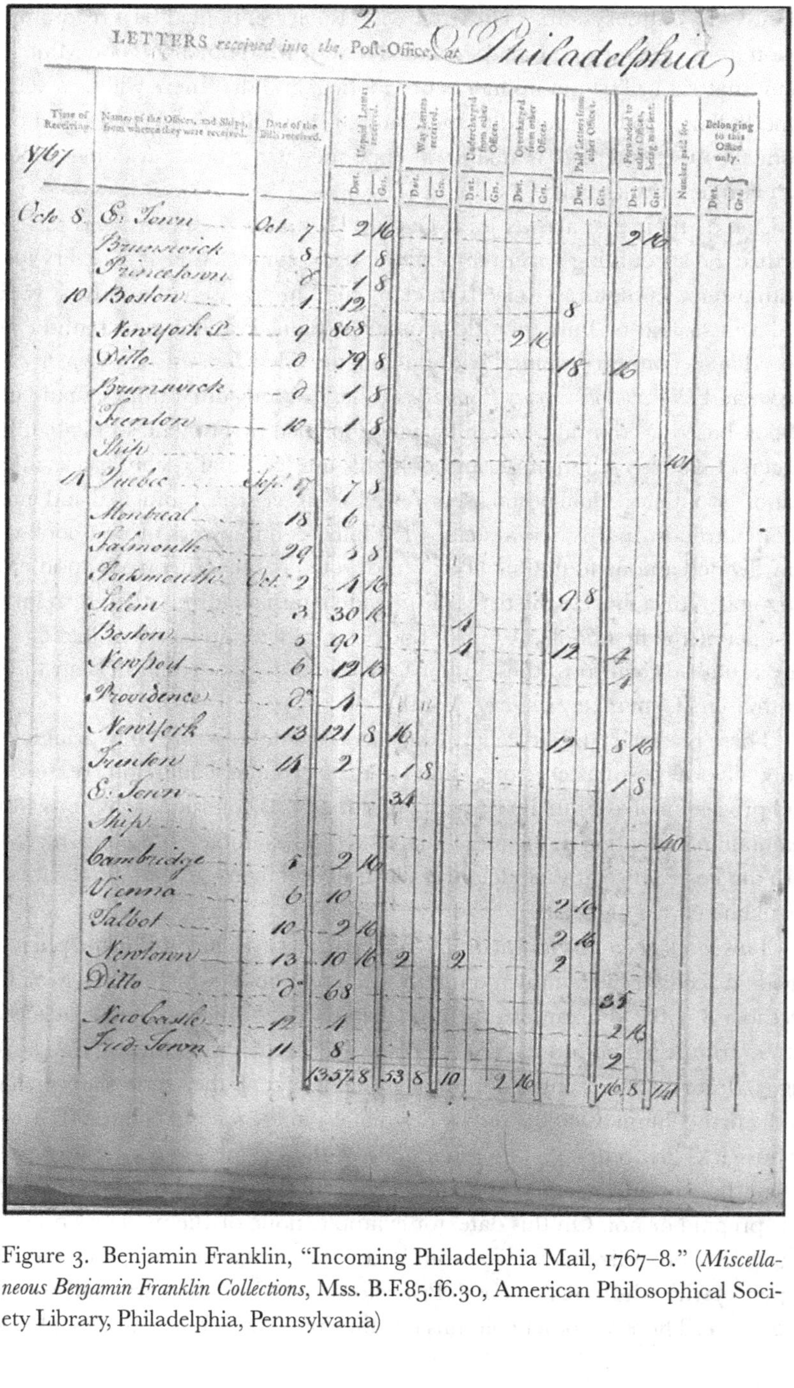

2

LETTERS received into the Post-Office at Philadelphia

Time of Receiving. 1767	Names of the Offices, and Ships, from whence they were received.	Date of the Bills received.	Unpaid Letters received. Dwt.	Grs.	Way Letters received. Dwt.	Grs.	Undercharged from other Offices. Dwt.	Grs.	Overcharged from other Offices. Dwt.	Grs.	Paid Letters from other Offices. Dwt.	Grs.	Forwarded to other Offices, being mis-sent. Dwt.	Grs.	Number paid for.	Belonging to this Office only. Dwt.	Grs.
Oct. 8	E. Town	Oct. 7	2	16									2	16			
	Brunswick	8	1	8													
	Princetown	d°	1	8													
10	Boston	1	12								8						
	Newyork P.	9	86	8					2	16							
	Ditto	d°	79	8							18		16				
	Brunswick	d°	1	8													
	Trenton	10	1	8													
	Ship														101		
11	Quebec	Sep. 17	7	8													
	Montreal	18	6														
	Falmouth	29	3	8													
	Portsmouth	Oct. 2	4	16													
	Salem	3	30	16							9	8					
	Boston	5	90				4										
	Newport	6	19	16			4				12		4				
	Providence	d°	4										4				
	Newyork	13	121	8	16						17		8	16			
	Trenton	14	2		1	8											
	E. Town				34								1	8			
	Ship														40		
	Cambridge	5	2	16													
	Vienna	6	10								2	16					
	Talbot	10	2	16							2	16					
	Newtown	13	10	16	2		2				2						
	Ditto	d°	68										25				
	Newcastle	12	4										2	16			
	Fred. Town	11	8										2				
			1357	8	53	8	10		2	16	76	8			141		

Figure 3. Benjamin Franklin, "Incoming Philadelphia Mail, 1767–8." (*Miscellaneous Benjamin Franklin Collections*, Mss. B.F.85.f6.30, American Philosophical Society Library, Philadelphia, Pennsylvania)

postriders on their routes) and intercity mail. In addition to tracking costs of mail packets and their place of origin as in Franklin's other books, this system had the added capacity to preserve the amount of time it took to deliver a single letter, thanks to information in the first and third columns. Mail from Trenton and New Brunswick benefited from same-day service in this account, whereas letters from Quebec and Montreal took nearly a month to arrive in Philadelphia. Like Franklin's 1748 Philadelphia book, this new system was organized around the temporal patterns of mail movement within a given municipality. In doing so, these books structure textual circulation according to its communal rather than individual rhythms.

This new accounting system offered Franklin and his collaborators a bird's-eye view of the British Colonial Mail in North America. Every three months, municipal postmasters would submit their quarterly accounts to Franklin and Hunter (and, later, John Foxcroft, Hunter's successor), who would study large-scale communications patterns. From these aggregated accounts, they could determine where letters were going and where they were coming from; they could gauge how heavy a postrider's portmanteau might be on a given route. Moreover, by asking every postmaster to record both incoming and outgoing mail with special attention to overcharged mail, this system instituted a widespread practice of double-entry accounting. In effect, this cut down on graft at post offices, kept costs low, and helped build greater public trust in the mail. According to William Beatty Warner, "the subtle interlocking character of these [books] helped to give the General Post Office crucial information about what was happening throughout the postal system."[22] With this information, the Postmasters General adapted routes and schedules to best suit the needs of the colonies. This attention to detail made the colonial post profitable for the very first time under their watch: by 1761, Franklin and Hunter had cleared a profit of more than £1400 (more than $370,000 today).

This particular plan did more than bring the colonial mail out of the red. It empowered Franklin and Hunter to make data-driven adjustments to postal operations to improve the speed, frequency, and reliability of textual circulation. For example, they used this information to schedule more frequent deliveries between New York and Philadelphia—two cities with strong economic and social ties. A notice in a 1755 issue of the *Philadelphia Gazette* proclaims: "This is to give notice that for the future the Posts will go *twice* a week between Philad. and New York, and for that purpose will set out from both those places precisely at *ten o'clock* in the morning on every *Monday* and *Thursday* and will come in on every *Wednesday* and *Saturday* noon throughout the year."[23] In effect, this change doubled the level of service between the two cities and thereby cut response times in half. Such adjustments not only ensured that the portmanteau would remain a reasonable weight for postriders, but these schedule adjustments, Franklin hoped, would increase intercourse between cities. Franklin and Hunter likewise doubled the service between Philadelphia and Boston in 1755: "It having been found very inconvenient to persons concerned in trade, that the mail *from Philadelphia to New England* sets out once a fortnight during the winter season: This is to give notice, that the New England mail will henceforth go once a week the year round, whereby correspondence may be carried on and answers obtained to letters between Philad. and Boston in three weeks, which used in the winter, to require six weeks."[24] This announcement illustrates the degree to which the postmasters believed communication and correspondence would increase if the infrastructure allowed it. According to Ruth Lapham Butler, they also opened up new routes between Philadelphia and Baltimore, New York and Quebec, and southward to towns in Virginia and North Carolina.[25] With this book-based information management system, they could track the use of new routes and make schedule adjustments as needed. Even though some offices had very little mail and operated at a deficit (like Quebec and Hobbs Hole, Virginia) the Deputy Postmasters General maintained consistent albeit less frequent service to them. Franklin's post office books were more than mere records of postal communication as it occurred; they were also sources to guide the oversight of the postal system.

These final Philadelphia records show the incredibly expanded postal reach of Philadelphians during Franklin's tenure as Deputy Postmaster General. Even though these standardized records exist only in fragments of their original codex form, a chronological period between 1767 and 1768 endures in its entirety to speak to this change. Between May and December 1767, Philadelphians corresponded with people in forty-six other towns, compared with thirteen towns from the entire period within the 1748 to 1752 book. The 1767 accounts show Philadelphians sending and receiving mail as far north as Quebec and as far south as Charleston, North Carolina, four times the geographical scale of the earlier book. The volume of mail between these geographically distant cities also increased substantially in those years. From the vantage of Philadelphia, Franklin's postal improvements—more frequent delivery, standardized rates, and a rate reduction—enabled colonists to send mail much farther and faster than ever before. These books illustrate that over the course of a few decades, colonists were corresponding more frequently and at a greater scale with people in distant places. These postal patterns suggest that economic and social ties increased and even flourished in the years leading up to the

American Revolution. The British colonial mail was an engine for reliable and secure long-distance communication.

One of the most significant changes in Franklin's accounting system between 1737 and 1767 is the shift in organization from individual postal patron to the chronological record of letters sent and received in a given community. The original emphasis on the individual took a different direction, tracking mail packets across a much wider geography at much faster speeds. Over time, Franklin came to see that textual circulation was best organized and understood through its communal and temporal rhythms. This information management system evolved from a record of postage debts to a timepiece that measured the movement of mail throughout the North American colonies. In doing so, it integrates the missives of individual postal patrons into a collective record, one that binds them together within a shared postal time akin to that anatomized by Benedict Anderson. In this way, the move toward collaboration, fundamental to the project of American Revolution, can be traced through the material forms of Franklin's post office books.

Analyzing Franklin's information management system opens up rich terrain to reconsider a host of other material factors that animated the circulation of texts in early America. To close this section, I highlight two important lessons these post office ledgers can teach us about the circulation of information in the eighteenth century: the first, based on what these ledgers overlook, and the second, based on information spread thin within the data itself.

For one, Franklin's post office books offer a less abstracted way to understand long-standing debates about the circulation of print and the formation of translocal communities in early America. For Americanist scholars like Michael Warner and Trish Loughran, the circulation of print had profound effects on the making and unmaking of the United States in the eighteenth and nineteenth centuries. Franklin's manuscript books stand as a fascinating intervention in debates that study textual circulation through the particular affordances of printed as opposed to scribal texts. Franklin's postal database—a central apparatus for determining the rhythms and geographical scale of long-distance textual circulation in the eighteenth century—did not differentiate between printed and scribal texts. There is no category for measuring a text according to its form. By contrast, in the nineteenth century, a text's printedness mattered, as printed texts were admitted into the postal system at a deep discount, and newspapers were sometimes carried for free. Before the founding of the US Post Office Department in 1792, however, the physical form of a piece of mail did not influence postal rates or protocols. Indeed, Franklin reinforces this indistinction between print and other materials in his "Post Office Instructions and Directions" manual: "you are to observe that every single Piece of Paper, however small, or large, is to be tax'd as a single Letter, unless there are wrote on it more Letters than one, or Bills of Exchange, Merchants Accompts, Invoices, Bills of Lading, Writs or Proceedings at Law; in that Case every Letter, Bill, Accompt, Invoice, &c. is to be rated and taxed as so many several and distinct Letters."[26] While the materiality of a text is fundamental for its interpretation within the field of book history, Franklin's instructions ask eighteenth-century postmasters to ignore many aspects of a text's physical form within their accounts. As this data was used to determine how often mail would be delivered in a given place, we can see how printed and scribal texts were necessary partners in shaping the ebbs and flows of the early American postal system.[27]

Then, these books illustrate the degree to which Franklin himself was economically invested in the colonial postal system. In my description of these books, I have emphasized Franklin's meticulous attention to postal debts of individual users; his system was the first to tabulate and record postage on every piece of mail. Such exacting attention to postage debts might suggest that Franklin was eager to collect each and every penny due to maintain the profitability of the system. The story the data tells is actually quite the opposite: Franklin very rarely collected the debts he recorded during his years at the Philadelphia Office. Instead, he subsidized the unpaid accounts of more than seven hundred Philadelphians with his own income. According to the accounting system I have described, Franklin paid over £800 (more than $192,000 today) out of his own income to ensure that Philadelphians would have access to their letters. Historians have long recognized that the early American post office often operated on credit because small currency was scarce in the colonies, but what has been less appreciated is the extent to which Postmaster Franklin himself absorbed these small debts with his own income. Moreover, when Franklin was preparing his will in 1786, he transferred these postal debts to his general account "Ledger E," which he donated to the Pennsylvania Hospital upon his death.[28] Even though he died with little money, he hoped to ensure the Pennsylvania Hospital a source of income by spurring Philadelphians to donate their decades old postal debts to the hospital.[29] Franklin's account books reflect his deep economic investment in intercolonial communication, and they speak to his understanding of an accessible and affordable postal system as a social good.

Twenty-first century scholars still have a great deal to learn from Franklin's post office books. Thanks to Cynthia Heider, Bayard Miller, and the rest of the digital humanities team at the American Philosophical Society Library, these records are openly available as high-resolution images and as transcribed data, ripe for analysis and study. This chapter has illustrated thus far that attention to the circulation and communication patterns within Franklin's books can point us toward different kinds of insights about the information landscape of early America. Franklin's post office books illustrate the need to consider the full range of media forms that existed alongside print, including manuscript account books and mail in its many forms. Doing so reveals the way in which Franklin's methods for organizing the movement of texts is interwoven with the values of intercolonial union.

Finding Narratives in the Book-based Database

The information management system of Franklin's post office books is fascinating in its own right, but what is perhaps even more compelling are these manifold narratives of systematized textual exchange exercised in each data point. Just beneath the surface, Franklin's books preserve the stories of thousands of ships, stagecoaches, horses, and people carrying the mail. They tell the story of protracted and uneven intercolonial union and territorial expansion through the slow but consistent ploddings of eighteenth-century communications infrastructure. The narratives within each piece of data were not lost on Franklin. He spoke with postal patrons on a daily basis in the Philadelphia Post Office; he learned about their lives and reasons for posting and receiving the mail. Franklin's post office (which shared a roof with his print shop and his home) was a busy, bustling place undoubtedly filled with life. Moreover, as Joint Deputy Postmaster General, Franklin twice traveled the full length of the British colonial postal system, meeting every postmaster under his employ, testing each road, measuring distances between offices, and laying mile markers. Although the post office books do not relay these stories to us directly, they would have been, for Franklin, inseparable from his authorship and interpretation of these accounts. The place names and mail quantities in these books would have represented a much wider range of human associations for Franklin. Informed by Katherine Hayles's formulation that narrative and database are "natural symbionts," I argue that Franklin's book-based database demands a narrative context.[30]

Up to this point, I have framed the increased circulation of mail in North America as a victory of Franklin's particular bookkeeping practices. Through these evolving records and their effects, Franklin helped colonists communicate across great expanses with dispatch and ease, and laid the groundwork necessary for the American Revolution. But this narrative has a double-entry, so to speak. As the British colonial mail became more orderly and efficient under Franklin's watch, other communications systems and their attendant infrastructures were being overwritten. Paths that had been forged by indigenous messengers were co-opted and controlled by colonial postriders under Franklin's employ. This account of communications usurpation in North America has been well told by Matt Cohen and Katherine Grandjean whose books animate the broader context around the postal system represented in Franklin's books. Early American communications systems, Cohen writes, "were both occasions for and sites of contest for control over social and economic power."[31] According to Grandjean, by the late eighteenth century these sites of contest were predominantly controlled by colonial authorities like the postal system; roads that had been "Indian pathways" were "adopted by English passengers who had gleefully clogged them with carts and beasts of burden."[32] The establishment of the North American postal system is indeed an unsettling of existing indigenous networks.

Even though their data structures do not speak to the narrative of colonization directly, Franklin's post office books helped colonial authorities enact territorial control through the circulation of texts. There are traces of this story within Franklin's other postal records. For example, Franklin and Hunter's "Post Office Instructions and Directions" betray anxiety around unexpected contacts during mail delivery. Franklin instructs postriders "to wind their Horns once every five Miles, and three Times in every Town or Village, and upon the Meeting any Passenger on the Road."[33] Here, Franklin asks postriders to make a spectacle of their mobility by sounding a horn at various points in their journey. The blaring horn would notify postal patrons of such routine postal matters as news, letters, and other mail that were soon to arrive or depart their office. Between arrivals and destinations, however, the blaring horn is an assertion of colonial authority on pathways that were much more difficult to control. By sounding the horn during a moment of encounter, postriders vest their passage with the authority of the British Colonial Mail—a practice that spoke to the rider's place within a colonial network. It also would have notified nearby others that a roadside contact had occurred, as, perhaps, a protective measure. Nearby listeners would know a postrider was proximate, and depending on the sequence and timing of the horn blasts, had encountered someone else on the road. A sounding horn enacted an imperial public that both authorized the passage of a postrider as a British official and served as a protective measure by calling attention to moments of contact. In this way and in many others, the strengthening colonial postal system exacted its authority through routine, standardization, and spectacle. Experiences like the blaring horn during an encounter on an open road do not find their ways into Franklin's database directly, but instead demand study of the broader communications and information landscape in which the post office books operated.

To understand early American communication solely through the data structures in Franklin's post office books would exclude other modes and systems of communication that animated the middle decades of the eighteenth century. To demonstrate the partiality of Franklin's database, I turn to his Gulf Stream map, an archival object that is similarly one-dimensional in its representation of eighteenth-century circulation. Historians have often made a passing connection between Franklin's postal work and his map of the Gulf Stream, the first of its kind in print, published in London in 1769.[34] Louis De Vorsey concludes that "it is obvious that at some time between 1746 and 1762 Franklin became aware of the general location and magnitude of the Gulf Stream," and he used this knowledge to collaborate on the map with Timothy Folger, a Nantucket ship captain.[35] Although the precise nature of his Gulf Stream education has been heretofore left to the imagination, Franklin's post office books may be the missing link. These books measured the time it took for postriders and mail packet ships to travel between various post offices and ports, providing Franklin with a veritable trove of oceanographic information. From these books, he would have learned that it took two weeks longer for mail packet ships to sail from England to North America than vice versa. These books also illustrate that ships leaving Virginia would arrive in England faster than those leaving from Rhode Island. As mail packets cut across the ocean on their postal routes, he would have been privy to their departure and arrival times. It is easy to imagine how each journey would have contributed data to Franklin's books, information that unexpectedly helped him better understand the ocean.[36]

Franklin's Gulf Stream map (fig. 4) is an instructive parable in the ways systems of knowledge are displaced by the authority of certain texts. Franklin sometimes gets credited as being the first to map the Gulf Stream, but he was merely a facilitator in his account of the map's publication. Timothy Folger, Franklin's cousin, used his expertise as a whaler to create the map itself. Captains and sailors, Franklin knew, were well aware of the river in the ocean and were likely the first to call it by its current name. Sailors, Franklin describes elsewhere, learned about the Gulf Stream by sailing through it, seeing steam rise off of it, and observing the change in whale behavior in its proximity. Beyond Franklin's map, this knowledge would have been the province of sailors around the globe who learned about it firsthand or spoke about it in conversations and exchanges with other sailors. Given the geography of the Gulf

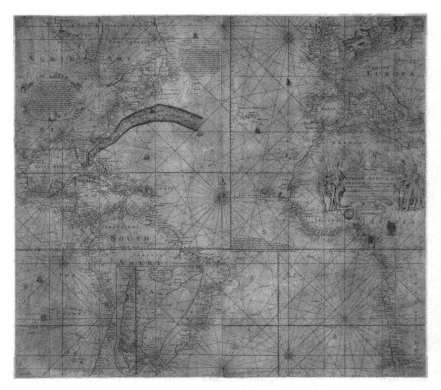

Figure 4. Benjamin Franklin and Timothy Folger, *Franklin-Folger Chart of the Gulf Stream*. (Library of Congress, Geography and Map Division)

Stream, it is likely that sailors from what are now Cuba, Jamaica, Florida, and the West Indies would have been well aware of the Gulf Stream, its location, and effects. Franklin himself recognizes the expertise of non-Western sailors in his own writings, describing "the islanders in the great Pacific ocean" as "the most expert boat-sailors in the world."[37]

The presence of Franklin's Gulf Stream map in the archive and its status as the first printed map of the Gulf Stream might tempt modern readers to overvalue its impact on eighteenth-century oceanic travel. Much to Franklin's chagrin, the map did little to change travel routes or practices. He describes his frustrations with British officials who refused to make use of his maps. For those with knowledge of the Gulf Stream, it is no wonder that his map was little used. It captures less than half of the river in the ocean—relaying information only about a portion of the stream from roughly Florida to Newfoundland. In actuality, flowing westward, the Gulf Stream originates off the coast of Central Africa, carrying warm water across the Atlantic into the Caribbean Sea and the West Indies. It then runs along the Florida coast and northeast along the Atlantic Seaboard before coursing across the Atlantic toward the European North Atlantic. Franklin's map, though it was the first and though it is famous, is only a partial account of this eighteenth-century circulatory system.

Franklin's post office account books are similarly partial. Their codex form, their red printed columns, and wealth of data suggest a kind of comprehensiveness, a tool that will allow us to understand how exactly the diffusion of information and the circulation of texts worked in the past. The colonial postal system preserved within Franklin's book-based database was only one means through which people communicated across distances. If we read Franklin's post office books as the most authoritative account of eighteenth-century circulation, we re-enact the same kinds of displacement that led to the loss of other systems in the first place. Instead, we should engage a mode of scholarship that accounts for the coexistence of other circulatory systems. Just as important as Franklin's post office books and the new networks that they trace, are the networks that were overwritten, suppressed, and eradicated by the colonial postal network.

Notes

1. Benjamin Franklin, "Autobiography," in *The Autobiography and Other Writings*, ed. Kenneth A. Silverman (New York: Penguin, 1986), 12.

2. Although, as Jim Green and Peter Stallybrass point out, "the cost and risk of publishing books was much greater, and for this reason Franklin printed very few books" compared to other printed forms. Among the books Franklin printed are Samuel Richardson's *Pamela* (1742–43), Isaac Watts's *The Psalms of David, Imitated* (1729), and *M. T. Cicero's Cato Major, or His Discourse of Old-Age with Explanatory Notes* (1778). James N. Green and Peter Stallybrass, *Benjamin Franklin: Writer and Printer* (New Castle, DE: Oak Knoll, 2006), 63.

3. See Michael Warner, "Franklin and the Letters of the Republic," *Representations* 16 (Autumn 1986): 110–30; and Green and Stallybrass, *Benjamin Franklin*.

4. Franklin, *Autobiography*, 84.

5. Stephen Ramsay, "Databases," in *A Companion to Digital Humanities*, ed. Susan Schreibman, Ray Siemens, and John Unsworth (Hoboken, NJ: Wiley-Blackwell, 2008), 177.

6. Michael Warner, *Letters of the Republic: Publication and the Public Sphere in Eighteenth-Century America* (Cambridge, MA: Harvard University Press, 1992); Meredith L. McGill, *American Literature and the Culture of Reprinting, 1834–1853* (Philadelphia: University of

Pennsylvania Press, 2007); Eric Slauter, "Reading and Radicalization: Print, Causality, and the American Revolution," *Early American Studies* 8, no. 1 (Winter 2010): 5–40.

7. See Heather Love, "Close Reading and Thin Description," *Public Culture* 25, no. 3 (2013): 401–34.

8. See Ann Blair, *Too Much to Know: Managing Scholarly Information before the Modern Age* (New Haven, CT: Yale University Press, 2010), and Kristen Case, "Knowing as Neighboring: Approaching Thoreau's Kalendar," *J19: The Journal of Nineteenth-Century Americanists* 2, no. 1 (2014): 107–29.

9. While the brick-and-mortar location where Bradford kept the Philadelphia Post Office was likely messy, too, Franklin did not inherit such a disorderly location. A Post Office was not a standalone institution until the middle of the nineteenth century. When Franklin took the position, the Philadelphia Post Office moved to him, as advertised in his 1737 newspaper: "Notice is hereby given, that the Post-Office of Philadelphia, is now kept at B. Franklin's in Market-Street."

10. Franklin, *Autobiography*, 103.

11. "Letter from Alexander Spotswood," *Pennsylvania Gazette*, December 11, 1740.

12. Franklin, *Autobiography*, 103.

13. Joseph M. Adelman, "'A Constitutional Conveyance of Intelligence, Public and Private': The Post Office, the Business of Printing, and the American Revolution," *Enterprise & Society* 11, no. 4 (December 2010): 709–52, 714–15; see also Ruth Lapham Butler, *Doctor Franklin, Postmaster General* (New York: Doubleday, 1928), and Richard R. John, *Spreading the News: The American Postal System from Franklin to Morse* (Cambridge, MA: Harvard University Press, 1995).

14. Warner and Soll's evaluation of Franklin's contribution to early American communication offers an important corrective to Richard John's dismissive assessment of Franklin's appointment as "a placeholder for the crown." William Beatty Warner, *Protocols of Liberty: Communication Innovation and the American Revolution* (Chicago: University of Chicago Press, 2013), 132, and Jacob Soll, *The Reckoning: Financial Accountability and the Rise and Fall of Nations* (New York: Basic Books, 2014), 153. John, *Spreading the News*.

15. These three books are part of a cache of Franklin's post office manuscripts housed at the American Philosophical Society Library in Philadelphia. Among the records are eight books of various sizes; early books tended to be thick octavo volumes, while later records were generally folio size. Some are covered in marbled wrappers, and others are bound in vellum. The later records are now unbound and fragmented but were originally bound together. The collection is as beautiful as it is materially diverse.

16. Franklin's second post office account book from 1742 to 1748 maintains many features of the first. It is organized alphabetically by Philadelphian, with a thumbprint index along the right side. Instead of listing post office debts from left to right as in the first account book, he listed debts in columns for faster calculation.

17. Under this new accounting system, Franklin implemented yet another new book, which totaled the accounts of individual postal patrons. At different times, Franklin drew out the accounts and listed them in a smaller book. This book, like the 1737 ledger,

was organized by individual postal patron, but instead of tallying each postage expense, Franklin listed the total owed by the patron. Franklin composed at least three of these books—and there are likely others that have since been lost. These drawn-out accounts were much smaller in size, and one is wrapped in vellum—suggesting that these books were kept in Franklin's pockets as he went around town. The books central to this study are much larger and were most likely kept in the post office.

18. The Digital Humanities team at the American Philosophical Society Library aggregated these totals as part of the Franklin Post Office Books project. They have transcribed Franklin's organization system into spreadsheet form that is open and available at https://github.com/AmericanPhilosophicalSociety.

19. Benjamin Franklin, "Letter to Peter Collison," Philadelphia, May 21, 1751, *Benjamin Franklin Papers Online* (Yale University Library), http://franklinpapers.org/franklin//framedNames.jsp.

20. Leo Lemay, *The Life of Benjamin Franklin* (Philadelphia: University of Pennsylvania Press, 2006), 338. Franklin also served as the comptroller of the British North American mail for two years prior to his promotion.

21. For a more robust examination of this system and effects, see William Beatty Warner's *Protocols of Liberty*.

22. Warner, *Protocols of Liberty*, 137.

23. Benjamin Franklin and William Hunter, "General Post Office," *Pennsylvania Gazette*, March 25, 1755.

24. Franklin and Hunter, "General Post Office," *Pennsylvania Gazette*, February 11, 1755.

25. Butler, *Doctor Franklin, Postmaster General*.

26. Benjamin Franklin and William Hunter, "Post Office Instructions and Directions," broadside, 1753. See also Trish Loughran, *The Republic in Print: Print Culture in the Age of U.S. Nation Building, 1770–1870* (New York: Columbia University Press, 2007.)

27. Although newspapers were omitted from this accounting system, the colonial mail did indeed deliver them. In 1758 Franklin issued additional instructions for postmasters that mandated prepayment of newspapers on a quarterly basis. For more on the close ties between newspaper delivery and the early American postal system, see John, *Spreading the News*, and Adelman, "A Constitutional Conveyance."

28. Benjamin Franklin, "Unpublished Will and Codicil," *Benjamin Franklin Papers Online* (Yale), http://franklinpapers.org/franklin//framedNames.jsp.

29. While this was a generous gesture, the hospital did not follow up on the debts in Franklin's book.

30. N. Katherine Hayles, "Narrative and Database: Natural Symbionts," *PMLA: Publications of The Modern Language Association of America* 122, no. 5 (October 2007): 1603–8.

31. Matthew Cohen, *The Networked Wilderness: Communicating in Early New England* (Minneapolis: University of Minnesota Press, 2010), 2.

32. Katherine Grandjean, *American Passage: The Communications Frontier in Early New England* (Cambridge, MA: Harvard University Press, 2011), 204.

33. Franklin and Hunter, "Post Office Instructions and Directions."

34. See Ellen R. Cohen, "Benjamin Franklin, Georges-Louis Le Rouge and the Franklin/Folger Chart of the Gulf Stream," *Imago Mundi* 52, no. 1 (2000): 124–42, and Philip L. Richardson, "Benjamin Franklin and Timothy Folger's First Printed Chart of the Gulf Stream," *Science* 207, no. 4431 (1980): 643–45.

35. Louis de Vorsey, "Pioneer Charting of the Gulf Stream: The Contributions of Benjamin Franklin and William Gerard De Brahm," *Imago Mundi* 28 (1976): 108.

36. Franklin also learned about the Gulf Stream firsthand during a transatlantic voyage. See Ellen R. Cohen and de Louis de Vorsey, "Pioneer Charting of the Gulf Stream," for a full account of Franklin's relationship to the Gulf Stream and its mapping.

37. Benjamin Franklin, "Letter to Julien-David LeRoy," February 1784, reprinted in Albert Henry Smyth, *The Writings of Benjamin Franklin*, vol 9 (London: MacMillan, 1906), 383.

Linking Book History and the Digital Humanities via Museum Studies

Jayme Yahr

Patrik Svensson asked early in the formation of the digital humanities if the DH "tent can naturally be taken to include critical work construing the digital as an object of inquiry rather than as a tool" and "whether there is room for research in the digital humanities that does not engage with tools or 'making'?"[1] The answer, nearly a decade later, is an affirmative "yes." While media studies shaped the primary approach to the digital object, the fields of Art History and Museum Studies provide fresh theories and frameworks to critically examine how visitors (in museum speak) visit contemporary digital images of historical printed material and users (in digital humanities speak) use them. In this essay I take as a case study Cornell University Library's Making of America Collection (MOA). This digital collection of primary source materials related to America's industrial and social history dating from roughly 1840 to 1901 is an early effort to link the history of printed information with a digital platform.[2] Using optical character recognition (OCR) and early funding from The Andrew W. Mellon Foundation, Cornell partnered with the University of Michigan to begin digitizing the collection in 1995, when digital humanities was better known as "humanities computing" and in many ways was not yet a formalized field of study.[3] There were continuous, yet often small changes made to the MOA site between the late 1990s and 2016. Following two years of inactivity, Cornell's MOA content, a collection that includes

267 monograph volumes and 100,000 journal articles with nineteenth-century imprints, is now being served by HathiTrust.[4] Cornell's MOA is a prime example of the ways in which museum structures can be applied to digital humanities collections and projects.

The MOA collection, when examined through a museum-based perspective, reveals a direct link between the challenges of user accessibility in the study of traditional print formats and the critical issues of visual/spatial juxtapositions in the digital humanities. What physical objects provide in their repositories, such as opportunities to make immediate visual and spatial links, are often lost in digital repositories. The digitized journals in the MOA collection provide solutions to these types of issues, namely the lack of accessibility, discoverability, and contextual organization. The central case study of MOA within this chapter affords us an opportunity to apply a Museum Studies framework to recent digital humanities collections and projects. Further, three Cultural Analytics Lab projects from the last decade, namely, Anna Karenina.viz (2009), *Science* and *Popular Science* (2010), On Broadway (2014–2015), and DIY History, provide additional examples of image-based projects that both succeed and fail to consider the issues that users face.[5]

Museum Framework

Museum Studies provides both a historical framework for understanding the role of the creator, or to use Stephen Ramsay's digital humanities term, "the builder," and the relationship between a creator's intended meaning and actual meaning from a user's perspective.[6] Cabinets of curiosity—considered to be the earliest examples of museums and often consisting of any number and type of objects, from a small collection of three or four tools or shells to an entire multiroom building filled from floor to ceiling with small sculptures and taxidermy—continue to inform exhibitions in the twenty-first century since they represent more than a disparate collection of things.[7] These eclectic collections were traditionally called *Wunderkammer*, or wonder rooms, which rose out of "the *studiolo*, a purpose-built chamber filled with antiquities, gemstones and sculptures, popular in Italy among men of both means and learning from the fourteenth century onwards."[8] What the curiosity cabinet provided to collectors and viewers from the seventeenth century on was an individualized way of conceiving of pertinent and critical links between tangible objects, visual stimulus, spatial juxtapositions, and the "tension between the object's affinities and differences."[9] Although seemingly unordered, these early museums reveal the importance of materiality and provide a way of viewing both book history and the digital humanities as part of a textual continuum, one that has a "long history of negotiating its relations with other arts."[10]

As opposed to many contemporary museum installations, which employ the white cube to limit visual noise and present objects in a minimalist and literal white-wall setting, the *Wunderkammer* allows visitors to make visual and spatial connections for themselves, as it is easier, in many ways, to forgo curatorial intent.[11] Linking disparate objects together to create meaning is often easier when there are dozens or even hundreds of objects in close proximity. A curator's argument or intent can more easily be obscured in a filled space than when a few objects occupy an otherwise blank room. These cabinets were often so full of objects that a singular visitor could link a jewel, a piece of coral, a globe, and a fossil together in a personal narrative that was entirely different from the perspective of another visitor looking at the same cabinet. Visitors, as determined by extensive research in Museum Studies within the last two decades, do not attend museum exhibitions to learn entirely new concepts, nor do collectors collect objects to own something they have never seen; rather, visitors visit to learn more about concepts with which they are already familiar, and collectors often endeavor to possess objects they have heard of or seen before.[12]

The first formal "cabinet-turned-public" museum in America was Charles Willson Peale's natural history museum, which opened to the Philadelphia public in 1786. The cabinet of curiosity was followed by salon-style hangs of artwork in the 1800s in which walls were covered floor to ceiling in an orderly manner with the most desirable location for a work of art being at eye level. The move toward a modified hang of artworks in double rows, rather than floor-to-ceiling, began at the turn of the twentieth century, and an eventual move toward, and implementation of, white cube minimalism took place in roughly the mid-1900s. By the early 2000s, the museum world saw a resurgence of interest in the cabinet of curiosity, giving credence to the adage "what is old is new again."

Given that digital humanities projects are often, but not always, visual displays of information, Museum Studies can provide a framework for questioning user design and how users visually and spatially make meaning. First, the same issues that a curator confronts with regard to exhibitions are faced by builders in the digital humanities. A curator and a digital humanities builder are content creators, making the initial links between objects (such as books), tools (such as mapping or textual analysis), and space (including physical spatial juxtapositions or issues of space syntax). Yet, there is no guarantee that visitors or users are making the same connections that a curator or digital humanities builder intends. The visitor controls the visit, although little has been written about the user in the digital humanities or the intersection of the digital humanities and Museum Studies. I add the caveat here that I do not mean the user as "collaborative curator" or "content builder" but strictly as the general user, the typical "public" that museum scholars often reference.[13] As Johanna Drucker argued in "Humanistic Theory and Digital Scholarship," as part of the initial 2012 volume *Debates in the Digital Humanities*, "To theorize humanities approaches to digital scholarship we need to consider the role of affect, notions of non-self-identicality of all expressions, the force of a constructivist approach to knowledge as knowing, observer dependent, emergent, and process-driven rather than entity-defined."[14] The constructivist approach to knowledge suggests that the learner, which in this study is akin to the user, is an active participant and creator of meaning.

Second, museums, and by extension in this study, digital humanities creators, cannot assume knowledge; yet, there is seemingly a great level of assumption that digital humanities collections or projects are accessible, useable, and understandable in ways that mirror the intent of the creator/builder.[15] It should be noted that the phrases "digital humanities collections" and "digital humanities projects" are often used interchangeably in scholarship; however, I employ these phrases according to each case study's online self-designation. As Sheila A. Brennan has suggested in "Public, First," the act of "going live" with a digital humanities collection or project online or through social media networks, "does not necessarily make a project discoverable, accessible, or relevant to anyone other than its creators."[16] User design, as explained by Charlie Edwards, is problematic in its assessment, as success is determined in a business setting by " . . . directing the user to a specific end: adoption of a site, retention on the site to view ads, seamless completion of commercial transactions."[17] This specific end, the business-oriented end, does not correlate with many digital humanities projects and collections in which the making of meaning, knowledge reinforcement, or sense of wonder and discovery are considered successful outcomes. Although a corpus of research related to user design exists, often referred to as UX or UXD, recent academic scholarship related directly to the digital humanities has devoted a minimal amount of space to a discussion of user design or the user as an autonomous figure in the same way that museum scholarship looks toward visitors as essential meaning-makers.[18] Many users of digital humanities projects/collections are truly visitors looking for an opportunity to make their own individualized connections between and across images, objects, or text based upon personal interest.

Case Study: Making of America

Taking the MOA collection as a case study, visitors alone must make the pertinent links between and across some 267 monograph volumes and 100,000 journal articles with nineteenth-century imprints as well as within the pages of each digitized monograph or periodical. The original MOA site was open to the public through the public domain as set forth in Cornell University Digital Library terms, immediately solving the issue of basic accessibility. No invitations, library subscriptions, specific software, or academic affiliations were necessary to access or use the MOA site or to download and use the digitized primary source material for personal and/or professional projects.

When considering the MOA collection, there is the question of the site's age. Although small changes to Cornell's MOA site were made from its inception in 1995 through 2016, the project is an example of an early digital humanities project.[19] Some may question why MOA is a relevant case study in 2021, especially given the recent shift of MOA holdings to HathiTrust. The answer to this question lies within the content and accessibility of the material, not in the date of creation. When applying the frameworks of book history and Museum Studies to digital humanities projects/collections as tools of critical analysis, the age of a project or collection is a relevant factor but not the *only* factor to consider. The MOA site is easily accessible online, is still used by scholars, and does represent an important collection of primary source documentation, including extensive periodical and monograph holdings, the age of the collection will be a secondary consideration within this chapter.

Given the MOA collection's age, it is essential to consider the technology upon which it originally relied. OCR technology was used extensively to scan its typeset texts allowing for full text searchability, which is problematic given that in certain instances historically, "the OCR was sometimes unreadable by the scanners and computers, starting with the obvious problems of older typefaces that the software could not recognize, most obviously the so-called long 's,' widely used before the late eighteenth century, that many modern scanners rendered as an 'f,' and ligatures that connected one letter to another."[20] Due to the reliance on OCR, users experienced the books and periodicals on the original MOA site through the basic functions of "search and browse." The user must depend upon personal meaning-making to link across texts and within texts, particularly with regard to search functionality. For instance, there were four options for searching the original site, which included, Basic, Boolean, Proximity, and Bibliographic. Although it may seem obvious, the Boolean search option, utilizing "and, or, not" shows associations between sets, a direct reflection of the user's choices, rather than the creator/builder's intent. Moreover, "and, or, not" allows the user to include and exclude (and, not) through search results or to choose one object *or* another. However, the searchability of the texts, even with OCR, is predicated on metadata and library cataloging systems, each of which is a form of curation often unrecognized by users.[21] In an effort to make visible the metadata structures that often limit search functionality, HathiTrust allows users to download metadata from search results, a distinct change for users working with the MOA collection. Although users have greater access to metadata, search options within the HathiTrust repository of the MOA collection have been further limited to the basic fields of title, author, subject, publisher, series title, ISBN, and full text. Gone are the options to search by Basic, Boolean, Proximity, and Bibliographic. Furthermore, the ability to search specifically within one periodical, an easy choice within the original MOA site, has vanished. Now, a basic search for *The Century Illustrated Monthly Magazine* (hereafter *The Century*), for example, produces nearly 1,000 results, the top twenty-five of which are issues of *Harper's New Monthly Magazine*. The search results are, no doubt, confusing for users attempting to find specific issues of *The Century* in a timely manner.[22]

The original MOA site tracked search history and offered the option of a "Bookbag," which would store links to pages and allow users to email, download, or link contents directly from the bag, akin to a simple version of an e-commerce cart, minus the product reviews and links to other sellers. Similarly, the new MOA site via HathiTrust allows users to create a collection with the option of logging into the site through a partner institution, or as a guest, to gain greater access to collections material, including advanced downloading and sharing options. However, if a user does not log into the HathiTrust site, the only options for sharing MOA materials are through social media links or a basic download of pages into a PDF file. The addition of tagging options, a comment box, or an opportunity to link with other users concurrently utilizing the HathiTrust site would greatly alter the user experience related to the MOA collection, while also increasing the opportunities for engagement across and between both texts and images. MOA's users continue to work within a structure that has limitations, rather than within a community-making framework that allows for different modes of participation. As Domenico Fiormonte explains with regard to the intersection of object and visitor in "Towards a Cultural Critique of the Digital Humanities": "One of the core assumptions of my own approach to digital humanities is that any human-born knowledge (including computer science) is subject to the cultural law of the artifact. This law affirms that both material and cognitive artifacts produced by humans are subject to the influence of its environment, culture, and the social habits of the individual and groups that devise and make use of them. The artifact influences and at the same time is influenced by its context; in other words, technology is always a part of culture, not a cause or an effect of it."[23] In taking Fiormonte's argument one step further, the cultural law of the artifact can be slightly adjusted in terminology from "artifact" to "object." When this word change is made, the link between Museum Studies and the MOA collection becomes clear. The sentence then reads: "The [object] influences and at the same time is influenced by its context; in other words, technology is always a part of culture, not a cause or an effect of it." When an object's context is altered, important cultural connections and a visitor's/user's understanding of the past are also affected.

Although the MOA collection, in its simplicity, is easy for users to browse through or utilize for academic work, its largest problem is that it has removed the primary sources from their original method and context of viewing. Instead of allowing visitors/users to view the books or periodicals in dual-page format, the original MOA site isolated each page. Viewing each page of a periodical individually separates text and image. No amount of collaborative transcription, curating, or building by users can remedy this problem. When the MOA holdings were transferred to HathiTrust, the page-viewing options were modified. Now a visitor/user has the option to view single, double, or many pages at once. Yet, these options are titled by their method of use, including scroll (single page), flip (double page), thumbnail (many pages), page by page (no connection between pages), and plain text (complete lack of original formatting), which is potentially confusing for users.[24] Furthermore, black-and-white digitization, an original MOA site feature that remains part of the HathiTrust collection, does little for the visual user, who is not afforded the opportunity to view the cream or brown pages of a periodical nor the book covers of the 267 monographs. This omission greatly alters the context of the object and the visitor/user experience.

The MOA collection is not alone in its lack of color digitization or side-by-side page viewing. A simple search for *The Century* between its first issue in 1881 and the turn of the twentieth century in the full, non-MOA, holdings of HathiTrust includes volumes of the periodical held by eight university libraries in digitized form, including Harvard University, the University of Michigan, Indiana University, the University of California, The Ohio State University, Michigan State University, Northwestern University, and the University of Minnesota. Of these holdings, however, there are *no* options to view a pre-1900 issue both in color (or grayscale) and as an open magazine, with two pages side by side. There are zero opportunities to view the magazine as readers would have experienced the text in its original printed form. When removing objects from this original context, whether through digitization and/or lack of access to digitized pages that replicate typical ways of reading during a historic period, there is inherently a restricted user experience, which can range from the lack of ability to flip quickly through pages to a lack of "annotations and marginalia."[25] Miguel Escobar Varela noted that there is a paradox between the access afforded users through digitization of primary sources and nineteenth-century newspapers in particular, and "the very experience of casually browsing through the pages of an essentially disposable publication [that] has become increasingly remote and difficult to reconstruct.[26] Varela's argument regarding nineteenth-century newspapers can easily be extended to nineteenth-century magazines. The casual browsing of a magazine's pages including images is lost in the digitized single-page format. The spatial juxtapositions of text and image are nonexistent. Meaning-making is altered by the removal of physical and historical context.

Varela's argument becomes particularly clear when using digital collections and projects that do offer the user the option to view periodicals in dual-page format, to flip through a magazine in color, and to connect different issues of a single title at the same time. The Internet Archive, which has built a digital library freely available to the general public with internet access, has multiple options for viewing copies of *The Century* in this context. Users can flip from the front cover to the middle of the magazine, view marginalia, and easily recognize differences in the discoloration of pages without lengthy load times or paywalls. Moreover, much like an e-commerce site, the Internet Archive provides suggestions for similar items that a visitor might be interested in viewing based upon metadata. Each digitized periodical in the similar items series clearly lists the document's number of views, stars (similar to "likes"), and comments. Reliant on libraries around the world to contribute digitized versions of their holdings to the Internet Archive, the site provides the user with an opportunity to construct meaning within and across objects.

As a final note on the MOA collection, the object's context is further limited by the scope of its original digitization efforts as the collection cut off at 1901 even though many of the periodicals continued to be produced decades into the twentieth century. For example, *The Century* did not cease to exist until 1930, and *Harper's New Monthly Magazine* is still in print as *Harper's Magazine*. In MOA's new HathiTrust location, the pre-1901 holdings are supplemented with additional volumes. *The Century* holdings include fifteen volumes dating between 1907 and 1922, an incomplete record. There is no indication to the user that the periodical had an uninterrupted print run between 1881 and 1930.[27] Therefore, the user must piece together digitized volumes from different sources or access the tangible objects in special/library collections. Much like a visitor to a *Wunderkammer* who devises a personal narrative based on a display of objects, meaning and purpose related to text and image in the digital realm is made personal by the user. Additionally, the user is limited in the creation of a personal narrative across objects. Tagging, or another kind of collaborative note-taking, could reveal thematic connections across objects, but these digital tools are currently not offered to users of the MOA collection within HathiTrust.

The case study of MOA points to the limitations of some digital humanities collections and projects. Although MOA provides accessible, digitized issues of monographs and serial volumes, it does little to aid the user in understanding the creator's/curator's choices, including black-and-white digitization or the original cut-off point of 1901. Of course, some of these restrictions are inherent to early digital humanities collections and projects, but the experience of the user is still largely lacking in scholarship and project design, even in recent years.

Recent Digital Solutions

However accessible the MOA collection is to users across the globe, it is *not* an ever-evolving or collaborative endeavor such as the University of Iowa Libraries' DIY History project, in which users can transcribe, translate, and discuss primary source documents by registering on the publicly accessible site.[28] DIY History boasts that 104,451 pages have been transcribed through crowdsourcing, which is defined as "engaging volunteers to contribute effort toward large-scale goals," and that the project ultimately makes specific primary source information available to researchers and general users.[29] The project is geared toward handwritten primary source documentation and thus cannot be scanned with OCR technology. The human eye and mind are needed to account for variations in script, including cursive text, and to tag photographs that cannot be read via OCR. The DIY History project also acknowledges a second, visitor-oriented, outcome on its homepage, the importance of an expanding audience-base, explaining that "With DIY History, we're also hoping to attract new users interested in more active engagement with the collections."[30] There is, additionally, a note that "Anyone is welcome to contribute to the site—no special expertise is required."[31] The University of Iowa Libraries is therefore employing a multimodal approach to the user. First, the visitor/user can browse the documents, read the transcriptions, and passively engage with the library online. Second, the visitor/user can turn into an active user by registering on the site and transcribing documents, becoming what Museum Studies scholars describe as a participatory visitor/ideal visitor.[32] Third, the DIY History project further encourages participation and community-building by including a "Digital Collection" link under "More Information" on each digital document page that has been transcribed or is available for transcription. Users can become discussants and join a community of interested visitors, scholars, and hobbyists simply by posting a tag or comment on the digital collection page. The University of Iowa Libraries has leveraged its role as a curator of digital experience related to primary source documents to create a successful structure, one in which users can make meaning across texts and between objects. The simple step of engaging visitors through participatory opportunities recognizes the multifaceted potential of a user.

Like DIY History, three Cultural Analytics Lab (CAL) works—Anna Karenina.viz (2009), *Science* and *Popular Science* (2010), and On Broadway (2014–2015)—reflect many of the same issues present in the MOA collection case study regarding accessibility and flexibility of visitor/user meaning-making. The CAL was developed in 2007 and now operates out of the California Institute for Telecommunication and The Graduate Center, City University of New York.[33] The lab is "using data science to analyze cultural trends" and poses a number of research questions on its "About" page including the question "How to best democratize computer vision and machine learning so they can be used by researchers and students without technical backgrounds"?[34] By posing this question clearly on its website, the CAL is effectively calling for a greater understanding of and emphasis on digital accessibility for the user. However, this question does not address how the user creates meaning or actually uses—for research, teaching, or personal enrichment—the digital project. What CAL's various projects do provide the visitor/user are a number of ways of visualizing data differently than the MOA collection in its original format or through its new host, HathiTrust. The goal of MOA was to digitize periodicals and monographs in such a way that users could read individual pages of printed material. Oppositely, CAL's projects use printed material, images, and objects in new ways. For instance, finding visual patterns within social media images or within the cover pages of magazines over a specified number of decades are just two examples of the ways in which CAL analyzes and visualizes thematic collections. The projects that CAL has created over the last decade have shifted decidedly from data visualization of a singular or small number of objects to interactive media and large-scale image analysis. Moving from the use of Flickr to newly designed websites and mobile apps, CAL projects provide a counterpoint to MOA while also suggesting that a Museum Studies framework is applicable but not always successful in the twenty-first century.

Two early CAL projects, Anna Karenina.viz and *Science* and *Popular Science*, provide the user an opportunity to make connections across pages of original printed material within a flexible structure but offer little insight into how a user would physically use, educationally implement, or conduct research with the project. Anna Karenina.viz is a visualization of the novel *Anna Karenina* by Leo Tolstoy.[35] Typical for the time, the novel was read by way of installments between 1873 and 1877 in the periodical *The Russian Messenger*. In the CAL visualization, authored by Lev Manovich, a program was designed that "reads the text from a file and renders it in a series of columns running from top to bottom and from left to right as a single image; it also checks whether text lines contain particular words (this version checks for the word 'Anna') and highlights the found matches."[36] The extensive lines of text, rendered unreadable in the CAL project, are visually interesting and provide a unique view of the "Anna" repetition. This allows a user to visually see patterns throughout the entire publication in just one image, yet the project does not extend beyond the visual patterns. There are no other versions of *Anna Karenina* for users to examine and no other visualizations for comparison, hence no opportunities to make meaning across or between texts. Besides a quick visual tour of the text-turned-image, it is unclear how a visitor/user would utilize this project. As Julia Flanders has argued with regard to the differences between print and digital, there is a "discomfort" with some digital models that seem to replace the "real thing."[37] Flanders expands upon this notion by explaining that "as our tools for manipulating digital models improve, the model stops marking loss and takes on a clearer role as a strategic representation, one which deliberately omits and exaggerates and distorts the scale so that we can work with the parts that matter to us."[38] Applying Flanders's argument to the Anna Karenina.viz project, there is some discomfort in the visualization of the entire novel as a single image complete with specific "Anna" underlines, a deliberate curatorial choice by Manovich, the author-curator of the digital project. However, what the project offers, beyond any discomfort, is an opportunity to image or digitally re-create physical markings and manipulation of the text. This is an example of the "strategic representation" of exaggerating and distorting scale that Flanders contends is necessary for users to "work with the parts that matter to us."

Small shifts in the consideration of the visitor can be found in *Science* and *Popular Science*, which makes visible the changing image/color strategies of those specific magazines between 1872 and 2007.[39] The visualizations, one for each magazine, reveal the disappearance of illustrations over time in favor of photographs, a typical change for periodicals of the era given technical advancements, cultural taste, and altered budgets. In fact, CAL describes the project as being as much about the invisible as the visible, although this shift in periodical structure from the late 1800s to the 2000s is not unique to science-oriented magazines.[40] Unlike Anna Karenina.viz, *Science* and *Popular Science* provides the user an opportunity to compare across objects and to make meaning based upon prior knowledge, interests, and images. In large part this is because the *Science* and *Popular Science* visualizations can be easily compared against one another, and details of each visualization are accessible online. The authors of the CAL project, William Huber, Tara Zepel, and Lev Manovich made curatorial choices regarding which specific magazine issues were included in the project: one issue for every five years of *Popular Science* between 1887 and 2007, and the third page of every issue of *Science* between 1880 and 1906. Much like metadata that creates curatorial structures within the MOA collection and is subsequently presented as a framework within which users must operate, the curatorial structures of the CAL project provide a set of limitations to the user's making of meaning. The use of *Science* and *Popular Science* as a historical tool, one that references changes in periodical structure, layout, and emphasis, has value for some researchers but is lacking a clear pathway to engagement, evidenced by the press the project received, which essentially deems the visualizations interesting without additional analysis or review.[41]

Within the last five years, there has been a distinct change in the size and scope of CAL's projects and an increased emphasis on user engagement. On Broadway, which became an interactive museum exhibition in multiple locations in Europe, Asia, and the US, encourages multimodal visitor experiences.[42] Described as an "interactive installation" that "represents life in the twenty-first-century city through a compilation of images and data collected along the 13 miles of Broadway that span Manhattan," On Broadway utilizes a wide array of data to image urban life.[43] The project was created collaboratively by artists Daniel Goddemeyer, Moritz Stefaner, Dominikus Baur, and Lev Manovich, in partnership with contributors Mehrdad Yazdani and Jay Chow of the Software Studies Initiative, along with Brynn Shepherd, Leah Meisterlin, Agustin Indaco, Michelle Morales, Emanuel Moss, and Alise Tifentale.[44] Unlike Anna Karenina.viz and *Science* and *Popular Science*, which relied on single publications or a range of issues from specific periodicals, images and data for On Broadway were sourced from Instagram, Twitter, Foursquare, Google Street View, the NYC Taxi and Limousine Commission, and the American Community Survey as part of the US Census Bureau's data.[45]

The shift from single perspective to multiperspective content and curation is a structure that museums have been slowly implementing in the past two decades. A move away from a single authoritative voice and experience, which often follows a Eurocentric history in museum spaces, has increased opportunities for collaboration, diversified voices and experiences, and given visitors a greater number of chances to view themselves and their interests within exhibitions.[46] Much like a multivoice museum exhibition, On Broadway presents the viewer with "a new visual metaphor for thinking about the city," one that has layers of data.[47] The layers of data include: Landmarks & Anecdotes, Google Street View Facades, Facade Colors, Taxi Statistics, Google Street View: Sky View, Social Media Statistics, Median Income, Colors in Instagram Photos, Instagram Photos, and Neighborhoods.

There are a number of images available on the project's website, many of which were taken at various museum and gallery exhibitions that featured On Broadway, exemplifying how touchscreens allowed visitors to interact with the On Broadway app. Without the app, however, users do not have the ability to engage with the layers of data, which limits the accessibility of the collection. If one has the ability to open the app, which does require both a large display and high speed, users are provided the flexibility to visually link disparate objects. Users must work within the established/curated framework, similar to the metadata of the MOA collection, but the visual and spatial juxtapositions yield near endless possibilities for meaning-making. In addition, the creation of community through the project, both in terms of depicting a specific physical place and analyzing user-generated content, is a distinct difference between early digital humanities collections and projects, such as MOA and Anna Karenina. viz, and recent/ongoing projects including DIY History.

This brief exploration of three Cultural Analytics Lab projects is by no means exhaustive; instead, this overview suggests that the role of the user within digital humanities collections and projects that offer a link to book history is as essential in the 2020s as it was in the 1990s. Although technology has changed, the one constant across all the digital humanities projects and collections discussed throughout this study is the visitor/user and the visitor's/user's ability to choose how to engage.

Conclusion

Often, new digital works are lauded for their creative elements, the ingenuity of authors, and interesting visual components. However, if users cannot access or make meaning of a collection such as MOA or a project such as Anna

Karenina.viz, the value of these digital humanities efforts is unclear. Creators of digital humanities projects and collections must consider not only computer scientists or tech-savvy academics as users but also the typical or general user during the creation and implementation of a digital humanities project and/or collection. To put it simply, visitor/user experiences drive the implementation, utilization, and success of digital humanities projects and collections.

When book history/digital humanities projects are viewed through the lens of Museum Studies, there is an opportunity to engage with meaning-making from the perspective of a visitor. Yet, as mentioned throughout this chapter, the role of the user as akin to the museum visitor has been underresearched, if not undervalued, within scholarship related directly to digital humanities projects and collections. Furthermore, the user remains the one constant across the MOA collection, DIY History, and CAL examples no matter the historical context in which the digital collection or project was conceptualized or the context of the research questions and goals that drove the creation of the collection or project. As Daniel Price, Rex Koontz, and Lauren Lovings have argued with regard to digital exhibitions, "The basic assumption that installations matter implies that the discursive power of the objects in relation to one another can and often does outstrip the limits and categories of the original criteria that brought the corpus together."[48] These authors continue by explaining how users experience digital projects in a relational, back-and-forth, human-to-object, process of engagement.[49] Much like the constructivist model, users must connect new ideas and objects with knowledge and meaning already established by other experiences to make both sense and use of digital projects and collections. Once a project or collection is complete and available online, the creation of meaning shifts from author/curator to user. By engaging with Museum Studies when developing or writing about digital humanities collections or projects, builders and researchers can better address issues of access and usability.

Cornell University Library's MOA collection demonstrates the challenges related to visual/spatial juxtapositions in early digital humanities collections and projects. Although problematic in many of its offerings, MOA does, alternatively, provide accessibility and an opportunity for continued research as a case study in early digital collections of print culture. When compared to the University of Iowa Libraries' DIY History site and CAL projects, MOA, even within its current HathiTrust location, provides a less flexible framework and fewer options to make meaning across or within objects. Yet, the field of Museum Studies offers an important lens for analysis with regard to the implementation of image-based projects that both succeed and fail to consider visitors/users, even within the last decade. In sum, the case studies of MOA, DIY

History, and CAL provide other ways of thinking about the intersection of Museum (visitor) Studies, book history, and the digital humanities. The user plays the most powerful role in making digital humanities collections and projects both meaningful and relevant.

Notes

1. Patrik Svensson, "Beyond the Big Tent," in *Debates in the Digital Humanities*, ed. Matthew K. Gold (Minneapolis: University of Minnesota Press, 2012), 41.

2. See Cornell University Library's Making of America Collection (MOA), "About the Project," accessible from http://ebooks.library.cornell.edu/m/moa/about.html.

3. For a brief overview of recent digital humanities scholarship, including a crash course in DH definitions, see Steven E. Jones, *The Emergence of the Digital Humanities* (New York: Routledge, 2014); Melissa Terras, Julianne Nyhan, and Edward Vanhoutte, *Defining Digital Humanities: A Reader* (Burlington, VT: Ashgate, 2013); Gold, ed., *Debates in the Digital Humanities* (2012).

4. MOA, http://collections.library.cornell.edu/moa_new/index.html. The MOA collection moved to HathiTrust in March 2018.

5. DIY History is a crowdsourced transcription project hosted at the University of Iowa Libraries. See https://diyhistory.lib.uiowa.edu/.

6. See Stephen Ramsay, "On Building," in Terras, Nyhan, and Vanhoutte, *Defining Digital Humanities*, 243–45. Originally published on January 11, 2011, at http://stephenramsay.us/text/2011/01/11/on-building.html.

7. Andrew McClellan, *The Art Museum: From Boullée to Bilbao* (Berkeley: University of California Press, 2008), 116.

8. Philipp Blom, *To Have and to Hold: An Intimate History of Collectors and Collecting* (New York: Overlook Press, 2002), 17; McClellan, *Art Museum*, 116.

9. Dagmar Motycka Weston, "'Worlds in Miniature': Some Reflections on Scale and the Microcosmic Meaning of Cabinets of Curiosities," *Arq: Architectural Research Quarterly* 13, no. 1 (2009): 41.

10. Meredith L. McGill, "Literary History, Book History, and Media Studies," in *Turn of Events: Nineteenth-Century American Literary Studies in Motion*, ed. Hester Blum (Philadelphia: University of Pennsylvania Press, 2016), 35.

11. Sue Shellenbarger, "Why You Can't Concentrate at Work," *Wall Street Journal*, May 9, 2017. Shellenbarger defines "visual noise" as "the activity or movement around the edges . . . [of one's] field of vision."

12. John H. Falk and Lynn D. Dierking, *The Museum Experience Revisited* (Walnut Creek, CA: Left Coast Press, 2013), 39, 78. See also John H. Falk and Lynn D. Dierking, *Learning from Museums: Visitor Experiences and the Making of Meaning* (New York: Rowman & Littlefield, 2000); John H. Falk, *In Principle, in Practice: Museums as Learning Institutions* (New York: Altamira Press, 2007); Elizabeth Wood, *The Objects of Experience: Transforming*

Visitor-Object Encounters in Museums (New York: Routledge, 2013); Peter Samis and Mimi Michaelson, *Creating the Visitor-Centered Museum* (New York: Routledge, 2016); Doug Woodham, *Art Collecting Today: Market Insights for Everyone Passionate About Art* (New York: Allworth Press, 2017).

13. See Steven E. Jones, *The Emergence of the Digital Humanities* (New York: Routledge, 2014), in which Jones discusses the idea of a collaborative curator (this term was coined by Martin Mueller). See also McClellan, *Art Museum*, 116. Falk and Dierking, in *Museum Experience Revisited*, extensively examine the roles visitors play in museums and how museum structures often limit or define the visitor's experience in both successful and unsuccessful ways.

14. Johanna Drucker, "Humanistic Theory and Digital Scholarship," in Gold, *Debates in the Digital Humanities* (2012), 87.

15. Charlie Edwards, "The Digital Humanities and Its Users," in Gold, *Debates in the Digital Humanities* (2012), 216. Edwards explains, "Oya Rieger's newer research supports Mueller's conclusions. . . . She found, moreover, that scholarly practices of the participants were unaltered, aside from the adoption of generic tools such as search engines—technology as conduit, to use Bradley's term. Meanwhile, many tools and techniques that are being associated with sophisticated digital practices, such as data mining or visualization, remain accessible and relevant to only a handful of scholars." For additional discussion of the phrase "technology as conduit," see John Bradley, "What You (Fore)see Is What You Get: Thinking About Usage Paradigms for Computer Assisted Text Analysis," *TEXT Technology* 14, no. 2 (2005): 1–19, http://texttechnology.mcmaster.ca/pdf/vol14_2/bradley14-2.pdf.

16. Sheila A. Brennan, "Public, First," in Gold, *Debates in the Digital Humanities* (2012), 384.

17. Edwards, "Digital Humanities and Its Users," 214.

18. Searching for references to the "user," "user design," "UX," or "UXD" in academic scholarship related directly to digital humanities collections and projects produces varied and limited results. For instance, in Terras, Nyhan, and Vanhoutte, *Defining Digital Humanities*, there are three instances when the word "user" appears in the entire edited volume and zero results for "user design," "UX," and "UXD"; in Gold, *Debates in the Digital Humanities* (2012), Sheila A. Brennan's brief chapter "Public, First" addresses ways in which digital humanities project creators can benefit from engaging with users, including such examples as utilizing light mobile frameworks and conventional naming schemas (387). Other chapters in the same edited volume reference the term "user" but engage only minimally in a discussion of meaning-making by users; see Brian Greenspan, "Are Digital Humanists Utopian?" and Andrew Stauffer, "Sweethearts: On Digitization and the Future of the Print Record" as two examples from the volume. Furthermore, a simple search for "user design" in the peer reviewed, open access journal *Digital Humanities Quarterly* produces just one result, the article "Building Better Digital Humanities Tools: Toward Broader Audiences and User-Centered Designs" by Fred Gibbs and Trevor Owens from 2012, while a simple search of "UX" returns just four results and "UXD" in the same journal produces zero results for articles published between 2007

and 2018. However, if the search is broadened to "user," there are 263 hits within the same publication timeframe of 2007 to 2018, yet these results reveal only the use of the term and not an in-depth engagement with issues related to the use of digital humanities projects and/or collections or with frameworks for understanding users. Similarly, a simple search of the now defunct *Journal of Digital Humanities* provides varied results depending on search term, including a fairly large array of published research posters, and the *International Journal of Humanities and Arts Computing* produces 222 hits for "user" but just one result for "user design," and no results for "UX" or "UXD" in articles published between 1994 and 2018. See *Digital Humanities Quarterly* (http://digitalhumanities.org/dhq/), *Journal of Digital Humanities* (http://journalofdigitalhumanities.org/), and *International Journal of Humanities and Arts Computing* (https://www.euppublishing.com/loi/ijhac) for articles and search results. In summary, these examples reveal that a focus on user design and a user's meaning-making in scholarly publications related directly to the digital humanities is tenuous at best.

 19. See Cornell's MOA holdings on the HathiTrust site at https://babel.hathitrust.org/cgi/mb?c=1930843488;a=listis.

 20. Jones, *Emergence of the Digital Humanities*, 90.

 21. The idea of metadata as curatorial process was suggested to me by attendees of the conference "BH and DH: Book History and Digital Humanities" at the Center for the History of Print and Digital Culture, University of Wisconsin–Madison, September 22–23, 2017. Conference information is available from http://www.wiscprintdigital.org/bh-and-dh-conference/.

 22. See Cornell's MOA holdings on the HathiTrust site at https://babel.hathitrust.org/cgi/mb?c=1930843488;a=listis, including social media sharing tabs on the left-side toolbar and the basic search bar at the center. There are no clear or easily accessible links back to Cornell University Library or to the original MOA site.

 23. Domenico Fiormonte, "Towards a Cultural Critique of the Digital Humanities," *Historical Social Research* 37, no. 3 (2012): 60.

 24. See the MOA holdings on the HathiTrust Digital Library site at https://babel.hathitrust.org/cgi/pt?id=coo.31924079630350;view=2up;seq=16. Viewing options are located on a right-hand side toolbar.

 25. Miguel Escobar Varela, "The Archive as Repertoire: Transience and Sustainability in Digital Archives," *Digital Humanities Quarterly* 10, no. 4 (2016): 5.

 26. Varela, "Archive as Repertoire," 5. See also Shafquat Towheed, "Reading in the Digital Archive," *Journal of Victorian Culture* 1, no. 15 (2010): 142.

 27. See *The Century Illustrated Monthly Magazine*, listed as "The Century; a popular quarterly" at https://catalog.hathitrust.org/Record/012508493.

 28. See the University of Iowa Libraries DIY History site at http://diyhistory.lib.uiowa.edu/.

 29. DIY History, http://diyhistory.lib.uiowa.edu/. As of April 19, 2021, the total number of transcribed pages listed on the University of Iowa Libraries DIY History site was 104,451.

 30. DIY History, http://diyhistory.lib.uiowa.edu/.

31. DIY History, http://diyhistory.lib.uiowa.edu/.

32. See Margaret Lindauer, "The Critical Museum Visitor," in *New Museum Theory and Practice: An Introduction*, ed. Janet Marstine (Hoboken, NJ: Blackwell, 2008), 203–25, in which she discusses the definition of an ideal (critical) visitor to museums, including the types of questions critical visitors ask, what they look for in a museum space, and how they operate within museum structures. See also Nina Simon, *The Participatory Museum* (Santa Cruz: Museum 2.0, 2010), as well as Falk and Dierking, *Museum Experience Revisited*, in which the various roles that visitors assume within museums are discussed, including how visitor roles can change within a singular visit or with each new visit to a museum.

33. See the CAL website, including the "About" tab at http://lab.culturalanalytics.info/p/about.html.

34. Cultural Analytics Lab, http://lab.culturalanalytics.info/.

35. See Lev Manovich, Anna Karenina.viz (2009), available from https://www.flickr.com/photos/culturevis/5108274292/in/photostream/.

36. Lev Manovich, Anna Karenina.viz, https://www.flickr.com/photos/culturevis/5108274292/in/photostream/.

37. Julia Flanders, "The Productive Unease of 21st-Century Digital Scholarship," in Terras, Nyhan, and Vanhoutte, *Defining Digital Humanities*, 215.

38. Flanders, "The Productive Unease," 215.

39. See William Huber, Tara Zepel, and Lev Manovich, *Science* and *Popular Science* (2010), available from http://lab.culturalanalytics.info/2010/11/science-and-popular-science-magazines_23.html.

40. Huber, Zepel, and Manovich, *Science* and *Popular Science*.

41. Huber, Zepel, and Manovich, *Science* and *Popular Science*.

42. Daniel Goddemeyer, Moritz Stefaner, Dominikus Baur, Lev Manovich, Mehrdad Yazdani, Jay Chow, Brynn Shepherd, Leah Meisterlin, Agustin Indaco, Michelle Morales, Emanuel Moss, and Alise Tifentale, On Broadway (2014–2015), available from http://on-broadway.nyc/.

43. Goddemeyer et al., On Broadway.

44. Goddemeyer et al., On Broadway.

45. Goddemeyer et al., On Broadway.

46. See Mike Muraski, "Object Stories: Rejecting the Single Story in Museums," *Art Museum Teaching: A Forum for Reflecting on Practice*, December 26, 2012, available from https://artmuseumteaching.com/2012/12/26/object-stories-rejecting-the-single-story-in-museums/. See also Bryony Onciul, *Museums, Heritage and Indigenous Voices: Decolonizing Engagement* (New York: Routledge, 2015).

47. Goddemeyer et al., On Broadway.

48. Daniel Price, Rex Koontz, and Lauren Lovings, "Curating Digital Spaces, Making Visual Arguments: A Case Study in New Media Presentations of Ancient Objects," *Digital Humanities Quarterly* 7, no. 2 (2013): 2.

49. Price, Koontz, and Lovings, "Curating Digital Spaces, Making Visual Arguments," 6.

Access

Section II

Material and Digital Traces in Patterns of Nature

Early Modern Botany Books and Seventeenth-Century Needlework

Mary Learner

The digitization of special collections materials has made early modern books accessible to researchers and the public, but it also incites questions about when and how to be attentive to the surfaces of books mediated by screens. The textures of pages can reveal information about printers and various hands that turned a book's leaves, evidence that is often more legible in rare book rooms than are their virtual counterparts. Digital reproductions of individual copies and copy-specific metadata can radically alter our understanding of a diverse early modern audience, providing a more capacious view of the participants creating and transmitting knowledge. By allowing the fields of digital humanities and book history to inform each other, digitized copies help us reinterpret bibliographic narratives; moreover, online archives afford spaces that can represent these revised histories. With digital reproductions, scholars have the opportunity to see the similarities between different surfaces, drawing connections between books that have been falsely and anachronistically categorized as distinct by modern sensibilities.

Increasingly, scholars have considered surfaces by studying the information books provide besides content. As a critical approach, "surface reading" departs from symptomatic reading (which requires critics to delve into the deeper meanings of a text, often facilitated by psychoanalytic or Marxist theory) and opens avenues for considering the materiality of pages and, by extension, offers a suggestive framework for studying digital mediations of print and manuscript.[1] Stephen Best and Sharon Marcus introduce the idea of reading the "[s]urface as materiality," where similarities between texts arise from their shared physical qualities.[2] Their suggestion that book history and surface reading rely on a common methodology is indebted to the scholarship of Margreta de Grazia and Peter Stallybrass, who demonstrate what material-textual surfaces can unveil.[3] By literalizing the metaphor of "surface" in surface reading, I propose that trends between punctures, indents, and sketches in different copies are evidence that books have been artificially siloed according to modern disciplines. Attention to surfaces can indeed challenge separations between genres, but skating across surface-level characteristics of numerous copies allows hitherto unremarkable or peculiar copy-specific attributes to emerge as part of broader phenomena. Digitization facilitates these unprecedented comparisons, comparisons that amend how we think about available literacies and book use in the period.

The ability to compare idiosyncrasies of copies in digital archives makes finding page-level evidence of book production and readers' interactions more likely, broadening seminal work in book history that addresses the various people and forces involved in the circulation of material texts. Roger Chartier, expanding from D. F. McKenzie's sociology of texts that encompasses a book's production and reception,[4] has shown that there is much to be learned about the history of reading and the rebellious use of print.[5] The many interactions readers had with the printed page, unruly and otherwise, have been explored by William Sherman, who has made evident the readers' marks that lend insights into patterns of book use during the Renaissance.[6] More recently, scholarship by Andrew Stauffer has leaned into the serendipitous: chance encounters with material traces in books and modeled what interpretations can be made with such fragmentary evidence.[7] The contributors to *Interacting with Print* have observed how marks on the page "[make] visible the haptic process of reading, calling us to attend to the historical book as a physical interface, even as it suggests the presence that remains within, or even haunts, the books we have inherited."[8] Such scholarship that explores the varied participants in the sociology of texts—publishers, printers, readers, and users—has furthered our understanding of the life cycles of books and confronted historical assumptions about the circulation of information and the agents involved in that process.[9]

When viewing materials represented in digital resources, however, scholars find new obstacles to discern subtle marks of construction and use. Digital facsimiles made available through online repositories like *Early English Books Online* (*EEBO*) and the *Internet Archive*, or collections of scanned reproductions by holding libraries, such as the Folger Shakespeare Library's *LUNA* and the Bibliothèque nationale de France's *Gallica*, have often undergone transformations that alter the legibility of books' surfaces. For Sarah Werner, whether researchers "[can] move away from reading text to studying the physical characteristics of text [. . .] [that] reveal important information about the content of the text and the cultural and historical creation of the artifact" remains an essential question when it comes to analyzing digitized texts.[10] Taking up this call to rethink the traces visible in books and digital reproductions, and attending to surfaces—physical and digital surfaces, which exhibit patterns between pages, even those separated by time and space—provide scholars with an opportunity to explore connections between disparate texts. Findings based on these correspondences confront distinctions between genre and gender and expectations about discipline and expertise, all dichotomies that begin to break down as information about books and their readers emerge.

The potential payoffs for attention to surfaces and their digital mediations are substantive: shared traces on pages reshape scholarly narratives about early modern culture, enabling a more comprehensive account of print production and reception that highlights the associative thinking and visual echoes that would have been familiar to readers at the time. For example, in the case of seventeenth-century botany, a different version of the history of science emerges from the correlations between herbals, natural histories, and florilegia books based on shared printing conventions and trends among users' marks. The correspondences between genres force a reconsideration of suppositions related to gendered-divided literacies and disciplines, reorienting ways of seeing and ordering to show an affinity shared with embroidery patterns. The contribution of women's work to early modern studies of nature is overshadowed by a masculinized account of early experimental science. Through surface reading at the most literal, by examining the surfaces of pages in rare books rooms and as mediated in digital archives, scholars can rethink the history of botany and its indebtedness to compositions associated with women. By looking to surfaces, the genre of botany books becomes more expansive, taking in consideration florilegia as well as herbals and natural histories. Florilegia emerge as books that made later taxonomies possible, combatting their dismissal as aesthetic novelties rather than scientific illustrations and overcoming their disregard because of their associations with women's work. By thinking through archival materials and digital representations, finding traces of use—and highlighting their significance in the history of printing and of reading—reveals a history always present on the surface but ignored, a history that scholarship can bring to the forefront through comprehensive metadata and transparent digitization practices.

To that end, this essay first analyzes how florilegia, a subgenre of botany books, are typically dismissed as decorative rather than substantive despite similar surface characteristics to herbals and natural histories. I then point to examples of how expectations about florilegia have influenced digitization choices, altering or excising reader's marks that profoundly broaden the scope of participants in botanical study. Finally, based on traces indicative of a way of seeing indebted to women's literacies, particularly embroidery, I turn to well-known historical examples and literary depictions of women sewing nature. These instances are symptomatic of texts that demand new readings in light of this material and digital evidence, exploring a revised history of science facilitated by the mutual elucidations of book history and digital humanities.

Historians of botany have long separated herbals and florilegia, two genres that at first seem intended for different purposes, yet their pages suggest they share more in common than previously credited. Modern research focuses on the scientific nature of the former and the artistic value of the latter. The first seems like a text designed for utility, instructing how to cultivate a kitchen garden and select ingredients for medicinal remedies, whereas the second, which emerged in the seventeenth century, seems designed for aesthetic pleasure only.[11] At least, these are the premises for some scholars,[12] reductive notions based on the alleged expertise of the creators. Brian Ogilvie observes that florilegia were "written neither by nor for scholars," unlike the herbals and botany books designed for more scientific endeavors, and therefore argues that scholars consider the two genres separately.[13] He contends that florilegia were printed commodities aimed toward self-fashioning collectors, while as natural histories developed, writers elected to not include the detailed engravings in favor of rigorous descriptions.[14] However, these genres share typographical features, illustrations, and signs of use, evident on their surfaces, thereby refusing to fall neatly into distinct categories.

This division of herbals from florilegia obscures how flower miscellanies provide insight into the methods early modern people used to visualize and study botany, a time when writers, engravers, and printers were departing from previous approaches used in earlier natural histories. Copper engravings permitted sharp lines for precise contours of flowers, which were made even more lifelike as engravers used environmental samples to create their designs.[15] According to Pamela Smith, the emphasis on eyewitness studies of nature allowed for a "new visual culture" to emerge.[16] The artisans who played a role in this process were engaged in science through their art, and their craft shaped how others viewed and studied nature. The reluctance to include florilegia within this history derives from its ephemeral and feminine associations, resulting in their dismissal as "picture books" containing inaccurate patterns for popular applications. Florilegia illustrations, however, participated in shaping the development of botanical study. Even for Ogilvie, the development of scientific description relied on botanical illustrations, and genres that visualize vegetable life provide essential insights into early observational science.[17] Although Ogilvie stresses that visual examples became increasingly unrelated to scientific inquiry, examining their use is critical to understand methods of seeing that would influence later eighteenth-century collections categorizing specimens. Observations on the textures of nature, such as the patterns of leaf surfaces and insect wings, would become the criteria for classification in the Linnaean system, which consists of taxonomies based on comparing species based on similitude of physical characteristics.[18]

Illustrated botany books, including florilegia and herbals, proliferated in the seventeenth century across the European continent, developing from natural histories published in the sixteenth century; indeed, examples of both challenge any easy separation based on genre. One of the most famous English herbals, John Gerard's *The herball or Generall historie of plantes* (1597), includes woodcuts of the roots, leaves, and bulbs alongside Latinate and vernacular names, place and time of growth, physical descriptions, and classical and contemporary references and uses. Gerard attributes his sources in his letter to the reader, acknowledging Aristotle and Dioscorides as well as sixteenth-century humanists and botanists including Conrad Gessner, Pietro Mattioli, Rembert Dodoens, and Carolus Clusius. As a close observational study of plants, Gerard's herbal describes the nuanced differences between flora and follows generic conventions used by other English herbals, like those by William Turner (*A new herball*, 1551) and John Parkinson (*Paradisi in sole*, 1629; *Theatrum botanicum*, 1640).[19] Their shared conventions drew from Continental precursors with supplemental illustrations of plants common to England. Especially remarkable about the 1633 edition of Gerard's herbal is that his editor, Thomas Johnson, emphasizes the importance of the printed illustrations. The prefatory material stresses that Johnson re-examines Gerard's sources and evaluates the images he believes artists sketched from dried specimens rather than fresh ones.[20] Johnson infers that this edition seeks to remedy some of the earlier visualizations' flaws by appropriately modifying descriptions and, occasionally, images.[21] Although herbals prioritize verisimilitude and accuracy, they are also works of artifice: drawn from nature, they often depict plants as they would never occur, with flowers, buds, shoots, and fruits all existing simultaneously.

Florilegia, or a "gathering of flowers," is a misleading name for the botanical genre that developed alongside these herbals because the term can refer to both figurative and literal floral compilations. In medieval manuscripts and incunabula, florilegia referred to a text that gathers the choicest flowers of rhetoric, collecting ideal excerpts from classical and theological works just as the bee accrues nectar from select flora to make honey.[22] However, the second type of florilegia—books illustrated with varieties of flowers in a literal collection of flora—emerged as a popular pictorial genre in the early seventeenth century.[23] These florilegia share characteristics with herbals. Such books feature paintings or engravings of specimens, often designed from live examples. Sometimes, they also incorporate text about the locations, physical attributes, and medicinal properties of the flowers, again, much like herbals. According to Ilia Veldman, engravers of florilegia imagined an encompassing audience for their books. Veldman notes that Crispijn van de Passe's *Den Blom-hof*, the Dutch version of *Hortus Floridus*, is dedicated to thirty-two people including flower enthusiasts, doctors, apothecaries, botanists, gardeners, and two women "who had displayed an interest in the publication, perhaps in the hope of using Crispijn's flowers as models for embroidery or paintings."[24] Although often characterized in scholarship as extravagances, these books and their illustrations were designed not only for aesthetic but also for practical use.

As a result of their emphasis on aesthetics, then, florilegia books are dismissed from scientific histories; but the distinction between florilegia and herbals was never clearly defined, especially not when studying women's involvement. Printed herbals relied on women's knowledge, as explored by Rebecca Laroche and Wendy Wall,[25] and florilegia books were both used for and shaped by women's embroidery and paintings. Because of their botanical illustrations, natural histories and herbals were also a source of "some inspiration for the embroideress," suggesting women's contributions to depicting and studying nature.[26]

The embroidery of women's work was indeed derivative of botany books; it was also a useful metaphor for scientific descriptions of biological life. Emphasis on textures and textiles in descriptions of nature was a common trope in the early discourse of the new science. Francis Bacon, often recognized as the father of experimental science, describes the use of "*Patternes* and *Samples*" in his utopia, the *New Atlantis* (1627).[27] Bacon's phrasing surprisingly resonates with the domestic image of embroidery and textile work, which is evocative in terms of studying the textures of bodies. The word "[p]atternes" is reminiscent of pictorial pattern books, which feature printed pages designed to be used and copied for artwork or embroidery, and "samples" evokes the process of sampling that results from using pattern books. For early modern people, "sampling"—my term for their copying and adapting of material—was a means of collecting and redeploying media; in embroidery, this can take the form of a sampler or of an embroidered panel containing sewing examples, which can then be altered or reused for future projects.[28] Gendered definitions for patterns and samples did not solidify until the eighteenth and nineteenth centuries, when both terms were more exclusively linked to women's needlework and moral education.[29] The effect of this gendering has meant that the connection between scientific "*Patternes* and *Samples*" with the patterns and samples associated with embroidery has gone unexplored, although the separation originated from modern assumptions.

Bacon's depiction of the scientific community in his utopia, and perhaps the requirement of "*Patternes* and *Samples*" to create new knowledge, informed the foundation of the Royal Society in 1660 and the language used by its members in descriptions of their experimental observations. Participants in the Royal Society published their experiments for *virtuousi*, or gentlemen-scholars, to follow and determine their own results, and thereby continue the growth of scientific knowledge. In other words, they provided patterns for followers to sample. In addition, their observations included textile-related terminology. For example, Robert Boyle and Robert Hooke, early members of the newly founded society, both use the language of the "textures" of bodies, usually within the context of describing microscopic surfaces and the combining of particles.[30] Their experimental patterns drew from a similar visual culture and shared textile metaphors, and form an essential component of these early scientific studies.

As a term to reconsider ways of seeing and perceiving evident in early modern science, then, "sampling" allows figures—particularly women—to come to the fore. Attention to sampling builds on the work of Pamela Smith, Tomomi Kinukawa, and Janice Neri who have clarified the roles of artisans and women in scientific inquiry, especially in the study of visualizations in natural histories.[31] Women artists and embroiderers, amateur and professional alike, contributed to natural histories through their sampling, and the signs of use that remain in individual copies of books show how botanical studies took shape in another media. Scholars overlook evidence of sampling for a few reasons: because now sampling is gendered, and women's roles in early modern science are often downplayed; because sampling is associated with needlework, and therefore usually relegated to the realm of "women's work"; and, finally, because evidence of sampling in pattern books is hard to find or illegible in both material texts and digital reproductions. The traces of sampling in books tell a story, however, about seventeenth-century investigations of the natural world. While the names of readers who sewed from pages are overwhelmingly missing. and the pricks and tracing are impossible to date with certainty, surviving embroideries that reflect the influence of print are highly suggestive of the remnants of female readership. I argue that continuing scholarship on patterns and textiles is a way to reconsider the canonical male archive of the history of science and to imagine the incorporation of women's "counterarchives."[32]

My focus is to investigate the affordances and limitations of digitized reproductions concerning a search for evidence of sampling, apparent in the traces of pinpricks and outlines, to draw attention to the readers' marks that appear or disappear in the process of digitization. One kind of sampling evidence is the constellation of tiny holes left by the process of "pouncing," which consisted of using the point of a needle to prick along the outline of a design and then dusting charcoal or chalk through the holes and onto a piece of cloth in order to transfer the shape of the pattern in preparation for embroidery.[33] Evidence of tracing with a pen on versos, or of coloring illustrations, reflects similarly purposed engagement with visual elements of books related to the study of botany. As Sherman notes, "used books" can convey much information to scholars; seventeenth-century readers were encouraged to "mark" their texts, both by being observant and by engaging with the material page.[34] The prick marks of needles are a form of use that Sherman does not mention, but if needles are effeminized pens, as Susan Frye claims, then their marks merit scholarly notice as well.[35] Frye's exploration of the pen and needle (and needle-as-pen) fruitfully expands the notion of women's work but still marks their employment as feminine. Other studies about women's labor in book production and composition note connections between textile and text, like work by Whitney Trettien and Jeffrey Todd Knight, which explore needlework as a mode of composition beyond a feminized sphere.[36] Building on Heidi Brayman's work, I seek to take women's marks in books seriously, as evidence of their involvement in the study of the natural world.[37] Just as manicules and marginal notes signify an engagement with the text, sampling and tracing represent sustained attentiveness to illustrations on the page.

Since this particular form of use requires pricking the page in the process of creating an embroidery, which leaves the page more delicate and liable to be removed or destroyed, what evidence of tracing remains is suggestive of a larger cultural phenomenon. Scholars such as Margaret Swain, Nancy Graves

Cabot, and J. L. Nevinson have all observed instances of surviving embroidery work that relied on printed engravings as patterns.[38] Additionally, samplers in museum collections reveal trends in content across the needlework of young women. Although many are anonymous, the inclusion of flora and fauna in samplers and panels, often alongside biblical references or scenes, suggests that florilegia books often served as inspiration for embroidery designs.

Crispijn van de Passe the Younger's *Hortus Floridus* (*The Flower Garden*) serves as an ideal case study for the correlations between botany books and florilegia, and the traces of use left behind are suggestive of a broader readership. The engraving on the title page features portraits of two botanists, Rembert Dodoens and Carolus Clusius, who were famous for their illustrated books on medical botany in the sixteenth century.[39] Crispijn van de Passe deliberately evokes professional expertise for his engraved prints through these portraits, much like the citations in contemporaneous herbals, and in the text accompanying *Hortus Floridus*, he gestures to earlier botanists such as Conrad Gesner and Leonhart Fuchs.[40] Tulips are the kind of flower most frequently depicted in the *Hortus Floridus*. Indeed, van de Passe published this text amid the Dutch tulip mania, perhaps in anticipation of growing demand for the flower as a trade and artistic commodity.[41] Crispijn van de Passe the Younger learned his trade from his father, the engraver Crispijn van de Passe the Elder, who was born in Zeeland and worked as a printer in Antwerp, Cologne, and Utrecht during his lifetime. The Younger brought the family business to Amsterdam following his father's death, and he continued engraving books similar to those his father made.[42] Not just Crispijn, but all of van de Passe the Elder's children were trained in the art of engraving, and their family was known for designing many plates, chiefly of English portraits.[43] The Dutch workshop's market extended well beyond Amsterdam, and many of their engravings were intended for an international audience, particularly with an eye toward the English print market. Different states of the *Hortus Floridus* include Latin, German, French, Italian, and English paratexts, and several florilegia, especially those printed in England, copied images from *Hortus Floridus*.[44]

The elaborate production and reception history of *Hortus Floridus* provides unique challenges and opportunities in digitizations due to the variations between individual copies, both in their construction and use. The book is constituted primarily of prints from copper plates and is sometimes accompanied by Latin text. Spencer Savage has explored the variations in surviving copies that arise from changes during the book's production or made by later collectors who "made up" versions.[45] Savage's strictly bibliographical approach provides great insight into the plethora of idiosyncrasies between copies—indeed, he

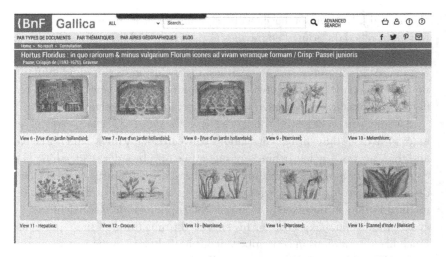

Figure 5. Crispijn de Passe, *Hortus Floridus: in quo rariorum & minus vulgarium Florum icones ad vivam veramque formam* (Arnhem, 1614). (Bibliothèque nationale de France, dèpartement Estampes et photographie, 4-JD-22; screenshot of reproductions in *Gallica*)

refers to the production as a "continuous process" of alterations, to the extent that the term "edition" does not apply to the variations between copies. However, although he investigates the many states of existing texts, he does not explore or interpret the repercussions of these variations, especially not in terms of florilegia as a genre and signs of their use, signs that reveal how readers, particularly women, may have used the pages to see nature differently.[46]

The material traces and subtle marks on the pages of florilegia are often difficult to discern in digital spaces. For instance, the copy reproduced in *Gallica* contains high-resolution images but does not include the versos of each page (see fig. 5). Of course, the resources required for digitization can mean that libraries need to make difficult choices, particularly in the face of financial or time restrictions. The efforts to make materials available to audiences who cannot travel to repositories is admirable work and requires prioritizing what will serve the majority. Nevertheless, giving precedence to content and focusing only on the printed illustrations come at a cost. Although details on the recto side, like the indentation caused by the copper plate or the intricate lines that suggest the contour, are visible with zooming, any marks on the versos, or the back of a printed leaf—such as tracing, either with pen or needle—disappears.

Further, any evidence that this copy may be bound with a Latin text, as a copy in the *Internet Archive* makes clear, is missing (see fig. 6). The presence or absence of Latin text changes the circumstances around reception of the

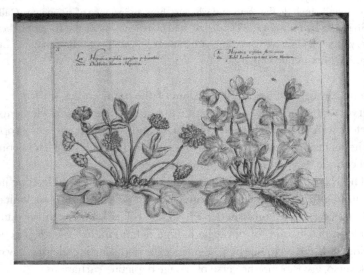

Figure 6. Crispijn van de Passe, *Hortus Floridus in quo rariorum & minus vulgarium florum icones ad vivam veramq[ue] formam* (Arnhem, 1614). (Getty Research Institute, Los Angeles [2898–803], Internet Archive, https://archive.org/details/hortusfloridusinoopass/page/n11/mode/2up)

Figure 7. Crispijn van de Passe, *A garden of flovvers* (Utrecht, 1615). Notice the first two images that do include the recto and verso to show an instance of pouncing. (Call number SB450 P2 F7 1615 Cage; STC 19459, used by permission of the Folger Shakespeare Library under a Creative Commons Attribution-ShareAlike 4.0 International License; screenshot of reproductions in *LUNA*)

content; Savage's bibliographic account of the many copies of *Hortus Floridus* observes that some copies are bound without the Latin textual elements, and therefore were more likely to reach different audiences. Because each copy varies, the inclusion of reproductions of each recto and verso, even beyond the floral content, becomes especially important.

The Folger Shakespeare Library, one of the foremost and leading institutions for digitizing materials, faces similar decisions that show these limitations. For instance, a copy represented in *LUNA*, the Folger Library's image database, includes reproductions of florilegia in high definition; like *Gallica*, it generally provides only the recto (see fig.7). Evidence for pouncing is easier to view on the blank verso, as visible in the verso of a page depicting carnations.

In the case of this *Hortus Floridus* copy, not including the versos means the Latin text is lost, whereas viewed in person or through the online catalog, it becomes clear that this copy includes textual descriptions. It is hard to perceive from these digital reproductions, then, whether women sampled from a book while encountering, if not reading, Latin text derivative of natural histories.[47] From the digitized recto, it is nearly impossible to tell if there has been sampling at all. For example, a high-resolution image shows how the pouncing is invisible on the recto, yet is legible on the verso, here tracing the leaves, moth,

Figure 8. Crispijn van de Passe, *A garden of flovvers* (Arnhem, 1614). (Call number 245-301q, used by permission of the Folger Shakespeare Library under a Creative Commons Attribution-ShareAlike 4.0 International License)

bee, and beetle (see figs. 8 and 9). Digitized reproductions, even ones of such remarkable image quality with high resolution and zooming capability as those on *LUNA*, render the marks of feminized users indiscernible without the digitized versos.

Digital reproductions on *Early English Books Online* (*EEBO*), a resource used by scholars far more often than *LUNA*, also raise vital book-historical questions. The difference between outlines, pouncing, copying, printing error, and imprints from a wet sheet can be even more indistinguishable in the digitized microfilm. Also, scans of the book sometimes blur the page to prioritize the printed content and diminish so-called extraneous marks, such as handwriting. As Jeffrey Todd Knight has argued, "'ghost images'" often go "unseen and uncatalogued," and that *EEBO* particularly reflects biases for high contrast images with a focus on textual content.[48] For example, an *EEBO* copy of *Animalium quadrupedum* (1630), with engravings by Simon van de Passe compiled by John Payne, is a florilegium of flora and fauna, which exemplifies spectral traces in digital reproductions. An associate of the van de Passe family, Payne had copied engravings from Crispijn van de Passe the Elder's *Congnoscite Lilia* and the Younger's *Hortus Floridus* for his earlier florilegia compilation, *FLORA Flowers*

Figure 9. Crispijn van de Passe, *A garden of flowers* (Arnhem, 1614). Verso of the previous image. The leaves, moth, bee, and beetle show evidence of pouncing. (Call number 245–301q, used by permission of the Folger Shakespeare Library under a Creative Commons Attribution-ShareAlike 4.0 International License)

Fruicts Beastes Birds and Flies exactly drawne.[49] In the digital reproduction on *EEBO*, an apparition graces a verso's surface opposite to the bird it imitates; based on its direction and location, this example is not evidence of pouncing, tracing, or the imprint from ink on another copy but is instead a sketch copying the image on the facing recto (see fig. 10). Like pouncing, this evidence of book use reveals attention to the textures of the bird and indicates a more significant trend for how these books were used to study nature.

The reproduction of a 1625 copy of the same book at a different library on *EEBO* does not include the versos, and so such tantalizing hauntings are omitted.[50] However, the versos in a copy at Cambridge University Library reveal a reader's marks that trace the faint lines from the impression (see fig. 11). These include a phantom outline of the same illustration another reader copied in the British Library example, this time facing the opposite direction as a trace on the verso of the page. The tracing pays particular attention to the textures of the tail represented in the pattern:

Learner / Material and Digital Traces in Patterns of Nature 75

Figure 10. Simon van de Passe, *Animalium quadrupedum* (London, 1630). (© British Library Board, General Reference Collection 462.b.18.(1.), as in *EEBO*; image published with permission of ProQuest, further reproduction is prohibited without permission)

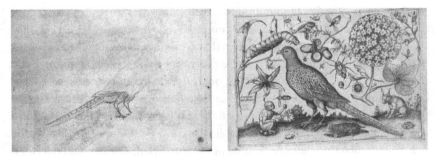

Figure 11. Simon van de Passe, *Animalium quadrupedum* (London, [1628?]). (Cambridge University Library, Syn.4.62.17)

While these instances show the limitations of online reproductions, digital spaces can also provide unique opportunities to bring together far-flung copies for comparison. As a result, nuances between states of the plates become apparent. For example, linking digital facsimiles from copies in various libraries can reveal pulls from different states of a particular plate. The hepatica flowers are later joined by insects, as evidenced by the alterations between copies (figs. 6 and 8). The plates appear to be identical, but on a closer look, the engraver added a moth, bee, and beetle later, balancing the composition and filling extra space. Both are labeled as created in 1614, and because these are prints from the same plates, modifications must have occurred between pulls. Savage believes that the engraver decided to incorporate additional insects to the "Spring" and "Summer" sections but not until after using the pre-modified plate for several impressions.[51] Digitization makes visible this artistic license during the printing process, a choice that crafts a natural scene that otherwise might be missed when viewing a single copy. Such an example is a reminder of the traces of artisans adjusting images, often making additions to cultivate a sense of balance or realism. In this case, the addition to the plate creates a more holistic vision and approaches depictions in women's embroidery samplers that included flowers and insects. Based on the sampling evident in the Folger copy of the same page, the supplemental insects not only imitated preexisting embroidered panels but also inspired women to sew.

This artisan work that included revision was necessary for creating visualizations, from drawing and painting to engraving woodcuts and copper plates for printing, and thus had a direct effect on the reception of prints as scientific.[52] A century before florilegia and copper-engraved flora, Conrad Gessner (1516–1565), the prolific humanist author and editor who specialized in natural history, was working on his botany compilation, *Historia plantarum*, until his death.[53] Sachiko Kusukawa has argued that Gessner's collection of illustrations in preparation for that book reveals his process of botanical observation, as he drew from previously printed herbals, other woodcuts, and samples sent from collaborators.[54] The book was to include detailed woodcuts carved from drawings based on live specimens, along with descriptions based on text by premier classical and modern writers. To compile these images, Gessner worked with a network of correspondents, including physicians, apothecaries, and collectors, who sent pressed plants and pictures created by hired artists.[55] His project of "completing," that is, correcting, earlier printed illustrations required that he paint modifications and add fruits, seeds, and roots by hand. Gessner augmented images so that the plants were drawn "in its color and with all its lines" [*suo colore et lineamentis omnibus*] to appear as they did in nature.[56]

In many ways, Gessner's process—comparing figures between natural histories, sketching specimens, and adding color to printed illustrations to better study flora and fauna—is not so different from the way other, less famous (in fact, overwhelmingly anonymous) users who marked the printed pages of florilegia. Some copies of *Hortus Floridus* include coloring instructions, which were occasionally followed by readers, as in a copy of *A Booke of Flowers Fruicts Beastes Birds and Flies* at the British Library, following the same method of learning as the influential sixteenth-century humanist.[57] The artistic rendering of nature was an essential component of determining the textures of minute details, which extends to popular, feminine readers as well as the humanists who used the same methods.

So, in fact, literacies typically associated with women's embroideries and artistry informed the development of natural histories. A hundred years after Gessner's method for "completing" botanical depictions, the artist and embroiderer Maria Sibylla Merian (1647–1717) devised a procedure for illustrating insects, plants, and their life processes, which relied on literacies associated with women's work. Her detailed botanical illustrations have firmly situated her as one of the leading contributors to pre-Linnaean botany, a role that has been celebrated and recognized by scholarship.[58] A study by Stephanie Schrader, Nancy Turner, and Nancy Yocco on Merian's printing techniques reveals her innovative use of counterproofs, or the process of placing a paper on top of still-wet prints made from copper plates, to create faintly printed undercopies that were then hand-colored. Merian's invented technique resulted in more aesthetically pleasing prints and allowed her to capture more naturalistic detail. She found a way to print from engravings that "closely resembled her original *modelli* of watercolor and gouache."[59] Her experimental technique of printing with copper plates offers a window into her way of seeing the world, which drew from methods indebted to her training in embroidery.

Merian's interest in entomology originated from her childhood sewing, which inspired her to raise and study silkworms, the creatures responsible for her thread.[60] The trades of both her engraver father and painter stepfather related to the creation of florilegia patterns, and their artisan training likely influenced Merian's practice as an artist and embroiderer. Her father, the engraver Matthäus Merian, is credited by Savage as having created the "most notable" later copy of van de Passe's *Hortus Floridus* in his *Florilegium Renovatum* (1641).[61] Because Matthäus Merian died soon after Merian's birth, her stepfather, Jacob Marrel, a still life painter who specialized in flowers, is typically ascribed with informing her development as an artist. Merian's father's engravings, which emulated popular florilegia books from the period, may have also influenced her experimental printing methods later in her life when she designed patterns from nature.[62] Her aesthetic sensibility comes from an interest in the textures of organisms and capturing these textures in artistic renderings. Considering that Carl Linnaeus cites Merian more than one hundred times in his *Species Plantarum* (1753) and *Systema Naturae* (1758), her way of seeing reveals a scientific legacy of viewing that portrays nature as a pattern to be sampled from and rendered through art as a means for botanical study.[63]

Digital spaces provide an opportunity to compare reader interactions with florilegia books: patterns of use emerge from the traces left on the surfaces of surviving copies and are suggestive, if deeply underacknowledged, parts of the history of science. Because of their variability in print, the capacity to compare digitized copies allows the genre to be perceived differently. Seen freshly within this context, pinpricks and tracings offer crucial evidence about women's work and seventeenth-century embroideries that demonstrate the influence of these patterns. Exceptional women like Maria Sibylla Merian appear to be more representative of the extent of women's labor in the early modern period. Tracking the traces of pens and needles, in metadata or spreadsheets produced by researchers, may create unforetold connections, connections that also collapse false distinctions between art and science in early modern culture. Moreover, these connections demand that scholars revisit the surfaces of books and texts to investigate what vestiges of evidence were present all along.

An awareness of these features on the surfaces—the pouncing, pricking, sketching on pages—invites a return to literary examples that contain, hiding in plain sight, on the surface, glimpses of women's pens and needles working directly from nature. Embroidery requires attention to the textures of nature, and pictures of women's work and the study of the natural world permeate some of the most canonical texts. For instance, in the case of Michel de Montaigne's *Essays*, the influential collection first published in 1580 that popularized the essay genre across continental Europe, scholars have documented how Montaigne perpetuates misogynistic sentiments on a variety of topics, including friendship, marriage, and household dynamics.[64] Yet Montaigne also takes on female personae in his writing and dedicates a few of his most literary self-aware essays to women, however, such as his "Apology for Raymond Sebond," an essay that Robert Cottrell has described as "central to Montaigne's literary project," thus complicating his representations of women.[65] John Florio's 1603 translated "Of the Caniballes" brings a female persona mediated by a male lover's song; the essay concludes with the report of an "amorous canzonet" about a Tupinambá woman's sewing that draws from the pattern of snakes: "Adder stay, stay good adder, that my sister may by the patterne of thy partie-coloured coate drawe the fashion and worke of a rich lace, for me to give vnto my love; so may thy beautie, thy nimblenesse or disposition be ever preferred before al other serpents."[66] With all veracity of the account and Montaigne's representation aside,[67] the imagery of the sister's sewn study of nature converted into a commodity for a curious European audience is a striking example of knowledge mediated by women's needles. The narrator emphasizes that this refrain reflects the dignity of the cannibals and remarks that "this invention hath no barbarisme [. . .] but is altogether Anacreontike," relating their music to the erotic lyric poetry of the ancient Greeks.[68] Although the passage suggests phallic resonances, mainly since the song immediately follows an account of the cannibals' practice of polygamy, nonetheless the lyrics situate a woman as an ideal arbitrator between nature and the would-be suitor. The woman's ability to study the adder and use its skin as her pattern to create lace by emulating its "partie-coloured coate" is a form of knowledge limited to her, knowledge directly tied to her needlework. Her gendered skillset situates her in a privileged position to see and create. The sister's lace is a natural history project in demand, which travels between media and across oceans for an eager European audience: the commodified pattern will be passed from the brother to a lover, transforming the snake's skin into an organic love token. Through Montaigne's account, her pattern also becomes a tantalizing glimpse of the New World in print. Just as the song becomes an "amorous canzonet" in the hands of Florio (the first English translator of Montaigne, more closely resembling the popular poetry of Renaissance Europe than the song's alleged origins in the Americas) the pattern of New World fauna is transformed into a recognizable luxury item. In his translation of the refrain, Florio extends the Tupinambá woman's practice of seeking designs and sampling from nature, and translates it into "the fashion and worke of a rich lace," a commodity familiar to Continental Europe and one for which printed pattern books provided new designs. For instance, Frederico de Vinciolo collaborated with publishers to create some of the earliest printed patterns for lace in the late sixteenth century, books that quickly spread to presses in other countries.[69] Here Florio's translation, first printed twenty years after Vinciolo's lace pattern book arrived on the market, where it remained continuously in print until 1605 in cities spanning Paris, London, Torino, and Lyon, gestures toward a novel pattern of the Americas presented to an English audience, already primed for opulent laces.[70]

    William Shakespeare, the most famous reader of Montaigne's "Of the Caniballes," also creates a rendition of "sampling women" who best understand the patterns of nature in *A Midsummer Night's Dream*. First acted before the 1603 first edition of Florio's Montaigne translation, Shakespeare's female characters enact a similar scene of sewing from nature. A distraught Helena reminds Hermia of their early education and intimate friendship, lamenting:

—oh, is all forgot,
All schooldays' friendship, childhood innocence?
We, Hermia, like two artificial
Have with our needles created both one flower,
Both on one sampler, sitting on one cushion,
Both warbling of one song, both in one key,
As if our hands, our sides, voices, and minds
Had been incorporate. So we grew together

> Like to a double cherry, seeming parted,
> But yet an union in partition,
> Two lovely berries molded on one stem.[71]

As young women, Helena and Hermia learn about feminine virtue, natural history, and needlework as a unified subject. They become "two artificial gods" whose knowledge of botany allows for artistic creation on par with the divine. Much like the translation of Montaigne, their insights into the natural world result from seeing through sewing. With the label "artificial gods," Shakespeare sets up an irreconcilable difference: Hermia and Helena use their human skill in embroidery to create a flower as though they were deities.[72] Their two needles collaborate on a single creation, unified in the repetition of the *one* flower, on *one* sampler; like the many women pricking floral designs, Hermia and Helena see and comprehend the fruits and flowers through sewing, and through this education, understand the world. In this metaphor, their shared botanical knowledge emphasizes their alikeness, until Helena's speech culminates in the women themselves being combined in one "incorporate" fruit, as two female bodies becoming "a double cherry" on one stem, embroidered together in their shared perspective of flower-crafting gods. Shakespeare's objective in this speech is to provide insight into the intensity of this feminized friendship, but he also gestures toward a cultural practice of a gendered studying of nature, facilitated by the use of the needle. He elevates his female characters' way of seeing to the level of gods, albeit ones constrained by their synthetic tools.

Helena's needlework metaphor in this play anticipates the poet and playwright Margaret Cavendish's complex (and at times, contradictory) representation of needlework in her philosophical writings. Cavendish begins her *Poems, and Fancies* (1653), which treats subjects of natural philosophy ranging from atomism to plant and animal sentience, with an image of women's work. She describes elements of women's sewing practices, with "their curious shadowing, and mixing of Colours, in their Wrought workes, and divers sorts of Stitches they imploy their Needle, and many Curious things they make, as Flowers, Boxes, Baskets with Beads, Shells, Silke, Straw, or anything else."[73] By equating women's "thoughts" with their needlework, "imploy[ing]" their "Fancies" as they do their needles, she correlates their sewing designs with the study of the natural world. Her embroidery metaphor for women's work—even to facetiously beseech herself to "[w]ork lady, work"—speaks to a way of studying nature that she advocates as she publishes original literary conceptions of seventeenth-century science.

These literary representations demand new attention in light of the punctured surfaces of books, traces suggestive of women's literacies that particularly lent themselves to studying nature. With the remnants in books connecting florilegia and botany books, scholars can return to sixteenth- and seventeenth-century texts with new eyes, revisiting passages that reveal what was there all along: women sampling, participating in scientific ordering and visualization.

In the meantime, the question remains: What can the shared surfaces of these needle pricks and tracings (the painting, the pouncing, the kinds of marks that may have been encouraged, but also those that were not) reveal about early modern experiments among the textures of nature? Helena and Hermia—those artificial gods, working in one sampler—and Cavendish's "[w]ork lady, work," a poetical wink that twists a modesty topos to mock those who believe her work should be "wrought" (sewn work) rather than written natural philosophy—suggest that women were part of a larger schema, contributors to the project of understanding the natural world through artistic study.[74] Digital reproductions can redirect focus to the physical surface, and digital archives can be space to bring disparate examples together, opening important counterarchives that radically change our perceptions of historical accounts. If we paid attention to pinpricks of needles and tracing of pens by ensuring florilegia are fully digitized, verso and recto, or by clearly describing partial digitizations, new narratives may emerge, ones that alter the history of botanical study. Metadata, versos, pouncing, and sketches: these are such stuff as counterarchives are made on, as we await future studies about the surfaces of pages.

Notes

1. Stephen Best and Sharon Marcus, "Introduction," *Representations* 108, no. 1 (2009): 2–3.

2. Best and Marcus, "Introduction," 9.

3. Margreta de Grazia and Peter Stallybrass, "The Materiality of the Shakespearean Text," *Shakespeare Quarterly* 44, no. 3 (1993): 255–83.

4. D. F. McKenzie, *Bibliography and the Sociology of Texts* (London: British Library, 1986).

5. Roger Chartier, *The Order of Books: Readers, Authors, and Libraries in Europe between the Fourteenth and Eighteenth Centuries* (Stanford, CA: Stanford University Press, 1994), 6, 28.

6. William H. Sherman, *Used Books: Marking Readers in Renaissance England* (Philadelphia: University of Pennsylvania Press, 2008).

7. Andrew M. Stauffer, *Book Traces: Nineteenth-Century Readers and the Future of the Library* (Philadelphia: University of Pennsylvania Press, 2021), 11, 18.

8. The Multigraph Collection, "Marking," in *Interacting with Print: Elements of Reading in the Era of Print Saturation* (Chicago: University of Chicago Press, 2018), 210.

9. Jeffrey Todd Knight, *Bound to Read: Compilations, Collections, and the Making of Renaissance Literature* (Philadelphia: University of Pennsylvania Press, 2013); Zachary Lesser, *Hamlet after Q1: An Uncanny History of the Shakespearean Text* (Philadelphia: University of Pennsylvania Press, 2015). Of particular importance to this article are scholars who have accounted for gender in their sociology of texts, such as Helen Smith's *"Grossly Material Things": Women and Book Production in Early Modern England* (Oxford: Oxford University Press, 2012), and Heidi Brayman's *Reading Material in Early Modern England: Print, Gender, and Literacy* (Cambridge: Cambridge University Press, 2005).

10. Sarah Werner, "Where Material Book Culture Meets Digital Humanities," *Journal of Digital Humanities* 1, no. 3 (2012): para. 12.

11. On the practical necessity of illustrations, see Sachiko Kusukawa, *Picturing the Book of Nature: Image, Text, and Argument in Sixteenth-Century Human Anatomy and Medical Botany* (Chicago: University of Chicago Press, 2011); Pamela H. Smith, "Art, Science, and Visual Culture in Early Modern Europe," *Isis* 97, no. 7 (2006): 88. On the development of the florilegium genre, see Brian W. Ogilvie, *The Science of Describing: Natural History in Renaissance Europe* (Chicago: University of Chicago Press, 2006), 47, 203.

12. Martyn Rix, *The Golden Age of Botanical Art* (Chicago: University of Chicago Press, 2013), 40; Rix describes some cases where the separation between florilegia and botany is less clear but classifies Crispijn van de Passe's engravings, discussed at length in this essay, as fitting within the category of entertainment. See also Wilfrid Blunt, *The Art of Botanical Illustration* (Woodbridge, Suffolk: Antique Collectors' Club, 1994), and Gill Saunders, *Picturing Plants: An Analytical History of Botanical Illustration* (Chicago: Kws Publishers, 2009).

13. Ogilvie, *Science of Describing*, 47.

14. Rix echoes this sentiment, although he adds that these were pattern books for court ladies as well as representations of renowned European gardens (Rix, *Golden Age of Botanical Art*, 34).

15. According to Sohee Kim's unpublished dissertation, Crispijn van de Passe the Elder's sketchbook contains evidence that he drew from nature, a practice his son, van de Passe the Younger, the artist of *Hortus Floridus*, most likely continued. "Jacques le Moyne de Morgues (c. 1533–1588) and the Origins of Seventeenth-Century Netherlandish Flower Still Lifes" (PhD diss., University of Maryland, 2009), 150–51.

16. P. Smith, "Art, Science, and Visual Culture," 83.

17. Ogilvie, *Science of Describing*, 1–24.

18. Isabelle Charmantier, "Carl Linnaeus and the Visual Representation of Nature," *Historical Studies in the Natural Sciences* 41, no. 4 (2011): 375–76, 401–2.

19. John Gerard, *The herball, or Generall historie of plantes* (London: Printed by Adam Islip Joice Norton and Richard Whitakers, 1633), ¶¶¶iv; William Turner, *A new herball* (London: By Steven Mierdman, 1551); John Parkinson, *Paradisi in sole paradisus terrestris* (London: Printed by Humfrey Lownes and Robert Young at the signe of the Starre on

Bread-street hill, 1629); *Theatrum botanicum: The theater of plants* (London: Printed by Tho. Cotes, 1640).

20. Gerard, *The herball*, ¶¶5r.

21. Gerard, *The herball*, ¶¶¶1v.

22. Ann Moss, *Printed Commonplace-Books and the Structuring of Renaissance Thought* (New York: Oxford University Press, 1996), 24–50. For the conflation between gathering herbs and poetic compilations in the sixteenth century, see Leah Knight, *Of Books and Botany in Early Modern England: Sixteenth-Century Plants and Print Culture* (Burlington, VT: Ashgate, 2009).

23. For arguments on how florilegia prints capitalized on the demand for still-life paintings, see Ilja M. Veldman, *Crispijn de Passe and His Progeny (1564–1670): A Century of Print Production*, trans. Michael Hoyle (Rotterdam: Sound & Vision, 2001), 212. An Ashmolean Museum catalog provides examples of this genre. Fred G. Meijer, *The Collection of Dutch and Flemish Still-life Paintings Bequeathed by Daisy Linda Ward* (Zwolle: Waanders, 2003).

24. Veldman, *Crispijn de Passe and His Progeny*, 209–10.

25. Rebecca Laroche, *Medical Authority and Englishwomen's Herbal Texts, 1550–1650* (Burlington, VT: Ashgate, 2009); Wendy Wall, *Recipes for Thought: Knowledge and Taste in the Early Modern English Kitchen* (Philadelphia: University of Pennsylvania Press, 2016).

26. J. L. Nevinson, "English Domestic Embroidery Patterns of the Sixteenth and Seventeenth Centuries," *The Volume of the Walpole Society* 28, no. 4 (1939): 4. Rozsika Parker similarly sees embroidery and botany becoming intertwined in the sixteenth century, particularly in their shared metaphors. Parker, *The Subversive Stitch: Embroidery and the Making of the Feminine* (London: Women's Press, 1996), 71–72.

27. Francis Bacon, *Sylua syluarum: or A naturall historie* (London: Printed by Iohn Haviland and Augustine Mathewes, 1627), 45.

28. "sampler, n. 1." OED Online, June 2018.

29. "pattern, n. and adj." OED Online, June 2018.

30. See, for example, Robert Boyle, *Experiments and considerations touching colours* (London: Printed for Henry Herringman, 1664), 38, 54; *New experiments and observations touching cold* (London: Printed for John Crook, 1665), 200. Robert Hooke's *Micrographia* (1665) explores the "*Textures* of Bodies" in illustrations derived from his viewings of nature under the microscope. Hooke, *Micrographia: or some physiological description of minute bodies made by magnifying glasses* (London: Printed for John Martyn, 1665), b2v.

31. P. Smith, "Art, Science, and Visual Culture," 87–88; see also P. Smith and Benjamin Schmidt's edited collection, *Making Knowledge in Early Modern Europe: Practices, Objects, and Texts, 1400–1800* (Chicago: University of Chicago Press, 2007), and P. Smith, "Science on the Move: Recent Trends in the History of Early Modern Science," *Renaissance Quarterly* 62, no. 2 (Summer 2009): 345–75; Janice Neri, *The Insect and the Image: Visualizing Nature in Early Modern Europe, 1500–1700* (Minneapolis: University of Minnesota Press, 2011); Tomomi Kinukawa, "Science and Whiteness as Property in the Dutch Atlantic World: Maria Sibylla Merian's *Metamorphosis Insectorum Surinamensium* (1705)," *Journal of Women's History* 24, no. 3 (2012): 91–116.

32. With "counterarchives," I use Natasha Korda's term. Korda invites researchers to draw from the counterarchives, that is, from the materials ignored in scholarship because of their alleged unimportance due to their feminized connotations. Korda, "Shakespeare's Laundry: Feminist Futures in the Archive," in *Rethinking Feminism in Early Modern Studies: Gender, Race, and Sexuality*, ed. Ania Loomba and Melissa E. Sanchez (New York: Routledge, 2016), 93–128.

33. Typically associated with writing and embroidery, "pounce" was the term used for the powder, which could be charcoal or pumice, used to prepare paper for writing, blotting excess ink, and transferring designs for sewing. Pouncing was the process of sprinkling the powder through holes onto a surface to copy an image and was a method used in other forms of artwork besides embroidery, including painting and tattooing. See James Daybell, *The Material Letter in Early Modern England: Manuscript Letters and the Culture and Practices of Letter-Writing, 1512–1635* (New York: Palgrave Macmillan, 2012), 41. See also Susan F. Lake, "A Pounced Design in 'David and Bathsheba' by Paris Bordone," *Journal of the Walters Art Gallery* 42 (1984): 62–65; Juliet Fleming, *Graffiti and the Writing Arts of Early Modern England* (Philadelphia: University of Pennsylvania Press, 2001), 90. For information about women's "pounce bags" used in this method, see Barbara Whitehead, *Women's Education in Early Modern Europe* (New York: Garland, 1999), n. 24.

34. Sherman, *Used Books*, 3–4; 16–17.

35. Susan Frye, *Pens and Needles: Women's Textualities in Early Modern England* (Philadelphia: University of Pennsylvania Press, 2010).

36. Whitney Trettien, "Isabella Whitney's Slips: Textile Labor, Gendered Authorship, and the Early Modern Miscellany," *Journal of Medieval and Early Modern Studies* 45, no. 3 (2015): 505–21; Jeffrey Todd Knight, "Needles and Pens: Sewing in Early English Books," *Journal of Medieval and Early Modern Studies* 45, no. 3 (2015): 523–42.

37. Brayman, *Reading Material in Early Modern*, 138–41.

38. Margaret Swain, "Engravings and Needlework of the Sixteenth Century," *Burlington Magazine* 119, no. 890 (1977): 343–45; Nancy Graves Cabot, *Pattern Sources of Scriptural Subjects in Tudor and Stuart Embroideries* (N.p.: Read Books, 2013); Nevinson, "English Domestic Embroidery Patterns," 1–13.

39. Spencer Savage, "The *Hortus Floridus* of Crispijn Van de Pas the Younger," *The Library* 4, no. 3 (1923): 181.

40. Kim, "Jacques le Moyne de Morgues," 152.

41. See Savage on the addition of twelve tulip plates to some copies ("The *Hortus Floridus*," 186).

42. Joaneath A. Spicer, "The Role of Printmaking in Utrecht during the First Half of the Seventeenth Century," *Journal of the Walters Art Gallery* 57 (1999): 112.

43. "Passe, Crispijn van de," in *The Oxford Dictionary of the Renaissance*, ed. Gordon Campbell (Oxford University Press, 2003).

44. Savage, "*Hortus Floridus*," 197. For information about later copies, see Robert A. Gerard, "De Passe and Early English Natural History Printmaking," *Print Quarterly* 14, no. 2 (1997): 174–79. The inclusion of the names of flowers in various languages was

necessary for the European botanical trade in the eighteenth century, as Dániel Margócsy has argued. Margócsy, *Commercial Visions: Science, Trade, and Visual Culture in the Dutch Golden Age* (Chicago: University of Chicago Press, 2014). Seventeenth-century florilegia could similarly serve as a catalog for collectors. See also Daniel Margócsy, "'Refer to folio and number': Encyclopedias, the Exchange of Curiosities, and Practices of Identification before Linnaeus," *Journal of the History of Ideas* 71, no. 1 (2010): 63–89.

45. Savage, "*Hortus Floridus,*" 185.

46. Savage, "*Hortus Floridus,*" 188.

47. Because pouncing is a method also used for artwork, it is possible that the transfers were for drawings and paintings. Since it would be impossible to know without a corresponding sampler or sketch, the materials created from pouncing must remain speculative. Nevinson fails to mention which specific embroidered object but indicates that "one such picture in the Victoria and Albert Museum has recently been traced to its original engraving by Crispin van de Passe (Pl. v *a* and *b*)," which evinces that there are some examples of van de Passe's prints in extant embroideries (Nevinson, "English Domestic Embroidery Patterns," 9). He may refer to an embroidered panel that depicts five portraits of the seven virtues, including a Fides from van de Passe, surrounded by flowers and animals (Victoria and Albert Museum, T.34–2002). Other cabinets with embroidered panels from van de Passe's prints include one at the Provinciaal Museum Voor Kunstambachten Sterckshof and another at Klooster Onze-Lieve-Vrouw van de Poterie Bruges, both in Belgium, as referenced on the Victoria and Albert Museums s catalog.

48. Jeffrey Todd Knight, "Invisible Ink: A Note on Ghost Images in Early Printed Books," *Textual Cultures* 5, no. 2 (2010): 60–61.

49. Kim, "Jacques le Moyne de Morgues," 149. According to Gerard, Payne was affiliated with Simon van de Passe, the younger brother of Crispijn the Younger (Gerard, "De Passe," 175). Because the plates so closely resemble the work of the van de Passe family, there is some debate about whether van de Passe or Payne engraved the plates. See the Folger catalog entry for the British Library's copy of *Animalium quadrupedum*. According to Veldman, John Payne was most likely trained by Simon van de Passe while he was in London, and this may account for the confusion due to similar style (Veldman, *Crispijn de Passe*, 245).

50. Simon van de Passe, *Animalium quadrupedum* ([London]: Are to be sold by Roger Danell, [ca. 1625]).

51. Savage, "*Hortus Floridus,*" 186.

52. P. Smith and Schmidt, *Making Knowledge in Early Modern Europe*, 7.

53. Ann Blair's work on Conrad Gessner's use of print to organize and manage information and to engage with a large audience about natural history—including details relating to his acquisition and emendation to illustrations—provides insights into his scientific methods. Blair, "Conrad Gessner's Paratexts," *Gesnerus* 73, no. 1 (2016): 73–122; "Humanism and Printing in the Work of Conrad Gesner," *Renaissance Quarterly* 70, no. 1 (2017): 1–43.

54. Kusukawa, *Picturing the Book of Nature*, 139–61.
55. Kusukawa, *Picturing the Book of Nature*, 143.
56. Kusukawa, *Picturing the Book of Nature*, 147.
57. Anonymous, *A Booke of Flowers Fruicts Beastes Birds and Flies exactly drawne* ([London]: And are to bee sold by P. Stent at the White hors in Guiltspur street without Newgate, [1661]).
58. William T. Stearn, "Maria Sibylla Merian (1647–1717) as Botanical Artist," *Taxon* 31, no. 3 (1982): 531–32.
59. Stephanie Schrader, Nancy Turner, and Nancy Yocco, "Naturalism under the Microscope: A Technical Study of Maria Sibylla Merian's 'Metamorphosis of the Insects of Surinam,'" *Getty Research Journal* 4 (2012): 164.
60. Stearn, "Maria Sibylla Merian," 529.
61. Savage, "*Hortus Floridus*," 206. Merian Senior expanded the *Florilegium novum* printed by his father-in-law, Johann Theodor de Bry, after his death (https://www.christies.com/lotfinder/Lot/bry-johann-theodor-de-1561-1623-florilegium-renovatum-5362349-details.aspx).
62. Meijer, *Collection of Dutch and Flemish Still-life Paintings*, 248. Meijer also mentions that Jacob Marrel created "a few etchings" in addition to "tulip books in watercolours" (248).
63. Stearn outlines references to Maria Sibylla Merian's texts in several of Linnaeus's works (Stearn, "Maria Sibylla Merian," 532). Linnaeus references Merian's work more than a hundred times.
64. See Floyd Gray's *Gender, Rhetoric, and Print Culture in French Renaissance Writing* (Cambridge: Cambridge University Press, 2000), 13, 115–21. Gray reads Montaigne as placing feminist and antifeminist text side-by-side in his *Essays*, thereby painting a relatively positive perspective on Montaigne's misogyny. Marie de Gournay's editorial interventions for her mentor's *Essays* after his death further complicate misogynistic passages from the text, although she does not make any changes in the passage discussed in this essay. Emily R. Cranford analyzes Montaigne's complex representation of women and use of feminine style, and her dissertation takes up the topic of Marie de Gournay's editorial interventions, including defenses made on behalf of the education of women. Cranford, "'Je Suis Moy-mesmes la Matriere de mon Livre': Sexual Ambiguities and Friendship in Montaigne's *Essais*" (master's thesis, University of North Carolina at Chapel Hill, 2006); "I Am Myself the Matter of My Book: Gender, Friendship, and Writing in Hélisenne de Crenne and Marie de Gournay" (PhD diss., University of North Carolina at Chapel Hill, 2015).
65. Robert D. Cottrell, "Gender Imprinting in Montaigne's *Essais*," *L'Esprit Créateur* 30, no. 4 (1990): 93.
66. Michel de Montaigne, *The essayes or morall, politike and millitarie discourses of Lo: Michaell de Montaigne*, trans. John Florio (London: Printed by Val. Sims for Edward Blount, 1603), 106. I am grateful to Andrew Keener for this reference.
67. Eric Cheyfitz dismisses the song as "quite far" from the probable origins of any music of the Tupi people. Cheyfitz, *The Poetics of Imperialism: Translation and Colonization*

from "The Tempest" to "Tarzan" (Philadelphia: University of Pennsylvania Press, 1997), 146.

68. Montaigne, *The essayes*, 106.

69. Vinciolo's pattern book was printed in at least twenty-five editions, mostly between 1587 and 1599. The woodcuts emulated the most popular embroidery pattern book on the Continent that went through twenty-four editions in seven different cities, translated into French, German, and English.

70. John Wolfe, the English printer of Vinciolo's patterns, printed John Florio's English translation of the Italian almanac *Perpetuall and naturall prognostications of the change of weather* in 1591; otherwise, the extent of their relationship is indeterminate, although both were simultaneously printing Italianate texts in England.

71. William Shakespeare, "A Midsummer Night's Dream," ed. Lukas Erne, in *The Norton Shakespeare*, 3rd ed., ed. Stephen Greenblatt (New York: W. W. Norton, 2016), act 3, scene 2, lines 203–11.

72. "artificial, adj. and n." OED Online. June 2018.

73. Margaret Cavendish, *Poems, and fancies* (London: Printed by T. R. for J. Martin, and J. Allestrye, 1653), A3r.

74. The meaning of "wrought"—"To make (a fabric, garment, etc.); to weave, spin, sew, knit, etc. Now chiefly: to embroider (a garment, tapestry, etc.)"—relates to the etymology of the word "work" to mean "to sew." "work, v." OED Online. June 2018.

Opening the Book

The Utopian Dreams and Uncertain Future of Open Access Textbook Publishing

Joseph L. Locke and
Ben Wright

In a 2013 interview with *Forbes*, Megan Smith, a Google executive and later Chief Technology Officer of the United States under President Barack Obama, identified "education and learning" as at the edge of a transformative technological shift. "Three billion people are joining the global conversation," she said. "We're just at the very beginning of that; you can see the cracks in the dam." New educational technology would rescue the globe, Smith argued. There would be no problem too big for new voices and new technologies. By 2030, children would have to visit "poverty museums" to understand scarcity and inequality.[1] Smith's utopian rhetoric suffuses Silicon Valley, but it echoes far beyond it. In particular, it continues to frame academic work in the digital humanities. The first lines of the collaboratively authored 2012 monograph *Digital Humanities*, for instance, asserts that "We live in one of those rare moments of opportunity for the humanities, not unlike other great eras of cultural-historical transformation such as the shift from the scroll to the codex, the invention of moveable type, the encounter with the New World, and the Industrial Revolution."[2] The rise of digital technology has created a new epoch in the production and distribution of knowledge. "How knowledge circulates has always been vital to the life of the mind," wrote John Willinsky, the Stanford historian and open access advocate, "just as it is vital, ultimately, to the well-being of humanity."[3] The printing press revolutionized knowledge and learning, he argued, and, "Today, it is easy to imagine that we are in the hands of a similar agent of social change."[4]

The wedding of utopian dreams with education is nothing new, but the nature of those utopian dreams changes. Modern-day champions of open educational resources (OER) want to push back against soaring costs and decades' worth of mounting economic and cultural inequality by creating freely available textbooks. A new era, ushered in by crushing textbook costs and the ready availability of consumer-facing technology, freighted with an ideology shaped alternately by New Left discourses about democracy, Silicon Valley utopianism, and neoliberal university governance, has witnessed a new utopian dream: the open textbook.

As this volume attests, digital tools have marked a notable shift in the history of the book. Recent changes in the publication of textbooks hint at dramatic transformations in the world of publishing. New technologies are challenging the historic influence of textbook publishers and the traditional models of textbook authorship. Scores of prophets have predicted a wholesale revolution in the history of the book. One Silicon Valley utopian predicted in 2014 that, in less than ten years, "people will look back at textbooks the way we look back at encyclopedias. The notion of carrying around this antiquated textbook will become very quaint, very quickly."[5] In recent years, new educational industries have risen and fallen with startling speed. Reconstructing this history—and the rhetoric surrounding it—reveals the shifting values of the digital humanities, changes in the economics of publishing, and wider trends in the neoliberal university. This is a history of the book that balances both political economy and cultural values, of technological transformation and shifting social relationships, and of ideological upheaval and institutional continuities. Critical awareness of the origins and evolution of OER is therefore essential to contextualize the shifting ideological ground and practical realities of textbook production.

Our goal in this chapter is to historicize and evaluate the production of OER, particularly textbooks, and reveal how shifting means of production are refashioning academic publishing and the field of digital humanities. Tracking both pessimistic technophobia and misguided utopianism, we critically explore the origins and evolution of OER while evaluating how new projects are not only fighting soaring textbook costs but also harnessing new strategies such as "massive collaboration" to redefine the possibilities of textbook production, design, and use. This chapter begins with the ideological and institutional foundations of the open access movement before examining the crisis of textbook costs and educational inequality. The field of American history is then presented as a case study, one that reveals both how OER have been created and disseminated in the past and how new collaborative models of authorship are now pushing the field forward. Finally, we analyze how universities, libraries, and academic presses are attempting to connect the idealism of the OER movement with the values of traditional humanities scholarship.

Ideological Origins

Trends associated with the open access movement—decentralized collaboration, anti-corporate cultural identity, and extra-institutional status—were apparent in the earliest years of computer programming. In the 1950s, for instance, a collection of volunteer programmers working with IBM machines, operating together with little formal direction or organizational oversight, established and spread a free library of operating systems that culminated in the release of the SHARE Operating System in 1959.[6] A larger and more defined open access movement built upon decades of developments in academia, pedagogy, and computing, but now accelerated with the widespread adoption of personal computers in the early 1990s. Open and informal networks such as SHARE flourished among programmers, but the ideological commitment to openness was made explicit only in the 1980s.

Richard Stallman, an activist programmer, formed the GNU Project and its open-source operating system in 1983. In 1985, he launched the Free Software Foundation. In a manifesto published that same year, Stallman explained that he wanted "to use computers without dishonor" and contribute to a "postscarcity world, where nobody will have to work very hard just to make a living."[7] The use and development of free and open materials would thereafter be framed as a public good. Stallman's manifesto set a bar that was difficult to reach: while he interpreted openness as an essential step toward a broad and participatory form of social justice, later manifestations of open access advocacy would more narrowly emphasize cost alone. Nonetheless, the work of Stallman and others associated with the Free Software Foundation imbued the free and open access movements with a moral idealism that would endure even when projects ended up more often addressing practical, rather than political, problems. Meanwhile, it would take more than a decade before these programmer-driven initiatives would be copied and modified by scholars in higher education.

Whatever the self-congratulatory, anti-institutional rhetoric of the OER movement and the wider field of digital humanities that grew alongside and nurtured OER, both developed and existed within very real structures. As Amy

Earhart, a digital humanities scholar, noted that the academy, with all of its institutionalized contradictions and inequalities, determined the rise and development of the digital humanities. Similarly, the political economy of higher education steered the development and distribution of open educational resources.[8] The early OER movement, therefore, relied on the support of university systems and their funding sources. In 1997, for instance, the California State University system launched MERLOT (Multimedia Education Resource for Learning and Online Teaching), a shared repository for the creation and distribution of free, online teaching resources. Drawing inspiration from a National Science Foundation project, "Authoring Tools and an Educational Object Economy,"[9] MERLOT won the buy-in of other university systems, including the University System of Georgia, University of North Carolina System, and the Oklahoma State System. By 2000, the number of subscribing institutions had reached twenty-three.[10] MERLOT, thus, became and remains the most important repository for free and open materials. Moreover, MERLOT's stable of open projects testified to the major advances in the production and distribution of OER at the turn of the century, which were driven, in part, by a sudden deluge of foundation funding.

The William and Flora Hewlett Foundation loomed large in the early history of OER. In 2001, Hewlett made a grant to MIT in support of its OpenCourseWare initiative. In describing the initiative, MIT's president Charles Vest revealed the relationship between programmer culture and the rise of OER in a *New York Times* interview: "We've tried to open up software infrastructure in a variety of ways and that's what unleashed the creativity of software developers; I think the same thing can happen in education."[11] Other institutions followed the lead of MIT. Utah State University drew on Hewlett funds to create the Open Learning Support initiative. Carnegie Mellon went a step further than simply sharing course materials by attempting to create a full online learning experience, the Open Learning Initiative (OLI). By 2005, the Hewlett Foundation financed the creation of the OpenCourseWare Consortium that included members in the United States, Japan, and China.

Universities and grant-making organizations had begun to support open learning, but why? Advocates made a moral case: "Open access was born from a technological utopian vision to make traditional research output available to everyone," wrote Marguerite Avery, Alex Holzman, and Robert Brown[12]; the 2002 Budapest Open Access Initiative attempted to codify that vision and offer guidance to a broader movement; "An old tradition and a new technology have converged to make possible an unprecedented public good;" Academic research—the old tradition—and widespread internet access—the new technology—could make the intellectual fruits of academic labor available to all; "Open Access" would be the clarion call.[13] And if research could be available to all, why not educational materials? Five months after the Budapest declaration, the United Nations Educational, Scientific and Cultural Organization (UNESCO)-sponsored Forum on the Impact of Open Courseware for Higher Education in Developing Countries met to discuss possible avenues, and, in a declaration, "express[ed] their satisfaction and their wish to develop together a universal educational resource available for the whole of humanity, to be referred to henceforth as Open Educational Resources." The forum "hope[d] that this open resource for the future mobilizes the whole of the worldwide community of educators."[14]

"Open," it should be said, has a distinct meaning: OER are more than traditional materials posted online, and as such they must forgo traditional copyright restrictions by using an open license or by being released into the public domain. According to David Wiley, a Utah State University professor who pioneered open licensing, open material allows more than simple online access: it allows users to retain copies of the material, reuse the material, revise the material, remix the material with other content, and redistribute the material.[15] OER are not only free, they are adaptable.[16]

Much of the early access movement emerged from disciplines in science and technology.[17] By 2001, for instance, PLOS (the Public Library of Science) had pioneered the model of an open access journal.[18] MIT's leadership in creating the OpenCourseWare Consortium created particular pressure for institutions with strengths in science, technology, engineering, and math. In 2004, Richard Baraniuk, a Rice University engineering professor, officially launched Connexions, an open resource sharing platform that linked resources across multiple campuses.[19]

Open access is a newer idea in the humanities.[20] In a notice appended to their 2014 open monograph, *The History Manifesto*, David Armitage and Jo Guldi wrote, "Even two or three years ago, most academics in the humanities, and certainly most members of the non-academic public, had not heard much if anything about the Open Access movement."[21] But already, as the open access advocate Martin Weller put it, "openness is now such a part of everyday life that it seems unworthy of comment."[22] Publications in the humanities are following the sciences into open access publishing, and grant money is appearing for new open projects. In fact, according to Eve, "It is now more often the practicalities of achieving such a goal that are the focus of disagreement."[23] And it is in the practicalities where open textbooks had nearly stalled.

The primary push for the adoption of open educational resources is obvious: the cost of higher education has exploded over the past several decades. Academics have had to confront the ugly fact that universities are sites of profound inequality and that, against the best hopes and much conventional wisdom, academic institutions too often perpetuate and accelerate inequality instead of combatting it. Income achievement gaps in education, for instance, continue to advance.[24] Higher education is rife with seemingly intractable inequalities, and the utopian rhetoric of digital "disruptors" hardly gets at the roots of the neoliberal university, let alone the intransigent structural inequalities of twenty-first-century capitalism. Textbooks are, in other words, only one small component of a much broader and more complicated problem. But they are, nevertheless, a problem.

The Crisis of Cost

In a 2008 *New York Times* article, R. Preston McAfee, a Cal Tech economics professor, compared textbook publishers to pharmaceutical companies. Both, he said, benefit from "moral hazards—that is, the doctor who prescribes medication and the professor who requires a textbook don't have to bear the cost of either and therefore often don't think twice about price. The person who pays for the book, the parent or the student, doesn't choose it," McAfee said, and so "it's always O.K. to add $5."[25] According to the Bureau of Labor Statistics, textbook prices have jumped fifteenfold over the past forty years, three times the rate of inflation. The College Board found that the typical student spent $1,200 on textbooks and supplies in 2016.[26] A 2005 study found that textbooks accounted for more than a quarter of the cost of a four-year degree.[27] Even in the humanities, where textbook costs are historically lower, the costs of introductory textbooks still pose a financially onerous barrier to entry. Despite shifting technological and pedagogical trends, community colleges and other educational institutions catering to nontraditional or first-generation college students still rely heavily on traditional textbooks. The very students least able to afford ever-increasing costs are the most likely to bear them.

These costs affect students' education. According to the Education Fund, half of all students in American colleges and universities allow textbook costs to dictate the courses they take and the number for which they register. Graduation rates suffer. Two-thirds of students report not buying a textbook because of cost. Of those, 94 percent did so with the knowledge that it could hurt their grade. Put another way, more than 60 percent of students in Florida determined that they could not afford to earn an A.[28] The realities of unaffordable course materials present an existential threat to higher education.

If textbook costs are a problem, they are a problem with a solution. OER has shown the ability to alleviate the burden of textbook costs by creating high-quality, free, and open resources for all students. While open-source textbooks will hardly accomplish some kind of imagined utopian digital future, and their very production raises a whole new host of knotty problems, the uneven production of sophisticated, professionally curated academic textbooks nevertheless testifies to the many blind spots of the digital humanities.[29] As Adeline Koh wrote, the field's prizewinners privilege computation over argument, impact, or utility; she also suggested we treat pedagogy as central to the digital humanities. Doing so would require a reconsideration of textbooks[30]—traditional rather than disruptive, pedagogical rather than research-based, eye-glazing rather than grant-winning, textbooks are nevertheless the most widely used tool in humanities classrooms. Textbooks should indeed be ripe targets for the open access movement.[31] Nowhere else are current costs and potential savings quite so clear. Many outside academia have certainly recognized the democratic and cost-annihilating potential of open texts. For decades, scholars allowed responsibility for open textbook creation to fall upon for-profit education companies, unwieldy nonprofit bureaucracies, under-resourced lone wolves, and unregulated open wikis. A close look at the field of American history and the nearly universally required American history survey course is revealing.

Case Study: American History

Steven Mintz and Sara McNeil, for instance, pioneered a free (though not open) digital history text, *Digital History* (http://www.digitalhistory.uh.edu/), at the University of Houston in 2001, still in the early years of the digital age. Their work provides an enduring and valuable resource for instructors, with its impressive collection of media and other resources, but an intimidating interface, dead links, and an antiquated platform quickly made the surviving site unwieldy. Unfortunately, academic historians failed to follow Mintz and McNeil's pathbreaking model and produce a compelling alternative, one that harnesses the potential of open access and contemporary technology. The *Journal of American History*'s 2013 "Teaching and Textbooks" roundtable discussed the future of textbooks in American history courses, but rather than tout the promise of open resources, the forum cited only the unreliability of existing projects.[32] And so, where scholars failed, others outside of the academy were left to enter the fray.

Compelling but ultimately disappointing efforts emerged from well-funded, for-profit organizations. Founded in 2007, Flat World Knowledge took the open landscape by storm and raised more than $25 million by promising free online texts funded through premium paper and mobile offerings. But revenue lagged, and on January 1, 2013, Flat World's texts were no longer free or open. One of its two volumes of American history had been published by March 2012, and it lived as an open text for a full nine months. Boundless Learning arose in its wake and likewise raised millions, but its free model merely collects and repackages already extant open material, carving up Wikipedia articles and haphazardly peddling them as academic material. For example, in its opening chapter, *Boundless U.S. History*'s material on the "Pre-Columbian Era" is, well, the Wikipedia page titled "Pre-Columbian Era."

The creation of OER has not been an inexorable triumph. Flat World Knowledge evidenced the financial motives of much textbook production, and Boundless Learning revealed the difficulty of producing texts capable of competing with traditional products. A shift to open access textbook publishing is not easy—it requires a reconsideration of traditional funding models and profound shifts in organizational thought.[33] In the United Kingdom, the Learning and Teaching Support Network (LTSN) formed at the turn of the twenty-first century with government support for the purpose of disseminating free materials. "The 'not invented here' syndrome has prevailed for too long," wrote LTSN's director Cliff Allen, "and we can no longer afford to continue to spurn practices and developments conceived in other institutions or subjects that are clearly transferable."[34] The experiment, however, proved short-lived. Despite "the principle that the courseware produced through [the program] should be free," recouping costs to produce free resources meant that the organization encouraged cost recovery through fees and other barriers to access. The goal of openness remained unfulfilled.[35]

Cost recovery also marred much of the online educational movement in its early years. Massively Open Online Classes (MOOC's) grew out of the disruption-mania of Silicon Valley neoliberalism. In 2011, the venture capitalist Peter Thiel called for the disruption of higher education. "A true bubble is when something is overvalued and intensely believed," he said. "Education may be the only thing people still believe in [in] the United States. To question education is really dangerous. It is the absolute taboo. It's like telling the world there's no Santa Claus."[36] Venture capitalists could rescue education from itself, Thiel argued. Peer 2 Peer University (P2PU) and Khan Academy tried to do just that. Others, such as the edX corporation, partnered with university administrators, eager to harvest fees from large online courses so to launch their own university affiliated MOOCs. Professors fretted about the de-skilling of educators and the capture of education by venture capitalists. But the MOOC bubble burst. As Charles Vest stated before the bubble, the university can't be reduced to an online learning environment: "Our central value is people and the human experience of faculty working with students in classrooms and laboratories, and students learning from each other, and the kind of intensive environment we create in our residential university."[37] In 2020, the Covid-19 pandemic threw innumerable students and instructors rapidly into all-online learning environments. Although it will take time to analyze the effectiveness and implications of online pedagogy during the pandemic, anecdotal impressions hardly support an attitudinal shift away from traditional, face-to-face pedagogy.

The collapse of the MOOC model coincided with the difficulties of Boundless Learning and other private ventures to produce competent open textbooks in the humanities. In light of that failure, we conceived our own OER textbook, *The American Yawp*, in spring 2013 while teaching at various colleges in the greater Houston area. We approached the project with three overriding principles: first, to provide a free and truly open resource for students and educators; second, to maintain the highest standards of our discipline; and, third, to use collaboration and institution-free spaces to create a "living" resource that can ultimately expand the pedagogical horizons of traditional textbooks. We set out to balance the promise of open resources with the rigors of academic review. With the help of an advisory board composed of leading American historians and pioneers in the digital humanities, we recruited hundreds of scholars who were not only sympathetic to the project's mission but also willing to volunteer their expertise. We were overwhelmed by positive feedback. Many were surprised something like this didn't already exist. And so we went to work inviting more than 300 content specialists to submit short, mostly 300–500 word excerpts with the basic prompt, "What do undergraduates absolutely need to know about the subject of your expertise?"

The book title, *The American Yawp*, was chosen to capture a vibrant past. Even excellent textbooks struggle to encapsulate American history. Some organize around themes—*The American Promise, The Story of American Freedom*—while others surrender to the impossibility of synthesis and retreat toward generality—*America's History, The American People*. But in the oft-cited lines of the American poet Walt Whitman, we found as good an organizing principle as any other: "I too am not a bit tamed—I too am untranslatable," he wrote, "I sound my barbaric yawp over the roofs of the world." Long before Whitman and long after, Americans have sung something collectively amid the deafening roar of their many individual voices. *The American Yawp* offers both chorus and cacophony, together, as one. Without losing sight of politics and power, we wanted to incorporate transnational perspectives, integrate diverse voices, recover narratives of resistance, and explore the complex process of cultural creation. We wanted to look for America in sweltering slave cabins, bustling markets, congested tenements, and marbled halls. We wanted to navigate between maternity wards, prisons, streets, bars, and boardrooms. Whitman's America, like ours, cut across the narrow boundaries that strangle many narratives. We wanted a multilayered, democratic vision of the American past.

Or at least those were our ambitions, but first we had to write the text, and it is here that digital humanists can consider new models for the production of scholarship. How should scholars collaborate given the transformations wrought by the digital humanities?

Collaboration and New Models of Authorship

The impacts of the digital humanities have not been only technological but also social: perhaps no other development has encouraged a greater academic cooperation. In 2011, Anthony Grafton, then-president of the American Historical Association, argued against Wilhelm von Humboldt's idealization of academic "loneliness and freedom." Grafton wrote, "there is much to be gained by recognizing, and promoting, collaboration . . . and, with it, the elements of joy and creative fantasy that can too easily be lost as we go about our traditionally lonely craft."[38] Digital humanists have been ahead of their analog colleagues. Indeed, the so-called "digital turn" and the rise of the digital humanities have generated new opportunities and imperatives for collaboration that extend beyond traditional research opportunities.

Strikingly, much of this new collaboration is extra-institutional. Andrew Torget, who performed some of the earliest work in digital history at the University of Virginia, argued that "digital projects by necessity require collaboration." Torget nevertheless believed collaboration could be flexible and informal. "I see," he said, "a movement towards collaborative teams built around projects and problems that will last for as long as the project or problem does. You may have a home department, but you will also have collaborative teams that form and dissolve over time depending on what you're working on."[39] For example, Dino Franco Felluga's 2016 launch of COVE (Collaborative Organization for Virtual Education) drew on scholars from dozens of universities to produce peer-reviewed scholarship and pedagogical material on nineteenth-century British Literature.[40]

These new flexible forms of collaboration invite anxiety about uncompensated labor. The issue of free labor often confronts open-access projects. Of course, academics produce traditional articles, books, and other forms of scholarship even though doing so typically does not yield significant—if any—direct compensation. In 1994, Stevan Harnad advanced a "subversive proposal" that scholarly research papers should be available openly online. Harnad argued that academic salaries are already paid by universities and, as part of that compensation, they are expected to produce what he calls "esoteric" work: intellectual contributions made without regard to profits.[41] In this way, the rise of collaborative scholarship ought to reinforce the necessity of tenure and speak to the dangers of rising contingent academic employment. If the academy continues its movement toward precarious employment, creative, innovative collaborative work may be lost.

Copyright concerns also invite questions about intellectual property rights. But if few academics are profiting from their academic work, how many academics really require copyright protections? Martin Paul Eve asks, "why should academics retain the economic protections of copyright if they are not dependent upon the system of remuneration that this is supposed to uphold?"[42] The cost of reproduction is nearly nothing in the digital world. And so open access advocates such as John Willinsky and Creative Commons's Cable Green have argued that it is the intellectual as well as the moral responsibility of academics to share their scholarship as freely and widely as possible.[43] With students facing increasing economic pressures and the humanities increasingly devalued in public life, such work is essential.

Digital technologies should do more than facilitate the production of free resources; they should also facilitate the production of better resources. Toward that end, the *American Yawp* sought to reimagine the process of textbook production under the principles of massive collaboration.

We sought a narrative synthesis that would emerge through the many innovations of our profession's various subfields rather than through a preselected central theme or authorial agenda. Traditional textbooks usually begin with a single author or a small team of authors searching for synthetic threads to tie together a narrative; the work is then sent to reviewers for specialist vetting. Instead, we mirrored the way our profession already works. After years of conference presentations, journal and monograph publications, reviews, citations in related works, and historiographical evaluations, new research now disperses into our broad narratives of the past. Historical knowledge bubbles up from the work of researchers rather than flows down from the work of editors, publishers, or other institutional gatekeepers. We therefore gave the first draft to subfield specialists to ensure that the text reflected the cutting edge of scholarship. We relied upon a large and diverse yet loosely coordinated group of experienced contributors to construct a coherent and accessible narrative from all the best of recent historical scholarship.

After testing alternative models for collaborative online text creation, including traditional wikis, we embraced the promise of large-scale, managed crowd-sourcing. More than 300 historians ultimately collaborated during the 2013–2014 academic year to produce text and images, which a team of editors wove into cohesive chapters. The mediated model balanced the collaborative promise of many open-source models with the reliability of a traditional editorially controlled process, but this also demonstrated the value of tangible human networks and real-world connections to help sustain the otherwise anonymous world of digital content production. A static and impersonal "call to create" yielded little. A managed, cultivated creation process created a textbook. But how can scholars know which of these new digital projects are reliable? How does the essential academic commitment to peer review fit in the new digital paradigm?

Quality Control

University presses, who rightly remain the caretakers of academic standards, are increasingly turning toward open access while maintaining traditional practices such as peer review and institutional services such as editing, copyediting, and typesetting. In 2015 Neil B. Christensen, then the director of business development for the University of California Press, proclaimed, "If there ever was a time for a university press to go into open access, this is the time." That same year, the UC Press launched *Collabra* and Luminos, new digital platforms for publishing, respectively, open-access journals and monographs.[44] However, this open-access model requires author fees—in this case, $600 to $700—something that is commonplace in the sciences but, until recently, almost unheard of in the humanities. In 2012, the University of Minnesota's Center for Open Education, again through the Hewlett Foundation, launched The Open Textbook Network (OTN). The OTN requires participating universities to do three things on their campuses: host workshops where faculty hear how OER can improve their courses; train a permanent employee to serve as a campus facilitator for ongoing OER adoption; and gather data on OER use.[45] Additional data is gathered and analyzed by five Open Education Research Fellows drawn from the network.[46] The Open Textbook Network now includes more than 600 campuses. The University of Minnesota's Center for Open

Education also manages the Open Textbook Library (OTL), a collection of downloadable open textbooks. Reviews from qualified faculty are solicited for each textbook available through the OTL, and low-cost printing is also made available for each text.[47]

This new chapter in the history of the book extends beyond textbooks. In a 2011 reflection on new digital horizons in academic publishing, Kathleen Fitzpatrick concluded that "Access to the work we produce must be opened up as a site of conversation not just among scholars but also between scholars and the broader culture."[48] Four years later, Caroline Edwards and Martin Paul Eve won support from the Mellon Foundation and worked with various university libraries to launch the Open Library of Humanities (OLH), aiming to build new platforms to publish open-access humanities scholarship.[49]

In 2011, the Open Educational Quality Initiative attempted to take stock of the status of the OER movement, concluding that new quality-management approaches were required.[50] Again, university presses appear to be rising to the challenge. In 2006, Cambridge University Press published *The Orlando Project*, an exploration of women's writing in Britain. Cambridge's involvement brought legitimacy to open-source academic publishing—and to digital publishing more broadly—in the humanities. Other presses followed. The University of Virginia Press has been a leader in publishing projects online, however many retain copyright; MIT Press posted several field-defining books online with open licensing. From 2011 to 2013, the University of Michigan Press administered the open peer review and the eventual dual publishing of *Writing History in the Digital Age* at the same time the University of Minnesota Press similarly published the first volume of *Debates in the Digital Humanities*. Both were milestones not only as scholarly reflection on open publishing but also as prototypes for how open access platforms can extend traditional notions of "publication." And nearly a decade after first publishing *The Orlando Project*, in 2014 Cambridge University Press published *The History Manifesto*, a much remarked-upon exploration into the nature of historical scholarship by Jo Guldi and David Armitage, marking yet another highpoint in the academic respectability given to open access publication.[51]

Textbooks are building upon these developments. Projects like the Open Textbook Toolkit are linking university libraries and university presses in order to produce quality, open-source textbooks available for students and educators.[52] "Presses and libraries want the same thing," an Association of American University Presses report stated, "widespread, cost-effective distribution of scholarly products. They have shared problems and a shared future."[53] Similar textbook publishing efforts continue to multiply. The University System of

Georgia and Oregon State University are just two institutions that have committed themselves to producing and using open textbooks.[54] And the very nature of what "publication" means is changing. Rather than simply bringing traditional monographs online and pulling them into traditional press infrastructure, Mellon-funding is allowing Stanford University Press to bring peer-review to digital-native projects. Even though *The American Yawp* was not developed under that grant, Stanford University Press nevertheless published it in spring 2019 as a peer-reviewed, parallel digital/physical text. Both iterations operated under the same Creative Commons open license. In 2018, the University of Chicago Press launched *Building the American Republic*, a low-cost, copyrighted print book alongside a free—though not open—ebook.[55] With such efforts proliferating across the university press landscape, academic credibility can no longer be considered an obstacle to a more democratized access.

Things are changing quickly at the university level. Students, of course, are eager adopters. In one study, for instance, replacing a traditional textbook with an open resource led to greater student interest in the course and higher student evaluation of faculty in metrics such as kindness, encouragement, and creativity.[56] Studies continue to bear out the claims that OER increase student success.[57] Meanwhile, the shifting publishing landscape is coinciding with a rising acceptance of OER within the academic profession; OER are becoming mainstream among university educators.[58] After an influx of funding and a 2012 relaunch as the open textbook publisher OpenStax, the project since has commissioned and reviewed dozens of textbooks that have been accessed by hundreds of thousands of students. (Their American history textbook was released at the end of 2014.) Our own project, *The American Yawp*, has seen astonishing growth. In its beta release during the 2014–2015 academic year, the project attracted 32,980 unique users and 155,232 overall pageviews. In the 2020–2021 academic year, it brought in 1,564,198 unique users and 12,286,579 pageviews.[59]

Futures

The OER movement has created a new chapter in textbook production, but many continue to use textbooks as they have always used them. The last several years have brought an explosion of technological change and new pedagogical imperatives, but simply putting a textbook online misses the vast potential of the digital medium. The next step involves a critical reflection on the nature of the medium and strategies for the practical construction and use of new resources. Steven Mintz, who shepherded academia's first online American history textbook, *Digital History*, saw the future of digital texts in a "stage 2.0" that featured "hands-on inquiry and problem-based history projects designed to allow students to 'do' history," evolving into a "stage 3.0 in which the emphasis is on active learning, collaboration, and enhanced interaction," with a "stage 4.0" or "constructivist" future in which students explore and build their own paths into American history.[60]

OER can do more than annihilate costs for users. As Mintz suggested, the digital medium is fertile ground for new ways of writing, producing, and using traditional textbooks. In 2007, for instance, the Institute for the Future of the Book released their CommentPress platform, a Word Press–based tool that turned private margin notes into a social enterprise. "Text is meant to be a conversation," said Ben Vershbow, the institute's associate director. At the University of Michigan, the not-for-profit Ithaka organization realized the platform could be a new way to write and edit texts. Using the platform, it published "University Publishing in a Digital Age."[61] The platform offered publishers new experiments collapsing the relationships between book production and consumption. In 2012, the University of Minnesota Press used the platform to publish the initial *Debates in the Digital Humanities*.[62] The following year, the University of Michigan Press used it to publish *Writing History in the Digital Age*. Readers could witness book-writing in its formative stages. They could annotate socially and shape the construction of its text through comments. As the digital humanities scholar Matthew Gold put it, "any software engineer can tell you, the more eyes you have on a problem, the more likely you are to find and fix bugs in the system."[63] Review would no longer need to be limited to a few anonymous academic readers but could instead be opened to the entire profession. Even more radically, open review could dramatically expand the opportunities for collaborative knowledge production. To expand upon Gold's analogy, the more diverse the training and experiences of the eyes on the problem, the more likely you are to creatively refine and reshape intellectual work while finding and fixing bugs.

CommentPress is not alone. Connexions, an early proponent of open-source teaching materials, drew inspiration from the culture of digital music sharing—"rip, burn, and mash"—and built a collaborative writing platform via open-source software called Rhaptos.[64] Hypothes.is evolved from a platform to crowdsource translations of rap lyrics into, as the project described it, "a conversation layer over the entire web that works everywhere, without needing implementation by any underlying site." Launched in 2012, it offered a flexible platform for shared, user-end annotations as well as a medium for public review.

CommentPress, Hypothes.is, and other projects are a testament to the turn toward living, breathing texts that can adapt to both new content and new technologies. The field of digital humanities, eager to expand pedagogical horizons in ways that address the needs of students, remains full of creative energy. Recent innovations have created unprecedented challenges. For the first time, the greatest problem facing human knowledge is not an absence of information but a surplus. And yet reliable, curated information often remains inaccessible. In response, the open access movement has challenged not only the textbook cost crisis but the very values and assumptions that allowed for it. Digital technology may well offer solutions. Humanists have begun to embrace open texts and the promise of mass collaboration coupled with rigorous, traditional peer reviews. But despite such successes, an uncritical utopianism and the complacency it engenders must continue to be resisted. Quality code will not save us.

A critical evaluation of the history of open-access textbook publishing reveals the possibilities flowing from utopian dreaming while exposing the rigid structural limits to democratic change that persist in American higher education. Despite pedagogical trends that have de-emphasized their instructive utility, textbooks stubbornly persist as a central feature of higher education. Expanded access through OER has and will continue to level the playing field for disadvantaged students, while new methods of joint authorship and mass collaboration will not only improve textbook quality but will also redefine traditional notions of authorship and publishing. Democracy, however, isn't just about access; it's also about participation. Higher education exists within contexts and power structures buoyed by a neoliberal political economy. "Innovation and disruption are ideas that originated in the arena of business," wrote Jill Lepore, "but which have since been applied to arenas whose values and goals are remote from the values and goals of business."[65] At the mercy of cost-conscious administrators, "disruption"-minded donors, and institutionalized granting agencies, new publishing paradigms may only reinforce existing institutional inequalities while allowing OER and other ed-tech to justify the exploitation of contingent faculty and the de-skilling of the professoriate. Disruption is not liberation. Technology is entirely neutral. The digital revolution has enabled us to open the textbook, but only deeper and more-sustained structural change will allow digital humanists to live up to the democratic potential of disruptive technology.

Notes

1. Jessica Stillman, "The Future According to Megan Smith," *Forbes*, July 19, 2013.
2. Anne Burdick, Johanna Drucker, Peter Lunenfeld, Todd Presner, and Jeffrey Schnapp, *Digital_Humanities* (Cambridge: MIT Press, 2012), vii.

3. John Willinsky, *The Access Principle: The Case for Open Access to Research and Scholarship* (Cambridge: MIT Press, 2005), 207.

4. Willinsky, *Access Principle*, 189.

5. Gracia Lam, "Boundless Wants to Do to Textbooks What Wikipedia Did to Encyclopedias," *Boston Globe* (April 22, 2014).

6. For more on SHARE, see Share.org, "About" (https://www.share.org/about); and Donald L. Shell, "The Share 709 System: A Cooperative Effort," *Journal of the ACM* 6, no. 2 (April 1959): 123–27.

7. Richard Stallman, "The GNU Manifesto," https://www.gnu.org/gnu/manifesto.en.html.

8. Amy Earhart, "Digital Humanities Futures: Conflict, Power, and Public Knowledge," *Digital Studies* (2005), https://www.digitalstudies.org/ojs/index.php/digital_studies/article/view/347.

9. For more on the Educational Object Economy, see Edmond Gaible, "The Educational Object Economy: Alternatives in Authoring and Aggregation of Educational Software," *Interactive Learning Environment* 12, no. 1–2 (2004): 7–25.

10. "How We Got Started," MERLOT, info.merlot.org/merlothelp/topic.htm#t=How_We_Got_Started.htm, accessed July 10, 2018.

11. Carey Goldberg, "Auditing Classes at MIT, on the Web and Free," *New York Times*, April 4, 2001, http://www.nytimes.com/2001/04/04/us/auditing-classes-at-mit-on-the-web-and-free.html.

12. Marguerite Avery, Alex Holzman, and Robert Brown, "Special Issue on Open Access," *Journal of Scholarly Publishing* 49, no. 1 (October 2017): 1.

13. T. J. Bliss and M. Smith, "A Brief History of Open Educational Resources," in *Open: The Philosophy and Practices That Are Revolutionizing Education and Science*, ed. R. S. Jhangiani and R. Biswas-Diener (London: Ubiquity Press, 2017), 9–27.

14. UNESCO, "Forum on the Impact of Open Courseware for Higher Education in Developing Countries," July 1–3, 2002, http://unesdoc.unesco.org/images/0012/001285/128515e.pdf; see also Sally M. Johnstone, "Open Educational Resources Serve the World," *Educause Quarterly* 28, no. 3 (2005): 15–18.

15. David Wiley, "Defining the 'Open' in Open Content and Open Educational Resources," http://opencontent.org/definition/, accessed July 11, 2018.

16. Bliss and M. Smith, "Brief History," 13.

17. Beginning in 2008, for instance, the United States government mandated open access for all research that received the approximately $30 billion in annual funding from the National Institutes of Health. National Institutes of Health, "Open Access Policy and Funding Information," https://www.nature.com/openresearch/funding/nih-open-access-policy-funding/.

18. Bliss and M. Smith, "Brief History," 10.

19. Jade Boyd, "Connexions Project Officially Launches," Rice News, February 26, 2004, news.rice.edu/2004/02/26/connexions-project-officially-launches/.

20. According to Martin Paul Eve, "The term 'open access' refers to the removal of price and permission barriers to scholarly research." Martin Paul Eve, *Open Access and the Humanities: Contexts, Controversies, and the Future* (New York: Cambridge University Press, 2014), 3.

21. Jo Guldi and David Armitage, "Why Open Access Publication for The History Manifesto?" *Cambridge Open*, 2014, http://historymanifesto.cambridge.org/blog/2014/09/why-open-access-publication-history-manifesto#sthash.FYCNEiH9.dpuf.

22. Martin Weller, *The Battle for Open: How Openness Won and Why It Doesn't Feel Like Victory* (London: Ubiquity Press, 2014), 2.

23. Eve, *Open Access*, 7

24. For more on the achievement gap in education, see Sean F. Reardon, "The Widening Income Achievement Gap," *Educational Leadership* 70, no. 8 (May 2013): 10–16.

25. Noam Cohen, "Don't Buy That Textbook, Download It Free," *New York Times*, September 14, 2008, https://www.nytimes.com/2008/09/15/technology/15link.html?_r=1&ei=5070&emc=etal.

26. The precise amount was $1,298 in 2016. See https://bigfuture.collegeboard.org/pay-for-college/college-costs/quick-guide-college-costs.

27. Government Accountability Office, *College Textbooks: Enhanced Offerings Appear to Drive Recent Price Increases*, July 2005, GAO-05-806, http://www.gao.gov/new.items/d05806.pdf.

28. Ethan Senack, "Fixing the Broken Textbook Market: How Students Respond to High Textbook Costs and Demand Alternatives," Student PIRGs, January 2014, https://uspirg.org/sites/pirg/files/reports/NATIONAL%20Fixing%20Broken%20Textbooks%20Report1.pdf.

29. Elsewhere, we explore the contradictions between the democratic aspirations of digital history as an academic field and broader structural inequalities within the field, higher education, and the broader American economy. See Joseph L. Locke and Ben Wright, "History *Can* Be Open Source: Democratic Dreams and the Rise of Digital History," *American Historical Review* (forthcoming December 2022).

30. Adeline Koh, "A Letter to the Humanities: DH Will Not Save You," *Hybrid Pedagogy*, April 19, 2015, hybridpedagogy.org/a-letter-to-the-humanities-dh-will-not-save-you/.

31. Weller, *Battle*, 76.

32. "Textbooks Today and Tomorrow: A Conversation about History, Pedagogy, and Economics," *Journal of American History* 100, no. 4 (March 2014): 1139–69.

33. John Wright, "Open Access for Monograph Publishing: Operational Thoughts and Speculations," *Journal of Scholarly Publishing* 49, no. 2 (January 2018): 175–92.

34. *Times Higher Education Supplement*, October 13, 2000, http://www.timeshighereducation.co.uk/story.asp?storyCode=153788&sectioncode=26. In 2004, LTSN merged with the Institute for Learning and Teaching in High Education and the TQEF National Co-ordination Team to form the Higher Education Academy: https://en.wikipedia.org/wiki/Learning_and_Teaching_Support_Network.

35. http://www.hefce.ac.uk/learning/tinits/cetl/ipr/IPR_dissemination.pdf. See also David Kernohan and Amber Thomas, "Open Educational Resources: A Historical Perspective," 2012, available at https://oerknowledgecloud.org/content/open-educational-resources-historical-perspective.

36. Sarah Lacy, "Peter Thiel: We're in a Bubble and It's Not the Internet. It's Higher Education," *Tech Crunch*, April 10, 2011, https://techcrunch.com/2011/04/10/peter-thiel-were-in-a-bubble-and-its-not-the-internet-its-higher-education/.

37. Goldberg, "Auditing Classes at MIT, on the Web and Free."

38. Anthony Grafton, "Loneliness and Freedom," *Perspectives: The Newsletter of the American Historical Association* 49 (March 2011), https://www.historians.org/publications-and-directories/perspectives-on-history/march-2011/loneliness-and-freedom.

39. Scott Nesbit et al., "A Conversation with Digital Historians," *Southern Spaces* (January 31, 2012), https://southernspaces.org/2012/conversation-digital-historians.

40. Collaborative Organization for Virtual Education, Dino Franco Felluga, general editor, https://editions.covecollective.org/.

41. Stevan Harnad, "Overture: A Subversive Proposal," in *Scholarly Journals at the Crossroads: A Subversive Proposal for Electronic Publishing*, ed. Shumelda Okerson and James J. O'Donnell (Washington, DC: Association of Research Libraries, 1995), 11–12.

42. Eve, *Open Access and the Humanities*, 18; see also Peter Suber, *Open Access* (Cambridge: MIT Press, 2012), 9–15.

43. Willinsky, *The Access Principle*. As Cable Green, Creative Commons' Director of Global Learning, put it, "When the marginal cost of sharing is $0, educators have an ethical obligation to share." Cable Green, "Open Education: The Moral, Business & Policy Case for OER," Keynote Address, Affordable Learning Georgia Conference, December 11, 2014, http://www.affordablelearninggeorgia.org/documents/Cable_EveningPlenaryKeynote.pdf.

44. Carl Straumsheim, "'Paying It Forward' Publishing," *Inside Higher Ed*, February 10, 2015, https://www.insidehighered.com/news/2015/02/10/u-california-press-builds-open-access-publishing-model-around-paying-it-forward.

45. Open Textbook Network, http://research.cehd.umn.edu/otn/.

46. Center for Open Education, http://open.umn.edu/fellowship/default.asp.

47. Open Textbook Library, open.umn.edu/opentextbooks/.

48. Kathleen Fitzpatrick, *Planned Obsolescence: Publishing, Technology, and the Future of the Academy* (New York: New York University Press, 2011), 174.

49. See, for instance, Open Library of Humanities, "About," https://www.openlibhums.org/site/about/.

50. António Andrade et al., "Beyond OER: Shifting Focus to Open Educational Practices," OPAL Report 2011, https://oerknowledgecloud.org/sites/oerknowledgecloud.org/files/OPAL2011.pdf.

51. Jo Guldi and David Armitage, *The History Manifesto* (Cambridge: Cambridge University Press, 2014).

52. Mira Waller, William M. Cross, and Lillian Rigling, "The Open Textbook Toolkit: Seeding Successful Partnerships for Collaboration between Academic Libraries and University Presses," *Journal of Scholarly Publishing* 49 (October 2017): 53–65.

53. Mary Rose Muccie, Joe Lucia, Elliot Shore, Clifford Lynch, and Peter Berkery, "Across the Great Divide: Findings and Possibilities for Action from the 2016 Summit Meeting of Academic Libraries and University Presses with Administrative Relationships" (Washington, DC: Association of American University Presses, 2013), http://www.aaupnet.org/resources/for-members/data-collection-and-analysis/ library-press-collaboration-survey, cited by Waller, Cross, and Rigling, "The Open Textbook Toolkit," 55.

54. See, for instance, Jeff Gallant, "Librarians Transforming Textbooks: The Past, Present, and Future of the Affordable Learning Georgia Initiative," *Georgia Library Quarterly* 52, no. 2 (2015), http://digitalcommons.kennesaw.edu/glq/vol52/iss2/8; Shan C. Sutton and Faye A. Chadwell, "Open Textbooks at Oregon State University: A Case Study of New Opportunities for Academic Libraries and University Presses," *Journal of Librarianship and Scholarly Communication* 2, no. 4 (2014), doi:10.7710/2162-3309.1174.

55. Harry L. Watson, *Building the American Republic, Volume 1* (Chicago: University of Chicago Press, 2018), and Jane Dailey, *Building the American Republic, Volume 2* (Chicago: University of Chicago Press, 2018), http://press.uchicago.edu/sites/buildingtheamericanrepublic/index.html.

56. Gabrielle Vojtech and Judy Grissett, "Student Perceptions of College Faculty Who Use OER," *International Review of Research in Open and Distributed Learning* 18, no. 4 (June 1, 2017): 155–71.

57. J. Hilton III, D. Gaudet, P. Clark, T. J. Robinson, and D. Wiley, "The Adoption of Open Education Resources by One Community College Math Department," *International Review of Research in Open and Distributed Learning* 14, no. 4 (2013), retrieved from http://www.irrodl.org/index.php/irrodl/article/view/1523/2652; D. Wiley, J. Hilton III, S. Ellington, and T. Hall, "A Preliminary Examination of the Cost Savings and Learning Impacts of Using Open Textbooks in Middle and High School Science Classes," *International Review of Research in Open and Distributed Learning* 13, no. 3 (2012), retrieved from http://www.irrodl.org/index.php/irrodl/article/view/1153/2256; J. Hilton III, T. J. Robinson, and D. Wiley, "A Multi-Institutional Study of the Impact of Open Textbook Adoption on the Learning Outcomes of Post-Secondary Students," *Journal of Computing in Higher Education* 27, no. 3 (2015), 159–72, doi:10.1007/s12528-015-9101-x.

58. Rebecca Pitt, "Mainstreaming Open Textbooks: Educator Perspectives on the Impact of OpenStax College Open Textbooks," *International Review of Research in Open and Distributed Learning* 16, no. 4 (2015): 133–55; Eulho Jung, Christine Bauer, and Allan Heaps, "Higher Education Faculty Perceptions of Open Textbook Adoption," *International Review of Research in Open and Distributed Learning* 18, no. 4 (2017): 123–41.

59. *American Yawp* Custom Analytics Report, May 7, 2021, in the possession of the authors.

60. Daniel J. Cohen et al., "Interchange: The Promise of Digital History," *Journal of American History* 95, no. 2 (September 2008): 456.

61. Kathleen Fitzpatrick, "CommentPress: New (Social) Structures for New (Networked) Texts," *Journal of Electronic Publishing* (Fall 2007): n.p.; Brock Read, "Marginally Better: Software Uses Side Notes to Turn Books into Discussions," *Chronicle of Higher Education*, September 28, 2007. See sr.ithaka.org.

62. Lauren F. Klein and Matthew K. Gold, eds., *Debates in the Digital Humanities* (Minneapolis: University of Minnesota Press, 2016), http://dhdebates.gc.cuny.edu/.

63. Matthew K. Gold, "Whose Revolution? Towards a More Equitable Digital Humanities," *Lapland Chronicles*, 2012, blog.mkgold.net/2012/01/10/whose-revolution-toward-a-more-equitable-digital-humanities/.

64. Cohen, "Don't Buy That Textbook." For more on Rhaptos see "Connexions: Rhaptos Software Development," https://web.archive.org/web/20090724153058/http:/rhaptos.org/.

65. Jill Lepore, "The Disruption Machine," *New Yorker*, June 23, 2014, https://www.newyorker.com/magazine/2014/06/23/the-disruption-machine.

Books of Ours

What Libraries Can Learn about Social Media from Books of Hours

Alexandra Alvis

In an age of the democratization of information, special collections libraries can struggle to come to terms with the perceived conflict between collections care and access. More and more, those institutions with rare book holdings are turning to social media both to alleviate the conflict and to make their collections more accessible to new audiences, readers, and researchers. Some may argue that reaching a more general audience through social media should not be part of the core values of such specialized libraries and institutions. As Daniel H. Traister noted, some library staff "feel that a barrier between rare book collections and the public is a good thing."[1] While it may be true that maintaining a barrier reinforces the imperative that special collections items are to be handled with more care and respect than books on the open stacks, a social media presence does not magically unlock the vault doors and thus allow the public to stream into secure stacks.[2] If the wider public associates barriers—and "dust and irrelevance" as Colleen Theisen observes—with special collections, then there remains a great deal to be done in communicating the value and interest of special collections as well as generating excitement about them.[3]

Libraries must diversify the way they make their content accessible with a view toward maintaining existing user bases and appealing to new ones; social media is, quite simply, the most efficient way to provide access and engagement to the broadest audience in the twenty-first century.[4] The wider the net is cast, the more possibility there is of positive public engagement with a special collections' institutional social media presence. If done well, social media strategies enable the public to see not only those exciting items held in libraries but also to understand the opportunities for research studies. Social media can therefore act as a primer for the use of special collections. While a first-time viewer may not grasp the significance of the text and images posted by libraries, they will with sustained cultivation and connection-building.[5] Theisen believes the core purpose of special collections' social media use should be to give followers "the necessary knowledge, a reduction of anxiety, and a changed perspective."[6] This type of thoughtful marketing is inherent in the use and promotion of social media.

Rachel Pendergrass, CEO of scientific communications firm ScienceAF, extolls the relationship-building virtues of experts and nonexperts "riff[ing]" together, as well as "finding a shared language" between institutions and followers on Twitter.[7] These conversations rely on first-person communication norms to make "lifeless" entities more friendly to users, a form of interaction that some may not expect from institutions, which have traditionally pursued a "calculated" presence.[8] Deciding what content to Tweet or post about represents a conversation between a library and its followers: either the library is starting the conversation by posting something new and encouraging responses, or it is hopping into an ongoing conversation already taking place on a social media platform. At a party, for instance, different conversations are being carried out simultaneously. Some are serious and require measured responses; others are streams of jokes and playful ribbings. Whether starting or participating in a conversation, it is necessary to first read the room—see what others are talking about, figure out the different tones. This thoughtful communication encourages the establishment of relationships and trust between institutions and individuals.

Even though we tend to privilege the *platform* in discussions of social media, Daniel Miller et al. note, "it is the content rather than the platform that is most significant when it comes to why social media matters."[9] Different tones and levels of formality are more popular on different platforms. And though the flavor of the communication may change, the content writ large does not, especially when considering institutional content, with its grounding in the central mission of the organization it is meant to represent. Twitter—a social media platform that has gained influence in the world of special collections libraries—uses short-form posts and the inclusion of images where posts act as "hooks" to generate broader interest in the collection.[10] Thus, the platform is ideal for supporting special collections content since the most successful social media posts on any platform have both textual and visual elements.[11] Yet, as with any digital platform, it is important to consider the levels of access and engagement that a given platform affords as well as its limitations. In the case of Special Collection Libraries, the use of Twitter can make those collections perceived as "hidden" more visible and accessible, but in doing so, issues of content, context, and inherent inequity often arise.

#LibraryTwitter

It may seem that there are an infinite number of social media accounts with similarly infinite variations for users to follow, but the accounts can, in general, be sorted into two broad categories: personal accounts and brand accounts. Although some crossover exists between these two categories, it is generally fairly simple to make the distinction between them based on the content they post. Brand accounts, such as retail companies and heritage institutions like museums and libraries, are nearly as popular as personal accounts for social media users.[12] According to a 2016 survey, 48 percent of American social media users have interacted with brand accounts on at least one of their social media platforms.

A subset of special collections, which social media often use, is the phenomenon of "Library Twitter." This designation does not just refer to library presence on Twitter: within the #LibraryTwitter hashtag is everything from individuals calling for research assistance or opinions of colleagues to sharing interesting collection finds to general complaints from library workers. Institutions use the hashtag as well, but by and large this is a place for the library-adjacent and for librarians with personal accounts whose "opinions do not reflect those of [their] employer."

The library community is not limited to Twitter. It has a slightly less organized analog on Instagram, and it also seems to exist to a lesser extent on Tumblr. These are spaces where librarians can move relatively unrestrained by institutional standards and tones, and bluntly express their bibliographic passions and pains, to very warm receptions in some cases. On Twitter, John Overholt (@john_overholt), the Curator of Early Modern Books and Manuscripts at Harvard's Houghton Library, has around 8,500 more followers than the Houghton's institutional account (@houghtonlib). On Instagram, although I (@book_historia) only have 22,300 followers to my employer Smithsonian Libraries' (@silibraries) 49,100, in general my posts generate at least three times the engagement of theirs.

Techni-Calli
@Iwillleavenow

Btw, privacy law has brought me into the glorious world of #librarytwitter and if you're not friends with a whole bunch of librarians, you are MISSING OUT, these people are BADASS and I love them (plus, obviously, they have the best book recommendations).

4:00 PM · Mar 18, 2019 · Twitter Web Client

Figure 12.

At first glance, these statistics do not make sense: What could be a bigger draw to people than the content of prestigious institutions like Harvard and the Smithsonian? But Theisen pokes holes in the assumption that institutional status can engender more user engagement: she observes that "a known individual who is able to express . . . occasionally idiosyncratic opinions is perceived as more trustworthy than an anonymous institutional voice."[13] Although both the Houghton and the Smithsonian accounts make use of first-person pronouns, they remain literally faceless and tonally restrained. If they were to wade further into projecting individual identities, however, they run the risk of entering a sort of social media uncanny valley, where their efforts come off as disingenuous and perhaps creepy to their audiences. Is it possible for institutions to find a middle ground where they can build personal trust and still accomplish their core educational missions? Are librarians and the library-adjacent not also accomplishing this mission in a different way?

It may be useful here to think about special collections libraries and individual librarians as similar to the people involved in the production of medieval manuscripts, namely the scribes and illuminators of one Western European medieval "best seller," Books of Hours.[14] As special collections librarians use social media to represent both their institutions and their own personalities, scribes in those days were expected to copy text dutifully from an exemplar but had room for variation and a certain amount of personalization in that work. Illuminators also followed exemplars in most cases, but with differences evident when comparing illuminated miniatures of the same text side by side. Tweaks in the compositions of formulaic scenes abound, from differences in facial expression to the repositioning of figures. This is to say nothing of the mayhem that sometimes ran rampant in the margins around the miniatures, often filled with fantastic hybrid creatures and references to medieval jokes. Even in their variety, illuminations acted as an intermediary for readers in general to

Figure 13.

perform standardized devotions, and most recent scholarly interpretations understand marginal wackiness as content that supplements and contrasts with the central scenes rather than as non sequitur distractions. When combined, the work of the scribe and the illuminator amounts to the creation of a devotional object, one that is more than the sum of its parts. In a similar fashion, following John Overholt and the Houghton accounts offers a picture of a library inhabited by people passionate about their collections. The relationship between institutions and followers can be mediated by individuals, just as the relationship between the owner of a Book of Hours and its contents can be mediated by the personal input from scribes and illuminators.

Perhaps the most revolutionary feature of social media is the opportunity for *literal* dialogue between followers and the accounts they follow,[15] whether that dialogue is silly or serious. But, as Steven Escar Smith points out, the majority of social media users are not researchers, and some never will be; if the only audience that institutional social media caters to is that of the specialist, it will reinforce the negative stereotypes about special collections that Theisen draws attention to.[16] Therefore, connecting to social media users on their level—"riffing" with them in Rachel Pendergrass's words, or communicating "on the internet's terms" as described by Adam Koszary[17]—allows for ongoing engagement that makes the idea of archives and their holdings more accessible.

Just as Books of Hours encouraged readers to emotionally identify with the differentiated representations of text and image, a well-curated library social media presence can bring unfamiliar concepts to life and make them relevant to followers.[18] Institutional accounts can make use of tools such as livestreams to enable followers to see a book being actively used in real time, which, to some audiences, may be quite a departure from the static museum setting in which they are accustomed to seeing "old" books. This liveness may enable readers to engage with books in a manner different from their digitized copies. Even if followers have viewed digitized books, the majority of the images tend to be flat overhead views that can obscure the true size and shape of a book, giving it an immobile, two-dimensional feeling. By emphasizing the present and ongoing function of collections items through video, institutions can bring the past into the present and encourage users to understand books as dynamic objects to be used, and indeed show the proper methods of using them.[19]

In the same way that complex embellishments were outside the budget of many owners of Books of Hours, the activities prescribed for special collections to get the most out of social media—the time and technology needed to keep up with and contribute to current discourse, the showcasing of personal interests of employees, the livestreaming—come at a cost that some are not able to pay. Expecting or requiring librarians to tailor their personal social media presences in order to benefit their institution is an especially problematic path. Some people do not mind blurring the lines of their personal and professional lives to the point where they receive reference questions on personal accounts, but anonymity and a work-life balance are more important to others.[20] There is work to be done in the ethics of institutional first-person voice and what that means for the people amplifying that voice.

Decontextualization: Issues of Access and Inequality

The late Middle Ages saw a rise of the middle class in Western Europe, and the proliferation of manuscript Books of Hours came as a direct result.[21] Manuscript

Books of Hours survive in huge numbers in libraries and collections the world over; Christopher De Hamel estimates that they are "more widely scattered around the world than any other object made in the Middle Ages," attesting to the broad range of people that purchased, owned, and read these works.[22] Unlike complex liturgical manuscripts with a set function and audience, Books of Hours served multiple functions for their consumers, namely as devotional objects, as well as children's primers and even places to record family histories.[23] In comparison to Books of Hours, social media users can form personal connections through engagement with the platform and thus encounter people, places, and things that are not part of their daily lives. Following people and institutions on Twitter enables users to mentally situate themselves closer to things that they may never encounter face-to-face, with virtual participation bringing a "layperson" into perceived contact with a cultural heritage object, resulting in a beneficial effect for the reader/user.

Books of Hours were designed to be used as a whole codex with interdependent parts. When they fell out of favor in the mid-sixteenth century, many were broken up, scattered, and recycled for their strong and valuable parchment pages.[24] More still were dismembered during religious shifts such as the Reformation, and others dismantled by overly enthusiastic art historians, such as John Ruskin, in the nineteenth century. Creating extra-illustrated books by inserting leaves of illuminations cut from manuscripts was a common practice, as was the sale of visually interesting elements of books to buyers bedazzled by their bright colors and sparkling gold leaf.[25] In the twentieth century, Books of Hours were often broken up in order to sell the leaves at a greater profit individually than the manuscript would have made as a whole. For historians today, however, the desire to break books was, at the least, misguided.[26]

For social media users, this stripping of context can be seen occurring digitally in real time across various platforms. The @MedievalReacts Twitter account (now suspended) and other "aggregate" meme accounts use images from medieval manuscripts—often originally posted on social media with proper citations by scholars and libraries—presenting them with amusing captions without mentioning the image's host institution or origin. The goals of these aggregate accounts is to generate as many follows, likes, reTweets, or other forms of surface engagement in as short a time as possible in order to use the account as a vehicle for advertising.[27] These goals differ greatly from the core value of educational or institutional library accounts. The stakes are high: the founders of the @HistoryInPics Twitter account have raised more than $2 million in investments in this manner.[28] Determined viewers can use tools like Google Image Search to try to follow breadcrumbs back to the original source of the image, but this requires a degree of technical skill, some prior knowledge, and a time expenditure that many are not able to pay. Indeed, Theisen identifies skill, knowledge, and time as key to followers "envisioning [them]selves as a user of special collections."[29] Without these identifiers, special collections and the objects therein will remain a mystery. As Kate Wiles bemoans, it would not be that difficult for accounts that aggregate images to provide followers the option for further research and include context such as: "Understanding these images does not make them any less fantastic."[30] How viewers perceive access to special collections is fraught enough without the path to learning more about them being obscured by social media accounts, which are concerned only with profit.

Social media is so commonly touted as a medium that enables access that it occludes questions of both economic access and access on the basis of ability. Statistics show that while underprivileged populations today have a demonstrated "strong interest" in social media, they may not be able to access it on mobile devices due to economic limitations.[31] In addition to financial restrictions, participation in vision-based memes on Twitter, for example, that solicit images "with no further explanation" (such as book covers and initials) can leave the visually impaired behind; screen readers can only *dictate* the words that appear in a post. Without proper textual description or alt text, they—the visually impaired—remain unreachable. For the hearing impaired and deaf, live videos, unless they are captioned in real time, do not have the same impact. Certainly, viewing special collections books in motion is a beneficial experience, but the context offered by narration is often just as important as the visual element. This lack of digital accessibility sometimes mirrors physical accessibility: reading rooms, particularly in older special collections libraries, are not always wheelchair accessible. Although it would seem that within both institutional social media and Books of Hours, the differently abled are not top priorities, it is possible for special collections to be aware of this shortfall and adjust their content and accessibility accordingly.

Conclusion

> theory: medieval twitter's constant niche memes are a conspiracy designed to get people into medieval studies
> @ofmarginalia, January 8, 2019

The Tweet above by an undergraduate student in medieval studies in the UK neatly encapsulates many of the ideas presented in this essay. Although they specifically refer to Medieval Twitter (the collective term for the community of medievalists with Twitter accounts) and medieval studies, the sentiment also rings true for #LibraryTwitter and getting people into reading rooms. Embracing the fascinating and sometimes wacky elements of special collections through the use of a first-person voice and a humanizing tone does more than entertain: it generates interest among followers who have no prior experience with special collections and lets them know that using the collection is not beyond their reach. But overreliance on the social media format and shorter-form communication, or expecting the weight of the institution to be carried by pretty pictures, may leave users wanting more with no clear way to get it. It is important to "play the game of social media," balancing on the tightrope of educating while entertaining.[32] Too much of one over the other will alienate some groups, particularly those who do not have the means to further explore the content of institutional posts. With the help of certain parallels between Books of Hours and social media, we can begin to consider and uncover the potential of social media use in libraries so that the institution and librarians together can paint a fuller picture of their collections and the nature of human experience with the material world.

Notes

1. Daniel H. Traister, "Public Services and Outreach in Rare Book, Manuscript, and Special Collections Libraries," *Library Trends* 52, no. 1 (2003): 87–108, 91.

2. Traister, "Public Services and Outreach," 91.

3. Colleen Theisen, "Toward a Culture of Social Media in Special Collections," in *New Directions for Special Collections*, ed. Lynne M. Thomas and Beth M. Whittaker (Santa Barbara: Libraries Unlimited, 2017), 226.

4. Theisen, "Toward a Culture of Social Media," 226.

5. Theisen, "Toward a Culture of Social Media," 226.

6. Theisen, "Toward a Culture of Social Media," 227.

7. David Samuel Shiffman, "Silly Anatomy Lessons Take Biology by Storm," *American Scientist*, 2019, https://www.americanscientist.org/blog/macroscope/silly-anatomy-lessons-take-biology-twitter-by-storm.

8. Alyssa Bereznak, "Brands Who Stan: How Entertainment Companies Started Tweeting in the First Person," *The Ringer*, 2019, https://www.theringer.com/2019/1/16/18184386/netflix-mtv-hbo-tweeting-first-person.

9. Daniel Miller, Elisabetta Costa, Nell Haynes, Tom McDonald, Razvan Nicolescu, Jolynna Sinanan, Juliano Spyer, Shriram Venkatraman, and Xinyuan Wang, *How the World Changed Social Media* (London: UCL Press, 2016), 8.

10. Miller et al., *How the World Changed Social Media*, 155.

11. Adam Koszary, "Lowering the Tone: Doing Social Media at the Bodleian Libraries," *Art + Marketing*, 2017, https://artplusmarketing.com/lowering-the-tone-doing-social-media-at-bodleian-libraries-5c6c6d6287ca.

12. "Hootsuite Survey Highlights Importance of Social Media across the Customer Journey," *Hootsuite*, 2016, https://hootsuite.com/newsroom/press-releases/hootsuite-survey-highlights-importance-of-social-media-across-the-customer-journey.

13. Theisen, "Toward a Culture of Social Media," 230.

14. Books of Hours functioned as a connection for lay Christians to the pious lives of ordained members of the Roman Catholic Church, allowing them to participate, however sparingly, in the more regimented and frequent devotional practices of the clergy. For these Christian lay owners, this participation brought them spiritual comfort. Raymond Clemens and Timothy Graham, *Introduction to Manuscript Studies* (Ithaca, NY: Cornell University Press, 2007), 208.

15. Alexandra Newman, "Sharing, Not Shushing: Social Media and Rare Book Librarians," *TXT 2017: Navigating a World of Text*: 38–46, 43.

16. Steven Escar Smith, "From 'Treasure Room' to 'School Room': Special Collections and Education," *RBM: A Journal of Rare Books, Manuscripts, and Cultural Heritage* 7, no. 1 (2006): 31–39, 32.

17. Koszary, "Lowering the Tone."

18. Kathryn A. Smith, *Art, Identity and Devotion in Fourteenth-Century England: Three Women and Their Books of Hours* (London and Toronto: The British Library and the University of Toronto Press, 2003), 57.

19. Newman, "Sharing, Not Shushing," 43–44. Video, particularly when streamed live, also offers the opportunity for followers to virtually set foot in the reading room, by asking the book handlers to turn to a certain page or to get a closer view of something. This focus on handling and interaction allows nonspecialists to understand books in a human context, in the same way that use of first-person voice can be used as a means of connecting with followers.

20. I am referring to myself here, but based on professional and personal conversations this happens to other librarians with known social media presences.

21. Clemens and Graham, *Introduction to Manuscript Studies*, 208.

22. Christopher De Hamel, *A History of Illuminated Manuscripts* (London: Phaidon Press, 2014), 168. See also De Hamel, *Medieval Craftsmen Series: Scribes and Illuminators* (Toronto: University of Toronto Press, 2013).

23. De Hamel, *History of Illuminated Manuscripts*, 176 and 178.

24. John Harthan, *Books of Hours and Their Owners* (London: Thames and Hudson, 1982), 23; Roger S. Wieck, *Painted Prayers: The Book of Hours in Medieval and Renaissance Art* (New York: George Braziller, 1997), 9. See also Lawrence R. Poos, "Social History and the Book of Hours," in Roger S. Wieck, *Time Sanctified: The Book of Hours in Medieval Art and Life* (New York: George Braziller, 1988), 33–38.

25. Roger S. Wieck, "Folio Fugitiva: The Pursuit of the Illuminated Manuscript Leaf," *Journal of the Walters Art Gallery* 54 (1996): 233–54, 235.

26. Yet today, certain antiquarian book dealers with reputations as "breakers" take this same approach to profit over maintaining historical context.

27. Allison Meier, "How Viral History Accounts Are Hurting the Past They Purport to Celebrate," *Hyperallergic*, 2015, https://hyperallergic.com/198664/how-viral-history-accounts-are-hurting-the-past-they-purport-to-celebrate/.

28. Meier, "How Viral History Accounts."

29. Theisen, "Toward a Culture of Social Media," 227.

30. Kate Wiles, "Monetising the Past: Medieval Marginalia and Social Media," *History Today*, 2015, https://www.historytoday.com/monetising-past-medieval-marginalia-and-social-media.

31. Miller et al., *How the World Changed Social Media*, 128.

32. Koszary, "Lowering the Tone"; Newman, "Sharing, Not Shushing," 39.

Assessment

Section III

Whose Books Are Online?

Diversity, Equity, and Inclusion in Online Text Collections

Catherine A. Winters and
Clayton P. Michaud

Online text collections, such as Google Books, Open Library, Project Gutenberg, Wikisource, and others, have greatly expanded access to public domain books. These four projects in particular represent the four largest general collections and are free to use for anyone with an internet connection. These same services also have the potential to play a significant role in rectifying issues of exclusion by providing free, easily accessible texts that cover a more diverse range of authors and experiences through "liberation" from the constraints of the physical library.[1] While lesser-known and less frequently read books—such as noncanonical works, especially those written by women and men of color and white women—might have once been available in only a few academic libraries, now any text in the public domain can be scanned and made freely available.[2] With mission statements ranging from "choos[ing] etexts we hope extremely large portions of the audience will want and use frequently" to "giv[ing] everyone access to all knowledge—the books, web pages, audio, television, and software of our shared human culture. Forever."—it would appear that many of these online collections are not only aware of but are actively embracing this potential as a part of their organizational identity.[3] In reality, however, it remains unclear whether such online repositories have helped society move closer toward "digitization's democratic potential," or whether they continue to reinforce the same biases and expectations when it comes to traditionally underrepresented authors.[4]

This chapter asks if there is disproportionate representation in online repositories that correlates to authors' race and/or gender, or if the online repositories base their collections primarily on what people are interested in reading.[5] To test this, we create a methodology to predict the supply of readily available online texts as a result of demand, such that we can rigorously test if exclusion of texts is isolated from other causes, such as texts that are unknown or unavailable, or if these gaps exist despite reader demand. To that end, we use statistical regression analysis, "a way of mathematically sorting out which of those variables does indeed have an impact," to find whether the supply of texts in online repositories is determined solely by the demand for those texts or whether other factors, primarily the race and/or gender of the author, may play a role in the presence or absence of a text from the four major freely accessible online text repositories.[6] Our results suggest that despite the potential of online text repositories to promote greater inclusion, texts by women and authors of color are still underrepresented relative to equivalently sought-after texts by white male authors in these collections.

This research serves as a small but important step in acknowledging the continued effects of bias on the equitable availability of books for readers and expanding our understanding of online services. Concerns about public-facing internet operations include those raised in "Classics in the Million Book Library," in which the authors pointed out that "scholars have no way of understanding in more than the most general way how the services [such as Google Books and the Internet Archive] that extract information from that collection work."[7] While scholars and the general public alike often rely on services such as Google to find information, including access to texts online and through Google Books to read those texts, we have only begun to unearth and examine how these organizations operate, and when we do have a sense of *how* the collection was created, there continue to be gaps that need to be identified before they can be remedied. Crane et al. go on to ask "[W]hat is missed? What biases are embedded in the system?"[8] acknowledging that biases exist in the system both as a continuation of earlier systems, as we see in online text repositories that originally sourced their collection from physical libraries,[9] and through the decisions made to create a new system, such as the priorities and goals of the individual repositories to determine which texts to digitize and make available, perhaps based on their perception of "worthiness" or "quality." Our study provides a methodological framework for quantifying what these gaps are and therefore showing that there is a problem. We cannot begin to suggest solutions to a problem until we all agree that it exists and that these gaps reflect larger cultural patterns shaped by racism and sexism. While our statistical analysis focuses exclusively on nineteenth-century American literature and further work would need to be done to verify similar conclusions for other periods or national traditions, our findings suggest that these digital text collections continue to struggle in overcoming society's historical prejudices toward women writers and authors of color: overcoming those prejudices was not made a priority despite mission statements that might suggest otherwise.[10]

In this chapter, we lay out how we created our methodology and the results of our statistical analysis of the effect of author race and gender on the availability of texts in Google Books, Open Library, Project Gutenberg, and Wikisource. Later sections of this chapter detail these four repositories that we focus on here, creating our sample, collecting data on availability, the statistical model, and our statistical regression analysis.

Our methodology represents a collaboration between the humanities and econometrics, which is the application of statistical methods to data to quantify the relationship between multiple variables, and can be applied to other collections, time periods, or nationalities as a comparative tool, making it useful for determining inclusion and exclusion on any number of variables. It is our hope that continued use of methodologies such as these will help scholars understand these services until the point that continued inquiry begets further knowledge—not only of the extent of the exclusion but also of the causes and therefore solutions. This methodology can also be applied to other problems in which there is a perceived inequity between desire and representation that needs to be quantified for those who chose to treat it otherwise as anecdotal.

Online Repositories and the Supply of Digital Text Collections

Online digital repositories, as referred to in this chapter, are collections of texts, most frequently published books, accessible legally and without individual purchase through the internet. While the goals of each platform vary, generally these repositories focus on making texts more widely available through digital access. Some digital archives clearly define the texts that are likely to appear in the collection, such as Women Writers Project focusing on "early women's writing in English," while others are less transparent.[11] Project Gutenberg, for example, gives no indication of *how* books are selected for inclusion, simply stating that their mission is to make available "as many eBooks in as many formats as possible for the entire world to read in as many languages as possible."[12] The focus of this study is on four major repositories—Project Gutenberg, Wikisource, Google Books, and Open Library—based on the size and popularity of their collections and the stated missions of all four repositories that suggest *all* books are intended for collection.

Even though there are significant differences in how the collections are created, these four archives allow free access to texts to anyone. Not one requires an institutional license or individual membership to access texts in the public domain, and these sites can be found easily through online searches. The collections of these repositories are sizable, ranging from more than 60,000 free eBooks on Project Gutenberg to something over 10 million books free books available for download on Google Books. Furthermore, the mission statements of these organizations imply that any and every book could be a part of their collection. The information collected in this section is scattered across a number of pages on each site, and each repository appears to be falling short of its stated mission despite the staggering number of books across all four. To create a methodology that makes a fair comparison across these collections, we need to understand their differences.

The first repository, Project Gutenberg, relies on volunteer labor to create downloadable eBooks from scanned pages. After the pages are scanned, optical character recognition (OCR) software is used to convert the image file to a text file, after which each scanned page is read by volunteers to find and correct any misspellings or garbled words caused by the OCR. After several rounds of proofreading for each page, the books are then read as a whole before being released to the public, making each eBook the culmination of much labor. Anyone can volunteer for Project Gutenberg through their Distributed Proofreaders site, which is how we collected this information.[13] Books go through the lengthy preparation process based on decisions by project managers, volunteers who have formatted at least 400 pages and secured a mentor to vouch for their promotion to that level.[14] Project Gutenberg hosts most books on the English site and does not have different sites for different languages; the majority of texts on the main site are in English, but there are sometimes texts in other languages available alongside English-language eBooks.[15]

Similar to Project Gutenberg, Wikisource also uses volunteer labor and creates clean text copies, meaning each text is carefully proofread, if not retyped, to avoid any misrecognition by OCR software. However, rather than having a seniority system of volunteers who determine the texts to be included, as is the case with Project Gutenberg, anyone can choose to begin a page for a text on Wikisource, making it comparatively easy for individuals to add texts that are noted as absent. Wikisource is stratified by language, so only texts in English appear on the English-language site. Authors also have an author page, linking to the individual works to make it simple for users to find texts. Currently, multiple versions are rare in the Wikisource collection, with the few exceptions primarily including anthologies.

While Project Gutenberg and Wikisource are created and maintained by volunteers, Google Books works with a much wider network including business partnerships. Google Books is part of the Google suite, and the staff works with current authors and publishers and libraries.[16] However, these partnerships should not be understood as an inherent limit on the collection as Google Books has scanned more than 25 million books as of 2019.[17] Google Books includes books under copyright as well, some of which are available for download at the copyright holder's request,[18] unlike Project Gutenberg and Wikisource, which include only those books in the public domain. The stated goal of Google Books is to "create a comprehensive, searchable, virtual card catalog of all books in all languages that helps users discover new books and publishers discover new readers."[19] Whereas Project Gutenberg and Wikisource exist for people to download and read texts, Google views books as another thing to be searched.[20] This is further confirmed by the fact that most books appear as scanned facsimiles,[21] rather than plain text or as an eBook, and only some are available for download. Since the goal is to create a catalog of all books, there are also many versions of certain texts on Google Books.

Finally, Open Library is a project of the Internet Archive, best known for the Wayback Machine, founded by Brewster Kahle.[22] According to Kahle, the goal is "to give everyone access to all knowledge—the books, web pages, audio, television and software of our shared human culture. Forever."[23] This group aims to create an online "Library of Alexandria" and thus archive all books. Similar to Google Books, Open Library partners with libraries and other institutions and uses paid staff to scan books. Private individuals can also contribute books to the Internet Archive. Books that are not in the public domain are scanned but generally held privately, although some under copyright can be freely borrowed. Like Google Books, there are many versions of each title available, including a large number of facsimiles, but Open Library also provides plain-text versions of many books. These are not always clean-text versions, however, meaning that they have not been proofread, and sometimes include garbled text or other errors.

For those interested in determining the potential causes of disproportionate representation in these repositories as the next step in providing solutions, these differences are significant. For repositories that rely on volunteer labor, it is hard to say exactly where bias might be originating.[24] For example, Project

Gutenberg has a hierarchical system of deciding which books will be proofread and finalized.[25] This system is less than transparent, and the general philosophy "we choose etexts we hope extremely large portions of the audience will want and use frequently" is the most definitive statement of the selection criteria for this project.[26] Wikisource seems to be less seniority- and more volunteer-driven, but it is unknown if, as is widely acknowledged in the case of its parent company Wikimedia Commons, men are the dominant editorial force on the site.[27] Google Books and the Internet Archive rely on paid labor but also on their partner libraries. These collections can be seen, in part, as a reflection of which books are available in libraries, so it is not surprising that the most popular authors appear many times, while less popular authors have fewer texts available.[28] This closer look at the repositories and their differences highlights many potential avenues for biases to become embedded in the system.[29] However, before one determines why bias in text selection might exist, we first need to confirm that there truly *is* bias in representation within these online digital repositories, which is the focus of this study.[30]

Creating a Statistical Sample of Texts

Because collecting data on an entire population, in our case every book ever published, is an implausible task, we create a statistical sample of texts. For our purposes the ideal representative sample should meet the following criteria: First, it should be large enough to provide meaningful estimates yet manageable enough for one to collect the following data for each text: (i) its availability across all four collections, (ii) the race and gender of its author, as well as (iii) some way to measure the relative demand for each of our texts.[31] Second, our sample must include enough variation between the race and gender of the authors to provide meaningful statistical estimates but must be chosen in a manner such that each text's inclusion is as independent of race and gender as possible, meaning our sample needs to include men and women, white writers and writers of color, with as much of a mix between these factors as possible. However, we cannot handpick a sample of texts that evenly represents men, women, white writers, and writers of color because the sample of texts needs to be representative of our measure of demand. Last, all texts must be in the public domain so that variation across collections cannot be explained solely by copyright concerns.

With these criteria in mind, our sample consists of the most assigned text— that is, the book that was most often "assigned" or selected for each author, of the 100 most-assigned authors of nineteenth-century American literature. This sample was compiled using a sample of graduate exam reading lists.[32] By focusing on the nineteenth century, we ensure that all our texts will be in the public domain.[33] We choose to focus on nineteenth-century American literature to obtain a better balance of authors of color than would be obtained by including, for example, fifteenth-century British literature. We select the 100 most assigned authors as we found that less popular works often did not appear in any repository, nor could we find any meaningful measure of their relative demand. Likewise, focusing on the most assigned book for each author allowed us to simplify our data collection while still maintaining the level of demand associated with each author. Finally, while graduate exam reading lists are likely to exhibit bias toward traditionally canonical works of literature, they offer several distinct benefits for our research: importantly, as we need to estimate how many readers want to read a particular text, exam lists allow us to create a one-to-one relationship between the reader and the demand, whereas reading lists for both the general public[34] and course syllabi lack this relationship: one graduate student writes one exam list, while a college course might have 10 or 100 students, and often this information is not embedded in the syllabi; reading lists published for the general public could have thousands to millions of readers but may spur only a handful to read a particular book.[35] In the same vein, exam lists have about the same number of texts on each list and usually focus on texts published as books; therefore we can more safely assume that the entire book is being read.[36] Thus, exam lists provide a more clearly quantifiable demand that focuses on texts. Finally, while we accept that there is no example of pure demand that is removed from prejudice available to us because we cannot remove ourselves from the historical oppression of the field of literary studies or the world at large,[37] we chose this method of quantifying reader demand to reduce selection bias as understood in statistical sampling.[38]

The Importance of Controlling for Demand

Critical to our analysis is that we measure the relationship between the author's race and/or gender and the text's availability, which we refer to in our econometric model as its supply, *after* controlling for overall demand (i.e., the frequency with which each text appears on our set of exam lists). Controlling for the demand for each text is integral to isolating the true effect of author race and/or gender. It is to be expected that books that are assigned more frequently are more likely to be available online. For example, the fact that *Leaves of Grass* by Walt Whitman appears in more repositories than Harriet Jacobs's *Incidents in the Life of a Slave Girl* is not particularly surprising, nor is the availability of this text online necessarily the result of a race or gender bias within the repositories, because *Leaves of Grass* appears on 25 percent more exam lists.[39] A more statistically sound approach would be to compare *A Son of the Forest* by William Apess, a Native American writer, and *The Rise of Silas Lapham* by William Dean Howells, a white author, both of which were assigned on 18 of our 30 lists. *A Son of the Forest* appears in three of the four digital repositories queried, while *The Rise of Silas Lapham* appears in all four. This apples-to-apples comparison is an example of an author of color's text being less likely to appear in a digital repository, even though there is equal demand for both texts within the sample. By including the frequency with which a text is assigned in our statistical model, we can explicitly estimate differences in the probability of a text being available in a given digital repository based on author race and gender between books that we should expect to have equal demand.

Data Collection

We collected our data in September 2017. Our determination of the 100 most assigned authors was made by tallying the number of times that each author appears across a collection of 30 unique academic exam lists. We considered primarily PhD comprehensive exam lists that are designed to encompass the most significant texts in a field,[40] and our final sample consisted of 24 student-generated lists from the University of California Los Angeles (UCLA) and 6 department templates to be modified by students from UCLA, Columbia University, Sam Houston State University, the University of New Mexico, the University of Pennsylvania, and the University of Tennessee, Knoxville.[41] These particular lists were selected because the schools made the lists publicly available online, while many do not. At the time of writing, these 30 reading lists are the largest collection of data publicly available, exceeding the availability of other possibilities such as syllabi.[42] Furthermore, these universities represent a sampling of public and private universities across the United States. The balance of the departmental templates—which tend to be extremely canonical—with student-generated lists thus allows for greater potential variability, permitting a meaningful diversity of author identities. Each list has about 30 entries on it, therefore offering 900 possibilities of texts.

We found roughly 200 texts by 120 different writers throughout these 30 lists. Several authors are represented across the lists: for example, Walt Whitman's poetry is the only item on every single list. Other authors had multiple texts on most lists, such as Herman Melville, who appears 120 times on the

30 lists for an average of four texts by Melville on each list.[43] Having identified the 100 most assigned authors, we then identified each author's most cited work, thus providing us with a sample of 100 texts.

Having compiled our sample of 100 texts, we recorded the number of times each text appears on one of our 30 lists, hereafter referred to by the variable name *Frequency Assigned*. Because we can safely assume that the frequency with which a text appears in our sample is a reasonable approximation for how frequently a text is read and thus sought after, we can use this term as our measure of relative demand for each text. We then determined and recorded the race and gender of the author.[44] There are 28 writers of color represented, including 8 women of color, and 29 white female authors, meaning that about half of the writers in our sample are not white men. In examining our final data set, we observe the same general tendency presented by Maurice S. Lee: while there are a variety of writers represented on the lists, the traditional white male authors seem to be given more weight than women writers or writers of color.[45]

Finally, we searched for each text in each of the four repositories and recorded if at least one copy of that text is available in each repository.[46] As the final step in our data collection, this information represents our sample prior to statistical analysis and, while providing some insight into the issue, does not rigorously test our hypothesis.

Summary Statistics

Summary statistics for our data are presented in Table 1. We can see that not only are texts authored by white men the most frequently assigned, they are also the most likely to appear in a particular repository. On average, texts authored by white men are more frequently assigned, are more likely to appear in a single repository, and have more total digital versions available. The only measure by which texts authored by white men do not dominate is in terms of their probability of appearing in *any* repository, as all 29 texts authored by white women in our sample are in at least one repository. Aside from this fact, texts authored by white women have the second-highest value for all other measures after white men. Comparing texts by white authors and authors of color (ignoring gender), texts by white authors are more frequently assigned, more likely to appear in a single repository, more likely to appear in any repository, and have more total digital versions available.

These summary statistics might lead some to conclude that a bias exists against female authors and authors of color; however, this conclusion is based

Table 1. Summary statistics for our sample of popular texts by author demographics

	White man	White woman	Man of color	Woman of color	All (Pooled)
Average frequency assigned	9.95	8.38	6.20	5.13	8.36
Average number of archives available on	3.14	2.62	2.35	2.50	2.78
Probability of appearing in a single repository	0.78	0.66	0.59	0.63	0.70
Probability of appearing in any repository	0.98	1.00	0.90	0.88	0.96
Average total available digital versions	95.53	46.34	22.15	11.50	59.90
Total number of authors	41	30	22	9	100

	Man vs. woman		White vs. of color		All (pooled)
Average frequency assigned	8.76	7.68	9.32	5.89	8.36
Average number of archives available on	2.89	2.59	2.93	2.39	2.78
Probability of appearing in a single repository	0.72	0.65	0.73	0.60	0.70
Probability of appearing in any repository	0.95	0.97	0.99	0.89	0.96
Average total available digital versions	72.24	38.81	75.72	19.11	59.90
Total number of authors	63	37	72	28	100

Note: Wikisource only ever has a single version of any text. Values are rounded to two decimal places.

on supply data alone and does not account for differences in demand. As discussed earlier, a rigorous statistical analysis requires us to compare the availability of a text relative to other texts, which are equally sought after. This means that our statistical analysis needs to be able to isolate the effects of race and gender while simultaneously controlling for each text's relative demand. It is worth noting that texts authored by white women, men of color, and women of color appear less frequently in any particular repository, and writers of color are less likely to appear at all.[47]

Before moving on to the description of our statistical model and our quantitative results, it is worth considering some qualitative insights from our data collection. Many of the most popular writers from this period in American literature, such as Mark Twain, Edgar Allan Poe, Nathaniel Hawthorne, and Henry James, are widely available across all four platforms, potentially reinforcing their popularity and perceived significance. In contrast, many books by minority writers are harder to find. Some particularly significant works, such as Harriet Jacobs's *Incidents in the Life of a Slave Girl*, are widely available, but the availability of just a few texts authored by people of color may further reinforce the belief that only a small selection needs to be read to attain diversity in a reading list.[48] Likewise, some writers of color have published only one or two books, so it is difficult to say with certainty if these writers are being treated in the same manner because, inevitably, there are a smaller number of total texts available from these writers. Linked to this, is that more white men had the means and opportunity to publish in nineteenth-century America, potentially skewing our sample. Absences could also be an effect of books that went out of print at some point or were weeded prior to digitization, which is even more likely in now-recovered texts.

Finally, our method of generating a proxy for demand validated the findings of Maurice S. Lee regarding the lack of diversity in academic reading lists.[49] This information was a side effect of our study, but our compilation of exam lists aligns with Lee's conclusion that despite the canon wars, the same "representative" authors are overrepresented in academia producing at least an informal canon. Furthermore, while the demand of texts does show some diversity, our analysis of online text repositories shows that works by writers of color are less likely to be available online, whereas works by white male authors are abundant. In addition to showing that canonicity reproduces itself, it again shows how digitization projects can easily fall into a form of "retro-humanism" that attempts to appear neutral through new tools,[50] rather than grappling with cultural and critical critique and echoes the issues raised in the culture wars of the 1980s,1990s, and into the present.[51]

The Statistical Model

In its most general form, our statistical model takes the form

$$\Pr(Available_{i,r} = \text{True}) = F(Author\ Race_i,\ Author\ Gender_i,\ Frequency\ Assigned_i)$$

This states that we model the probability (Pr) of an individual text (i) appearing in a repository (r) as being a function of the author's race, gender, and the demand for that text—the frequency with which a given text is found on the reading lists. We start by modeling the probability of a text appearing in any one of our four repositories as a function of the natural log of the number of exam lists on which the text appears for each of our four author categories.[52] In order to estimate the slope and intercept of this function for each author category, we perform a 2-parameter (slope and intercept) Ordinary Least Squares regression (OLS) on each of the four race-gender based subsets of our data to estimate a line of best fit.[53] Based on these results, for our more integrated analysis, we combine texts by white women and texts by men of color into a single category (based on the fact that these two functions are remarkably similar)[54] and use OLS to estimate a 6-parameter model that estimates the slope and intercept for texts by white men (which serve as a baseline), as well as the difference in the slope and intercept estimates for our two remaining author categories.

Quantitative Results

The results of our statistical analysis confirm that both race and gender do indeed have a significant effect on which texts are available in online digital repositories. Figure 14 shows a graphical representation of the relationship between the probability of a text appearing in a given repository as a function of demand across our race and gender categories for authors: white men, white women, men of color, and women of color. The intercept of each line, where the line begins on the left side of the graph, represents the probability of appearing in a given repository for a corresponding text that appeared on only one list in our sample. The slope of each line represents the change in the probability of appearing in a given repository as a function of the percentage change in the number of lists on which it appears, such that a slope of 0.1 would indicate that a 100 percent increase in demand would lead to a 10 percent increase in the probability of appearing in a given repository. If the supply of texts were driven solely by demand, we would expect all four lines to appear similar—starting in a lower position on the left side of the graph to indicate

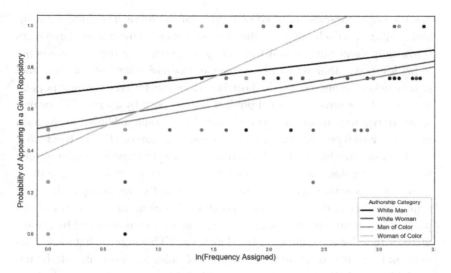

Figure 14. Probability of appearing in a given repository as a function of demand.

lower popularity with an upward slope as texts that are more frequently demanded appear more—regardless of the author's identity.

The first thing we observe in figure 14 is that the intercept for white men is higher than all other author identity categories—meaning that a relatively unpopular and infrequently demanded text authored by a white man is more likely to be available in any specific repository than a comparable text by a white woman, man of color, or woman of color. The intercept for texts authored by white men is 0.668, meaning that among our least popular texts (those that appeared on only one list), those authored by white men have approximately a 67 percent chance of appearing in a given repository. In contrast, similar texts by white women, men of color, and women of color had an intercept of 0.513, 0.471, and 0.390, respectively. This tells us that, on average, the least popular texts authored by white women and men of color are 17.5 percent less likely to appear in a given repository, and that similar texts authored by women of color are roughly 28 percent less likely to appear in a given repository than texts authored by white men.[55]

When we look at the slope of each line (that is, the increase in the probability of appearing in a repository as the popularity of the text increases), we see that the lines for white men, white women, and men of color increase at a roughly similar rate; however, the slope of the line is much steeper for texts authored by women of color. The slope for texts authored by white men is 0.062, and the slopes for texts authored by white women and men of color are 0.091 and 0.095, respectively (although the difference between these three slopes is not statistically significant). It is worth noting that even with the slightly steeper slopes for texts authored by white women and men of color, both of these lines remain below the line for texts authored by white men for even the most popular texts. In other words, our model predicts that if a text by a man of color or a white woman were to appear on every single list, it would still be less likely to appear in a given repository than a corresponding text authored by a white man.

The most striking result is the significantly steeper slope for texts authored by women of color, with an estimated slope of 0.242. Compared to a slope of 0.062 for texts authored by white men, this tells us that for an equivalent percentage change in demand, a corresponding change in the probability of appearing in a given repository is four times greater for texts authored by women of color than for texts authored by white men.[56] This implies that while relatively unpopular texts authored by women of color are more likely to be unavailable than their counterparts authored by white men, as these texts become relatively more popular, they also become more likely to appear than corresponding texts by white male authors. We can estimate that this threshold is reached when a text authored by a woman of color appears on roughly 17 percent of exam lists. While this percentage might seem surprisingly low, it is worth noting that only two of the texts authored by women of color in our sample appeared on at least this many lists, meaning that the negative bias (decreased likelihood of appearing) persists for all but the two most popular texts by women of color.[57]

For completeness, the quantitative results from our regression analyses are presented in Table 2. The standard error of each parameter estimate is presented in parentheses below the corresponding estimate and is used to calculate the level of statistical confidence (significance) for each estimated value.

One might make the argument that as long as each text appears in at least one of the four repositories, then no author category can be said to suffer from lack of representation in terms of the availability of their texts. However, even if it were the case that all 100 texts were available in at least one repository, this does not imply that each of the 100 texts is equally available. A text that is available in the first place you look can likewise be said to be more readily available than a text that is available only in the fourth place you look. Consequently, if two texts have the same demand and require the same inputs but one is available in only one of the four repositories while the other is available in all four, any additional factors that are driving this outcome can rightly be said to be affecting availability.

Table 2. Intercept and slope for each author category

	White man	White woman	Man of color	Woman of color
Intercept	0.668***	0.513***	0.471***	0.390**
	(0.076)	(0.064)	(0.100)	(0.138)
Diff v WM	—	-0.175*		-0.278**
	—	(0.091)		(0.131)
Slope	0.062*	0.091**	0.095	0.242**
	(0.036)	(0.033)	(0.061)	(0.097)
Diff v WM	—	0.033		0.180**
	—	(0.045)		(0.083)

Note: Standard errors are in parentheses. ***, **, * denote statistical significance at the 99 percent, 95 percent, and 90 percent level, respectively.

For the sake of completeness though, we do look to see if it is the case that all 100 of our texts appear in at least one of the four repositories. While we do find that 100 percent of white-female-authored texts appear in at least one repository, this is not the case for our three other author categories. In particular, two of the 20 texts authored by men of color (10 percent) do not appear in any of the four repositories, one of the eight texts authored by women of color (12.5 percent) do not appear in any of the four repositories, and one of the 43 texts authored by white men (2.3 percent) do not appear in any of the four repositories.[58] This suggests that texts by authors of color are between 4.3 and 5.3 times more likely to be unavailable in any of the four major repositories.

Conclusion

While this analysis relied, by necessity, on a form of the canon (whether one considers it a reformed or unreformed example of it) in the graduate exam lists, part of the appeal of these repositories is the implicit suggestion of their mission statements that by collecting all books, their collections—and therefore their users—can get beyond a canon of exclusion through sheer quantity. This is alluring whether one believes the canon encompasses the "most important" works of literature or not, the canon is "a supra-individual, shifting, and differential structural formation" that is beyond any one individual or institution to decide.[59] Part of the reason we see the logic of the canon being re-created in these repositories is that the logic of the canon is inherent in market-driven decisions, library collections, and the other deciding factors in what gets scanned, such as who has the money to pay for digitization services.

The sites we focused on are not explicitly Digital Humanities (DH) projects, but they are also not just resources we use.[60] In the same way that the library is curated and reflects subjective decisions about what should be included, so do these repositories, even as they claim to attempt to catalog all books, therefore creating a façade of neutrality. By critically engaging with these sites, we reflect "on their hybrid origins and dubious commercial and technological entanglements" with the recognition that especially public-facing sites such as these cannot help but have an impact on future scholars and the general public.[61] Many of these sites "are often a first, and occasionally only, stop for many members of the public when searching for information, [thus] it is incumbent upon scholars, as members of a specialist community often supported by public funds, to engage with the platform."[62] There is a definite tension between the mission statements of these repositories, to digitize all books, and the gaps in the representation of minority writers. There have been many successful scholarly DH projects that try to combat such underrepresentation,[63] such as the Women Writers Project, "imagined as leveling the production and preservation playing field."[64] However, these projects are often hyperspecific and/or behind paywalls, making them less accessible than these large open access repositories.

Our findings show that these gaps in availability are not based solely on reader demand but that there is a statistically significant and meaningful difference in representation as a factor of author race and/or gender. Specifically, we see a measurable difference in the way frequently comparably read texts authored by white men appear versus those by other authors within our sample through statistical analysis, which does not support the potential conjecture that some books are not being digitized because few readers would use the digital copy. The issue of what is and is not included is fraught and difficult, but these gaps across the board suggest that we need to be aware of these repositories and, as Miriam Posner says, we need to begin "ripping apart and rebuilding the machinery of the archive and database so that it does not reproduce the logic that got us here in the first place."[65] That this logic has been reproduced seems especially troubling, given that there was much hope that digitizing text would reduce the scarcity of books by marginalized writers. Maria Ramos offered this public comment during the Congressional Hearing on Libraries and Their Role in the Information Infrastructure in 1994: "As our society prepares to transform itself to accept and capitalize on the power of digitized information, our society should at least try to avoid the errors made in the past concerning the unequal representation in our archives of the different cultures that inform the nation."[66] These "silences of the archive" suggest that those biases have not been eradicated and that the power structures that lead to this scarcity in libraries are also in effect in online repositories.[67] Rather than being satisfied that the most "important" writers are in these collections or that a dedicated reader can find a text authored by a man of color "somewhere," we have the opportunity to bring light to the replication of traditional biases to allow others to focus energy on eliminating these gaps rather than spending their time endlessly proving that there is systemic bias. Furthermore, through attempting to validate the claims of large online text repositories and defining the gaps that exist within them, we can better understand these often opaque repositories. It is our hope that our methodology offered here can be a tool to provide quantifiable evidence of exclusion or inclusion and thus work toward a greater understanding of these public-facing platforms.

Notes

The findings and conclusions in this chapter are those of the authors and should not be construed to represent any official USDA or US Government determination or policy. This work was supported in part by the US Department of Agriculture, Economic Research Service.

1. David Finkelstein and Alistair McCleery, "The Future of the Book," in *An Introduction to Book History* (New York: Routledge, 2005), 120; Karen Attar, "Books in the Library," in *The Cambridge Companion to the History of the Book*, ed. Leslie Howsam (Cambridge, UK: Cambridge University Press, 2015), 17–35.

2. As of January 1, 2021, books that were published prior to 1926 are in the public domain. Unpublished or unregistered works may be protected under copyright if created prior to 1901. Peter B. Hirtle, "Copyright Term and the Public Domain in the United States," Cornell University Library Copyright Information Center, https://copyright.cornell.edu/publicdomain, last modified March 17, 2021.

3. Michael Hart, "The History and Philosophy of Project Gutenberg," https://www.gutenberg.org/about/background/history_and_philosophy.html, last modified August 26, 2020; Brewster Kahle, "430 Billion Web Pages Saved. . . . Help Us Do More!" https://blog.archive.org/2014/12/03/430-billion-web-pages-saved-help-us-do-more/, last modified December 3, 2014.

4. Tarez Graban, Alexis Ramsey-Tobienne, and Whitney Myers, "In, Through, and About the Archive: What Digitization (Dis)Allows," in *Rhetoric and the Digital Humanities*, ed. Jim Ridolfo and William Hart-Davidson (Chicago: University of Chicago Press, 2015), 237.

5. In other words, we examine whether certain author identities are given preferential treatment in terms of the frequency with which their texts appear in online repositories, or whether these collections are based primarily on readership demand.

6. Amy Gallo, "A Refresher on Regression Analysis," *Harvard Business Review* (2015), https://hbr.org/2015/11/a-refresher-on-regression-analysis, accessed April 8, 2021. This short article, while aimed at using regression analysis in business decisions, is a good resource for understanding the basics of how this statistical method understands relationships between potential variables.

7. Gregory Crane, Alison Babeu, David Bamman, Thomas Breuel, Lisa Cerrato, Daniel Deckers, Anke Lüdeling, David Mimno, Rashmi Singhal, David A. Smith, and Amir Zeldes, "Classics in the Million Book Library," *Digital Humanities Quarterly* 3, no. 1 (2009), http://digitalhumanities.org:8081/dhq/vol/3/1/000034/000034.html, accessed July 15, 2018.

8. Crane et al., "Classics in the Million Book Library."

9. In the next section, we discuss in further detail each of the four repositories and what we know about their collections. Although some repositories did start by digitizing large institutional libraries, none are currently affiliated with an academic institution, and none source their collections from a single institution or small group of institutions.

10. Currently, it appears that none of these four repositories collect or share metrics on the diversity of their text collections in terms of author identity. However, we still contend that the broad mission statements of the four repositories, as well as early expectations that the internet would "be a perfect libertarian space, free and open to all voices, unconstrained by the conventions and norms of the real world" make it reasonable to question if gaps are based on author race and/or gender rather than demand. Siva Vaidhyanathan, *The Googlization of Everything (and Why We Should Worry)* (Berkeley: University of California Press, 2011), 13.

11. "About the WWP," Women Writers Project, https://www.wwp.northeastern.edu/about/, accessed July 12, 2018.

12. Hart, "The Project Gutenberg Mission Statement."

13. "Home," Distributed Proofreaders, https://www.pgdp.net/c/, accessed July 12, 2018.

14. "Access Requirements—Content Provider, OCR Provider and Project Manager," DPWiki, https://www.pgdp.net/wiki/DP_Official_Documentation:CP_and_PM/Access_Requirements_--_Content_Provider,_OCR_Provider_and_Project_Manager, last modified October 6, 2016.

15. Additionally, several versions of the same text in the same language based on different scanned books were available until recently; for example, there were eight versions of *Uncle Tom's Cabin* in English as of this chapter's writing. However, since 2019, it appears that Project Gutenberg has flattened their collection to include only one version of each text per language.

16. The first libraries to partner with the project were Harvard, the University of Michigan, the New York Public Library, Oxford, and Stanford, with a combined total

of 15 million volumes. "Google Books History," Google Books, https://books.google.com/intl/en/googlebooks/about/history.html, accessed July 12, 2018.

17. For context, the largest library in the United States, the Library of Congress, holds "24,863,177 cataloged books in [their] classification system." "General Information," Library of Congress, https://www.loc.gov/about/general-information/#year-at-a-glance, accessed April 9, 2021.

18. Google Books offers restricted previews and a limited ability to search for most books under copyright.

19. "Google Books Library Project—An Enhanced Card Catalog of the World's Books," Google Books, https://books.google.com/intl/ms/googlebooks/library.html, accessed July 12, 2018.

20. Like a "giant phone book for the Internet." Karen Coyle, quoted in Vaidhyanathan, *Googlization of Everything*, 235.

21. In addition, these scans are frequently cited as being "too poor to serve the aims of preservation." Vaidhyanathan, *Googlization of Everything*, 156–57.

22. The Internet Archive is an affiliate of Project Gutenberg: "The Internet Archive was our long-time backup distribution site, and for several years our main site. They are actively working to produce more free eBooks, many of which become part of the Project Gutenberg collection" ("Partners, Affiliates and Resources," Project Gutenberg, http://gutenberg.org/about/partners_affiliates.html, accessed April 22, 2021). We could not find further information about the details of this relationship.

23. Kahle, "430 Billion Web Pages Saved."

24. More research, such as interviews with the creators of these projects and reviews of volunteer logs, would be needed to better understand the criterion by which texts are selected for online publication, for example.

25. While *Project Gutenberg (1971–2008)* by Marie Lebert (NEF, University of Toronto and Project Gutenberg, 2008) suggests that anyone can provide a scan to be proofread, the current DP Wiki indicates that in addition to proven dedication to Project Gutenberg, there are additional qualifications necessary for someone to become a "project manager," which appears to be the most effective way to make sure any book goes smoothly through the proofreading process ("Access Requirements," DP Wiki).

26. Michael Hart, "The History and Philosophy of Project Gutenberg," https://www.gutenberg.org/about/background/history_and_philosophy.html, last modified August 26, 2020.

27. Shyong (Tony) K. Lam, Anuradha Uduwage, Zhenhua Dong, Shilad Sen, David R. Musicant, Loren Terveen, and John Riedl, "WP: Clubhouse? An Exploration of Wikipedia's Gender Imbalance," paper presented at the 7th Annual International Symposium on Wikis and Open Collaboration, Mountain View, California, October 2011.

28. However, all books that we consider within this study are available at physical libraries, thus this is not the likely cause of the bias that we find in these two repositories. To gain a better sense, especially of the number of versions available, more data would need to be collected on what books are widely available in libraries and which books are

harder to find physically, and therefore are less likely to be in a partner library and digitized for inclusion in the collection. Furthermore, the motivation behind scanning multiple copies could be further examined. Annotations and marginalia are rarely being captured in these two repositories, unlike in *The Almanac Archive*, which "seeks to present and catalogue as many copies of the 'same' almanac as possible to facilitate comparison between readers and different modes of reading" (Lindsey Eckert and Julia Grandison, "The Almanac Archive: Theorizing Marginalia and 'Duplicate' Copies in the Digital Realm," *Digital Humanities Quarterly* 10, no 1 [2016], http://digitalhumanities.org:8081/dhq/vol/10/1/000240/000240.html, accessed July 15, 2018), but we could consider this duplication valuable to bibliographic research in that these repositories could become an aggregated record of "the material evidence of print culture" (Katherine Bode and Roger Osborne, "Book History from the Archival Record," in *The Cambridge Companion to the History of the Book*, ed. Leslie Howsam [Cambridge: Cambridge University Press, 2015], 219) through scanned facsimiles with associated metadata. For those interested in this thread of research, university library staff may be an additional method of data collection for which books Google Books is attempting to digitize, as universities that contract with Google Books are provided with lists of requested books and documents.

29. For those interested in more information about these repositories, Amaranth Borsuk reviews Project Gutenberg, the Internet Archive, and Google Books (213–29) in *The Book* (Cambridge, MA: MIT Press, 2018), and Christian Vandendorpe takes a close look at Wikisource in "Wikisource and the Scholarly Book," *Scholarly and Research Communication* 3, no. 4 (2013).

30. For our research question, the differences across these four repositories, primarily whether different editions of the same text can appear or not, necessitated that we evaluate simply whether a text is available on the site instead of how many copies of a given text were available. Especially given our focus on public-domain books, this flattening does not affect an individual's ability to access a text, as opposed to number of copies or licenses in considering physical collections or copyright-protected digital texts, respectively.

31. A lengthy explanation for why controlling for demand is critical to our analysis is provided later in this section.

32. We use the term "assigned" when considering the appearance of a text and author throughout this chapter. While one could say that at times students are independently selecting authors/texts, we consider this a self-assignment to read this text.

33. Hirtle, "Copyright Term and the Public Domain in the United States."

34. To verify that our data would not be skewed toward academic contexts while the repositories were responding to general public demand, we cross-checked our sample with reading lists aimed at the wider public—these lists did not offer detailed audience information, but rather directed themselves at the general public (such as "Have You Read the 200 'Best American Novels'?" PBS Newshour, September 2014, https://www.pbs.org/newshour/arts/have-you-read-the-200-best-american-novels)—and found no significant difference in the authors cited in academic contexts and popular contexts. It

is unclear if this similarity is due to the academy driving the majority of reading in historical texts, meaning that people are rating and buying books that are being read in primarily academic contexts.

35. We chose not to consider demand from the general public through an analysis of a site (such as Goodreads) because there was no mechanism to find the most popular books of a confined time period without scraping the entire database and then manually correcting the data. Although this might be a useful source for other researchers in the future, we viewed it as burdensome because we wanted primarily to test this methodology.

36. Whereas course syllabi have significantly more variations and may focus on excerpts taken from anthologies to cover a larger array of topics, which is especially difficult to control for in the cases where the syllabus lacks a course schedule.

37. Stephanie P. Browner, "The Canon: Revised, Repurposed, Unfrozen," *J19: The Journal of Nineteenth-Century Americanists* 4, no. 1 (2016): 155–60; Cecilia Konchar Farr, "The Canonical Apple Cart: Reloaded," *J19: The Journal of Nineteenth-Century Americanists* 4, no. 1 (2016): 150–55; Brian Quinn, "Collection Development and the Psychology of Bias," *The Library Quarterly* 82, no. 3 (2012): 277–304, 281–94; Cheryl Staats, Kelly Capatosto, Lena Tenney, and Sarah Mamo, *State of the Science: Implicit Bias Review* (Columbus, OH: Kirwan Institute for the Study of Race and Ethnicity, 2017).

38. Selection bias is bias introduced into the sample through the method of collection as opposed to bias that exists within the population itself.

39. We acknowledge that this likely does indicate a form of bias; however, it is bias that exists within the demand for the texts, rather than in the supply of online text repositories. As there is no unbiased measure of demand because we cannot separate ourselves from historical biases, we do not attempt to correct for potential biases in creating a proxy for demand but are seeking if there is additional bias that does not align with the demand in the supply of texts in the online repositories. Note that the numbers in this section are based on our data collection: more detail and summary statistics about which can be found in the following sections.

40. For our full dataset, visit https://github.com/catherineannwin/whose_books_data.

41. "Reading Lists," UCLA Department of English, https://english.ucla.edu/graduate-reading-list/, accessed January 13, 2019.

42. For our sample to be a robust measure of demand, we needed to have a large number of possible texts represented through the method of data collection. Thus, it was important that we had both a relatively large number of lists and that each list had a relatively large number of entries. Neither of these needs was met by syllabi publicly available online—as of April 2021, Humanities Commons CORE Repository has 18 syllabi under the subject of American literature, many of which cover primarily modern and contemporary materials, out of 359 syllabi in the repository. While one can find additional syllabi through general searches, these courses often cover periods broader than the nineteenth century, which dilutes the findings by creating a broader number of texts, and often rely on anthologies as the primary textbook, which introduces

uncertainty even when the course schedule is also available. Alongside the issues indicated, all these facts indicated graduate exam lists as a sound and viable choice.

43. It is worth noting that these two facts—Walt Whitman is represented on every list, and Herman Melville appears, on average, four times on every list—show some of the bias inherent in the exam lists. We are not suggesting that our measure of demand is unbiased; in fact, we believe that there is no unbiased measure of demand.

44. This data was recorded as three binary (0, 1) variables stating whether the author is identified as a woman, of color, and/or a woman of color. We collected data only on race and gender and did not collect data on ethnicity or other possible markers of diversity and inclusion. Furthermore, we did our best to consider how the author identified during their life and how scholars have located their identity.

45. Maurice S. Lee, "Introduction: A Survey of Survey Courses," *J19: The Journal of Nineteenth-Century Americanists* 4, no. 1 (2016): 125–30.

46. We also recorded this data as a binary, recording a "1" is at least one copy of that text is available in each repository, otherwise a "0."

47. While some may suggest that this is not an issue because keyword searching is the more common practice than looking within individual repositories, search engines can find only what is available online, and search engines are more likely to find what the searcher specifically wants, which in this case we assume are legally and freely available readable texts, when more people have vouched for a link as a trustworthy result. Google, which we take to be representative of other search engines, states "Search algorithms look at many factors, including the words of your query, relevance, and usability of pages, expertise of sources, and your location and settings" ("How Search Algorithms work," Google, https://www.google.com/search/howsearchworks/algorithms/, accessed April 22, 2021). As Siva Vaidhyanathan explains in more detail in *The Googlization of Everything (and Why We Should Worry)*: "Rank is assigned to a site [in Google search results] through a dynamic process of verification by communal affirmation. The instrument of that affirmation is the hyperlink. The secondary instrument is the click on the hyperlink" (61). Vaidhyanathan clarifies that this secondary measure considers "If a number of users doing the same search click on the third result instead of the first, then, over time, Google will raise the rank of that result. [. . .] Users thus believe that Google's rankings are honest expressions of probable importance and relevance" (59). Thus, while research on keyword search results is outside the scope of this study, these preliminary results do suggest that texts that are not included frequently in major open access repositories are likely more difficult to find regardless of the search method. For those interested in Google search, and search engine mechanics more generally, Vaidhyanathan's book offers a detailed explanation, especially on pages 20–26 and 59–64.

48. This is further reinforced by such worthwhile projects as "Just Teach One," which asks instructors to teach *just one* recovered "neglected or forgotten text" in their courses. Duncan Faherty and Ed White, "Welcome to Just Teach One," *Common-Place: The Journal of Early American Life*, http://jto.common-place.org/, accessed January 13, 2019.

49. M. S. Lee, "Introduction: A Survey of Survey Courses." Further aggregation and accounting of exam reading lists would continue the discussion of canonicity from the perspective of graduate education that Lee considers in the undergraduate survey course.

50. Jamie "Skye" Bianco, "This Digital Humanities Which Is Not One," in *Debates in the Digital Humanities*, ed. Matthew K. Gold (Minneapolis: University of Minnesota Press, 2012).

51. Roopika Risam, "Beyond the Margins: Intersectionality and the Digital Humanities," *Digital Humanities Quarterly* 9, no. 2 (2015), http://digitalhumanities.org:8081/dhq/vol/9/2/000208/000208.html, accessed July 15, 2018.

52. The reason we prefer the natural log is that it converts an absolute measure (number of list appearances) into a measure of percentage change, thus accounting for diminishing returns from popularity. The change in popularity is bigger between texts that are on one list and two lists (100 percent change), respectively, than between texts that are on 20 and 21 lists (5 percent), respectively. The natural log of some number, x, is denoted as $\ln(x)$.

53. This method estimates the parameters of the line (slope and intercept) in a way that minimizes the squared distance between the fitted line (line of best fit) and the observed data points, hence the name Ordinary Least Squares.

54. As our initial slope and intercept estimates for texts authored by white women and men of color are so similar, combining the two into a single author category has the benefit of increasing the statistical power of these estimates by increasing the sample size from 29 and 20 to 49.

55. These results are significant at the 90 percent and 95 percent confidence level, respectively. Statistical confidence is calculated based on the ratio of the parameter estimate, in this case the intercept, and the standard error of that estimate—a ratio of 1.645, 1.96, and 2.576 represent a confidence level of 90 percent, 95 percent, and 99 percent, respectively, and corresponds to the probability that this result should be replicable.

56. Even though the number of texts by women of color is relatively low, 8, this 0.18 difference in slope is statistically significant at the 95 percent level, even after controlling for this low sample size.

57. There are potentially a number of factors that may explain why more popular texts by women of color are overrepresented compared to texts authored by white men, white women, and men of color; the simplest explanation is that since this description only applied to two texts, it should not be surprising that these two works have been included in most repositories.

58. It is worth noting that our authors are categorized by race as opposed to ethnicity; however, the one white-male-authored text that does not appear in any of the four repositories is that of a Hispanic white man, meaning that all texts authored by non-Hispanic white men do in fact appear in at least one of the four repositories, possibly

suggesting that additional ethnicity-based bias may be occurring, though we would warn against drawing such an inference based on a single data point.

59. David Kazanjian, "Uncanon," *J19: The Journal of Nineteenth-Century Americanists* 4, no. 1 (2016): 140–46, 141.

60. For those interested in how race affects digitized material collection in DH projects, Amy E. Earhart's "Can Information Be Unfettered? Race and the New Digital Humanities Canon," in Gold, *Debates in the Digital Humanities* (2012), is an excellent piece.

61. Matthew Battles and Michael Maizels, "Collections and/of Data: Art History and the Art Museum in the DH Mode," in *Debates in the Digital Humanities 2016*, ed. Matthew K. Gold and Lauren F. Klein (Minneapolis: University of Minnesota Press, 2016).

62. Constance Crompton, Raymond Siemens, and Alyssa Arbuckle, "Enlisting 'Vertues Noble & Excelent': Behavior, Credit, and Knowledge Organization in the Social Edition," *Digital Humanities Quarterly* 9, no. 2 (2015), http://www.digitalhumanities.org/dhq/vol/9/2/000202/000202.html, accessed July 12, 2018.

63. As well as efforts that specifically aim to increase representation of underrepresented people in crowdsourced repositories such as those in the Wikimedia suite, frequently called "edit-a-thons."

64. Jacqueline Wernimont, "Whence Feminism? Assessing Feminist Interventions in Digital Literary Archives," *Digital Humanities Quarterly* 7, no. 1 (2013), http://digitalhumanities.org:8081/dhq/vol/7/1/000156/000156.html, accessed July 15, 2018.

65. Miriam Posner, "What's Next: The Radical, Unrealized Potential of Digital Humanities," in Gold and Klein, *Debates in the Digital Humanities 2016*.

66. Maria Ramos, "Please defend free e-texts," quoted in Jesse Mundis, "Library Services and Construction Act: Testimonies (1994): Speech 23," April 6, 1994, http://digitalcommons.uri.edu/pell_neh_I_53/19, 20.

67. Alexis Lothian and Amanda Phillips, "Can Digital Humanities Mean Transformative Critique?" *Journal of e-Media Studies* 3, no. 1 (2013), https://journals.dartmouth.edu/cgi-bin/WebObjects/Journals.woa/1/xmlpage/4/article/425.

Electronic Versioning and Digital Editions

Paul A. Broyles

The rise of digital editions has allowed editors to capture in ways previously impossible the multiplicity and mutability of texts. Freed from the economics of print publishing, digital editing projects have been able to present multiple versions of a text, giving readers access to many distinct stages of its manuscript development or print history.[1]

Digital editing projects have been less successful at dealing with their own textual multiplicity, the ways the editions they produce transform over the course of their lives. Digital resources, endlessly changeable in contrast to the fixity of printed books, can be expanded or corrected long after their initial releases. Indeed, this mutability is one of their defining promises. Jerome McGann, in his influential essay "The Rationale of Hypertext" (first published in 1995), contrasts the physical book, which "literally closes its covers on itself" when it is published, with the hypertext that "need never be 'complete'" and "will evolve and change over time, it will gather new bodies of material, and its organizational substructures will get modified, perhaps quite drastically."[2] And all who have tried to maintain a digital resource over any duration know that changes may not merely be possible but required in order to keep it operational.

Yet many digital editions and archives do not have clear public versioning practices; well-defined, citable version numbers still seem to be a rarity in the world of digital editions. And no consensus practice exists in the field regarding how different versions of an electronic textual resource should be identified, or what it is that version numbers should communicate.[3]

This lacuna is particularly surprising because textual studies, a field with which the textual digital humanities is closely aligned, has developed robust analytic frameworks for understanding the history of textual objects. Textual criticism and bibliography are both to a significant extent concerned with versioning texts—that is, with identifying and labeling the stages or layers of activity that make up a particular text's history.

Digital editions, composed of data files and software components, are also connected with software development, a field that has developed its own practices for managing the development of evolving resources. This chapter examines how software versioning practices relate to other attempts to describe the histories of resources and explores how these approaches might suggest versioning procedures for digital editions. I offer as a case study the development of a versioning policy for the *Piers Plowman Electronic Archive*, a long-standing scholarly resource that has published editions of multiple texts in evolving formats.

What Versioning Does

Versioning a resource is distinct from maintaining a revision history; both are necessary for the responsible management and publication of digital textual resources. A combination of technical and clerical procedures can do an adequate job of capturing a reproducible, reversible history of changes that records modifications to a resource and thus allows earlier states of the resource to be retrieved. The files themselves can be stored within a revision control system, like a Git repository, to record their state at any given time; metadata like the <revisionDesc> element in the header of Text Encoding Initiative (TEI) files, which allows projects to record narrative explanations of changes and the reasons and agents behind them. At a more basic level, many digital text projects provide revision lists, explaining in greater or less detail what has changed.

A number of digital editing projects maintain and publish revision histories that delineate the changes made to individual resources. The *Walt Whitman Archive*, for example, maintains a public changelog in the form of a blog that provides clear descriptions of modifications to the *Archive*, from corrections of typos to pervasive metadata updates.[4] In addition, individual XML files within the archive make use of the <revisionDesc> element provided by TEI to embed descriptions of changes to the file, along with the date and the responsible party. The *Whitman Archive*'s approach offers thoroughness and transparency in disclosing ongoing modifications to a digital resource. However, the

Archive's approach does not attempt to provide readers or users of the *Archive* with a clear identifier for the state of the file. Indeed, the *Archive*'s recommended citation format instructs scholars to cite the date of access. The *Whitman Archive* makes it possible to follow the history of a particular file but not to refer to any particular state of the text nor to understand how it relates to others.

The *Whitman Archive* also separates revision history from the reading environment provided on its website—probably the context in which most users will encounter the texts. The *William Blake Archive*, on the other hand, keeps version history tied to its texts: it extracts this revision history from data files and presents it in a human-readable format in an Electronic Edition Information section associated with each object in its collection.[5] This section makes the file history more directly available to readers conducting research within the *Blake Archive* and conceivably allows readers to cite the date of the last revision, but it still does not supply a specific identifier pointing unambiguously to a particular version of the file.

The increasing embrace of revision control systems (also commonly called version control systems) such as Git in the digital humanities suggests the possibility of automated, systematized methods for tracking revision history and providing access to specific versions of a file. Christian Wittern, for instance, has suggested that distributed revision control systems such as Git might furnish a new ecosystem for scholarly publishing of digital editions, allowing the maintenance of fine-grained revision histories as well as the coexistence of multiple revisions of a single file carried out by different scholars.[6]

Unlike the practices of maintaining external changelogs or recording revisions in file headers, revision control systems do provide unambiguous identifiers for a particular state of a file. In Git, for instance, each commit (act of saving changes to a repository) has an associated hash: a cryptographically generated key that can be used to identify and retrieve a particular state of the repository. In the context of a revision control system such as a Git repository, a particular version of a file—in fact, a state of the repository as a whole—can thus be identified through an associated hash.

Although such hashes are useful for identifying particular states of data, for ensuring the integrity of files, and for maintaining a reversible record of changes, they convey no information intelligible to human users. Git hashes, produced using the SHA-1 algorithm, take the form of forty-digit hexadecimal numbers (usually cited only by their first few digits). The hashes of successive commits bear no visible relationship to each other. Indeed, given two hashes but no access to the repository containing the data, it is not possible to determine which represents the more recent state of the data. Hashes are thus useful for retrieval and disambiguation, but not for understanding file histories.

Explicit, deliberate versioning of data can go beyond providing an arbitrary identifier for a particular state of a file, to communicate information that helps both humans and computers understand how that version relates to others and the context in which users should approach it. Adopting clear versioning practices aids both the preservation and the reuse of data, and the producers of digital editions can benefit from practices developed in both the fields of bibliography and in software development producing useful version numbers for digital editions.

The problem of versioning data is by no means unique to digital editions; it is a pressing issue of research data management and publication across disciplines. The World Wide Web Consortium (W3C) recommendation on "Data on the Web Best Practices" highlights the importance of versioning data and specifically indicates the value of standardized, meaningful version numbers that not only identify versions but also suggest how they differ.[7] But despite increasing recognition of the importance of clearly versioning research data, standard practices around versioning have yet to cohere in the research data community; a guide to data versioning from the Australian National Data Service, for instance, is replete with language like "no agreed standard or recommendation" and "no one way."[8] Still, emerging data infrastructures support a move toward more transparent and explicit versioning. For instance, the research data repository Zenodo introduced support for versioned Digital Object Identifiers (DOIs) in 2017, allowing depositors to update their data and permitting researchers to cite both specific versions and a whole concept independent of version.[9] Particularly within the Open Science movement, the growing emphasis on data publication has translated into attention on data versioning.

However, the textual digital humanities, and digital editing in particular, have been slower to adopt versioning practices. This reluctance may be due in part to a sense that digital editions are less sources of data than they are publications—a sense no doubt rooted in the bookish history of scholarly editing. Likewise, in contrast to the most commonly considered forms of research data—often seen as supporting materials to journal articles and archived or published as add-ons—digital editions are generally treated as full publications in themselves and may thus appear more similar to traditional print editions than to data publication of the kind increasingly discussed in the context of Open Science.

Books and Software Versioning

One role of bibliographic description of print-era books is to account for how a specific physical object fits within a printing history, which is, in effect, a history of changes. The classic bibliographic categorization of edition, impression, issue, and state offers a hierarchical model for understanding the sequence of textual, technical, and publishing processes that have produced a specific copy, and how it relates to others.[10] An edition of a book, in this schema, represents an act of composition, of typesetting; the characters that constitute a text are assembled and prepared for printing. An impression consists of a set of copies of a particular edition that are printed in the same act. An issue is a set of copies intended to be a single publishing unit, marked as such by the printed materials. Finally, the concept of state recognizes that even within the tightest publishing units there may be variation, such as cancels or stop-press corrections; parts of a book may exhibit different states from others in the same print run. This vocabulary serves bibliography by allowing any particular copy of a print book to be located precisely in relation to the book's entire publishing history.

Software version numbers also serve to situate the objects they describe in their developmental histories . . . but from the inside: rather than analytically describing objects after the fact, they are assigned during the development and release process to track development. Version numbers, at their most basic, delineate stages in the development of an object—for instance, a piece of software—by quantifying them and assigning ordered numbers to the object. It would be possible in principle to define version according to a single integer, which increases with every change.

This approach, which fails to distinguish the scope of the changes that have been made, is insufficient for dealing with complex software objects. It is instead common practice to subdivide the version number into parts according to the scale of the difference from what has come before. The most common approach is to segment the version number, using a period to divide the parts. A piece of software with version 2.7.4 would thus signify major version 2, minor version 7, revision or patch 4. (The meanings of the first two numbers are typically major and minor version; what, exactly, later numbers communicate is less consistent, but they often indicate small revisions intended to fix errors without adding features or altering behavior.)

The meanings of these sequences are not fixed; different software creators are free to construct their version numbers in different ways, and there are no universal criteria for distinguishing major and minor releases—although some recent efforts have attempted to make version numbers more systematically intelligible. But broadly, major version releases are likely to introduce significant changes to a product: for instance, a new user interface, a large set of new capabilities, or technical changes that make files produced with the new version incompatible with previous versions. Minor versions might introduce features that do not substantially alter the nature of the product or correct problems that have been discovered. Smaller releases, like patches, are likely to fix individual errors or update components that a user may not even notice.

This way of conceptualizing versions is at heart hierarchical, with each level in effect "containing" those below it. In general, bumping the version number at any level resets all the levels below it to zero, so that, for instance, the major release that follows 2.4.7 is given version number 3.0.0. Conceptually, the life of a major version consists of all the releases under that major version number, not just the original point zero release.

This hierarchy roughly parallels the way the edition-impression-issue-state model subdivides the bibliographic object. An edition, in bibliographical terms, is created whenever a given text is typeset; since bibliography as a discipline is concerned with books rather than texts, setting new type constitutes a fundamental change in the essence of the object even if the text remains unchanged. Bibliographically, a new edition is a kind of new major version, an object that on some level shares identity with what came before (it is not a new work) but also represents a significant break. Other categories are grouped beneath this, expressing different levels of identity change. Print runs even get "patches," specific changes correcting individual errors. In his attempts to distinguish issue from state, Fredson Bowers suggests that minor textual corrections, along with small supplements, produce only new states and not new issues because they are simply "delayed attempts to construct an 'ideal copy,'" much as software patches do not seek to extend functionality or change intended behavior but merely make the software conform to existing expectations.[11]

The point, of course, is not that software versioning and bibliographic description map the same procedures to different media. Each practice is informed by different practical needs, disciplinary contexts, and underlying technologies. Here, I wish to point to a broad correspondence in approach between the two procedures, even though they bear different relationships to their subject matter: both organize intellectual objects hierarchically, categorizing and subdividing around questions of essential identity and of imagined ideal state.

But bibliographic classification, as an analytical practice, is rooted in the evidence of specific changes. Software versioning, by contrast, is done by those creating the product. It has been accused of being arbitrary and inconsistent—and at times of being driven by market forces rather than technological logic. A few efforts to make versioning practices more consistently meaningful do indeed help clarify what version numbers can actually assert about an object.

Calendar Versioning

One approach, which has been called Calendar Versioning (hereafter CalVer), highlights the temporality of software releases.[12] This approach recognizes that knowing when a software object was released may be the most important way to identify and evaluate it. Microsoft has offered the most widely visible version of this practice, with releases like *Windows 95*, *98*, and *2000*. (It is worth noting that these are public release names and the software actually carries a different version number distinct from the release name.) But a variety of other software uses CalVer in less dramatic ways: the Ubuntu Linux distribution, for instance, offers what look like fairly traditional version numbers, but the first segment of the version numbers is the last two digits of the current year, followed by the month, so that as of the time of writing, the most recent version (released in April 2018) is 18.04.

In emphasizing date as what identifies an object, CalVer corresponds to some existing scholarly practices. Citation styles are in part calendrical: issues of a book might well be distinguished even in a non-bibliographical works-cited list by year, and many citation styles for electronic resources have recommended including a date of access, recognizing that the mutability of digital resources means that the same URL may yield different content on different dates (or even at different minutes, we might add, though typical citation practices do not extend to that level of precision).

Calendar Versioning privileges temporal sequence above all else; it suggests that when an object was produced is the most salient information for assessing it. It establishes a sequence of versions, chiefly by relating them in time. Thus, CalVer is effective for allowing users to assess the age of a particular resource, to understand which versions were produced earlier and later, and to determine whether a more recent version is available.

In privileging time, CalVer largely ignores the intellectual relationships among versions apart from the time when they were produced; CalVer establishes sequence, but not scope: it is impossible to tell from version numbers alone whether two versions are differentiated by the correction of a minor error or by a significant overhaul.

Semantic Versioning

Common versioning practices have tended to make the degree of difference among versions more prominent than in CalVer, differentiating major and minor versions according to the relative degree of change. These approaches have appeared inconsistent to some critics: different developers or companies make different decisions regarding what constitutes minor and major versions, and these decisions are sometimes driven by market forces as a new major version might generate excitement or drive customers to upgrade. The Semantic Versioning (hereafter SemVer) specification, created by Tom Preston-Werner, is an attempt to specify rigorously and technically what version numbers (or, more precisely, what *changes* in version numbers) actually mean.[13] Here, I dwell slightly longer on SemVer because it has provoked a debate that exposes a fundamental question not merely of how versions should be identified but what versioning is for.

This type of versioning is based on the traditional major.minor.patch format, but it attempts to codify something largely implicit in community practices for giving version numbers to software: how the different portions of a version number reflect different levels of change. Thus SemVer is most concerned with libraries and packages (that is, pieces of software designed to be used by other pieces of software), and specifically with what are called their APIs (Applications Programming Interfaces): the formal methods through which other programs interact with the package. (It is worth noting that the SemVer specification is itself semantically versioned; the application of these principles is not restricted to packages or libraries.)

Again, SemVer is primarily concerned with whether changes to a package break backwards compatibility. That is, have you changed the way your API works so that the same command, issued to the new version, will produce different results? The central principle is that any breaking change to the API (that is, one that will cause the same command to have different results) is a new major version. A release that adds new functions while maintaining backward compatibility is a new minor version, while a patch version is one that simply fixes bugs, provided the fix does not break backward compatibility. SemVer is designed especially for use with package managers: programs that can automate procuring and updating the packages needed to build or run a piece of software.

SemVer specification sits especially uneasily at the intersection of intellectual and mechanistic understandings of versioning. Jeremy Ashkenas, an influential JavaScript developer and vocal critic of SemVer, argues that the system "prioritize[s] a mechanistic understanding of a codebase over a human one. . . . It's alright for robots, but bad for us."[14] Ashkenas suggests that, in an environment where other developers may write source code relying on a project's bugs, the definition of a "breaking" change is subjective—a point others contest. Perhaps most significantly for Ashkenas and other detractors, minor function changes might under SemVer require an increase in the major version number (say, from 2.3.1 to 3.0.0)—a change that implies a major rethinking of the software that may not, in fact, exist (and can cause version numbers to balloon). Ashkenas agitates in favor of what others disparagingly call "Sentimental Versioning," and he playfully labels "Romantic Versioning" as a system under which a developer's understanding of the magnitude of the change and the relationship between versions defines the version number.[15]

The crux of the debate around Ashkenas's rejection of SemVer (which riled a community of software developers whose projects were affected by an update that Ashkenas declined to label a new major version) is whether version numbers are intended for human or machine consumption. Software processes that decide whether it is safe to update a given library do not care what a developer's sense of the change is; humans, on the other hand, may be misled by seeing a major release that actually consists of a conceptually minor change.

Why should scholars at the intersection of physical book study and digital scholarship be concerned with a several-year-old squabble among software developers, much of which involved how developer practices integrate with automated systems? The SemVer debate is particularly interesting for digital textuality because it draws attention to the different kinds of weight that version information can carry, and the different systems into which it integrates. The software developer Niels Roesen Abildgaard has attempted to nuance the SemVer debate by suggesting that software exists on a continuum between interfaces directly with users and interfaces exclusively with other software. User-facing software, like games or (to a lesser extent) desktop applications, is most suitable for Romantic Versioning, since human understanding is paramount, while software libraries would benefit from SemVer because relatively few humans will look at them directly, but they will often be included in other software systems.[16]

The Semantic/Romantic debate draws our attention to version numbers that provide an interface for understanding software changes; this interface is conditioned by purpose and audience—a key insight for considering how users of digital editions might interact with version numbers and what information they can convey.

The focus on versioning as a communicative interface, designed to work in a system with a clear audience to satisfy a defined purpose, helps us understand the complexity of digital editions as objects to be versioned. Digital editions operate within multiple systems at once. They are typically created first and foremost as objects for *reading*, to be studied closely by individuals. They are also sources of data, furnishing both character data and metadata that can be manipulated and analyzed in a variety of ways. And they are objects of citation, which must be unambiguously referenced in scholarly environments. Jerome McDonough et al. point out that people using and analyzing digital objects for different purposes may have profoundly different (though interrelated) needs in terms of how they are categorized.[17]

Moreover, digital editions are complex, layered objects. At base, they consist of one or more transcriptions (or constructed texts), which may have been collated or further analyzed to produce altered texts. In most cases, these texts have been encoded using a markup language to identify features, define structure, and incorporate metadata. And in most cases, they are accessed through a software interface for reading, which may well be unique to the edition or project in question. Even if the content of the edition was originally encapsulated in a manageable format like a single XML file, the reading interface will encompass a multitude of files and technologies, like CSS (Cascading Style Sheets) and JavaScript files executed on a user's computer in order to display the contents on the screen and other processes, such as XSLT transformations (Extensible Stylesheet Language Transformations), which may occur on a server entirely out of a user's sight, so that the user may not even directly receive the underlying data files without requesting them.

Describing Electronic Literature

Given the complexity of digital editions as textual objects, one place we might turn for more robust ways to describe them as temporal, bibliographic objects is work done by electronic literature scholars in classifying and categorizing their materials. (Digital editions are indeed a form of electronic literature, albeit one that has not attracted much study outside the field of editorial theory.)

In his 2002 article "Editing the Interface," Matthew Kirschenbaum postulated a set of terms for describing first-generation electronic objects inspired by Bowers's classic bibliographical typology. Layer, version, and release refer to the whole software object—another hierarchy. *Layer* refers to an integrated environment of software and data; adding a brand-new software interface might, for example, constitute a new layer. *Version* is somewhat subordinate to layer and describes the life sequence of the software; a new layer creates a new major version, while refining an existing layer creates a new minor version. *Release* seems to be primarily a matter of distribution channel: releases are "computationally compatible . . . but . . . not functionally integrated," and Kirschenbaum's example is of a work released both online and on CD-ROM (presumably with the same underlying software).[18]

Within the total software object so described are individual *objects*—individual digital entities. Kirschenbaum offers a file as an example of an object, but it is worth noting that Kirschenbaum's objects are independent of the data format in which they are stored. These are described by *states*: "the computational composition of an *object* in some particular data format."[19] For example, separate GIF and JPEG files representing the same image are different states of the same underlying object. *Instance* exists at the interplay between state and the software environment in which it operates: an image displayed in a particular program, which might (intentionally or inadvertently) render it differently from other programs. And finally, there is *copy*, a single instance of a state of an object, for example, the copy of an image that a web browser downloads and stores on a user's computer (as distinct from the copy on the server).

I describe this categorization at length because it represents a particularly thorough and robust attempt to think through the distinctive properties of electronic objects, and it also points to some of the properties we must consider when evaluating digital editions. Kirschenbaum's seven-part system is too detailed and cumbersome to be used as a versioning system in itself—although a refined version, adapted for the era of networked publishing, might ultimately prove valuable for future bibliographic accounts of digital editions. But Kirschenbaum's approach might suggest what sorts of features versioning needs to account for.

From the perspective of the publication of digital editions, the central insight of Kirschenbaum's proposal is his distinction between the whole software environment and the individual components that compose it. An electronic publication—consisting of both data and a technical environment in which that data is remediated for a reader—cannot usefully be described in total; media objects simultaneously precede their instantiation in a particular technical environment and become entangled in the systems that display them.

Kirschenbaum applied this schema to works of electronic literature; those discussed in his account appear to have evolved in relatively well-defined, separable releases that can be thought of as an issue of all parts at once. His descriptive vocabulary seems to reflect this tendency: terms addressing the whole software environment are concerned with evolution, while those concerned with individual objects are concerned with instantiation.

This particular division would work well for describing digital editions of the CD-ROM era, where the production of physical copies created a distinct issue of the whole, including both data and display software. But versioning all the parts together appears less appropriate for the "continuous publishing" practices of the web era, where individual components (and most importantly individual documents) may be updated independently, not to mention the prevalence of digital editions in large archives containing many documents, and even in semi-distributed systems like Jeffrey Witt's Scholastic Commentary and Text Archive, which promises to aggregate related, interoperable editions.[20]

Accordingly, rather than versioning entire systems of software and data as a single unit, I suggest that we offer separate accounts of objects and environments. Objects, here, are the edition content: the texts or other resources being presented online. Environment describes the whole system within which these objects are rendered and consumed: a web of server-side and client-side electronic processes that work in tandem with a user's local computer environment to display an edition.

This model has both intellectual and practical benefits. Versioning objects and environment separately means that our versioning practices can recognize the intellectual identity between an encoded document (for example, an XML file in the TEI vocabulary) and its rendering (for example, its rendering as an HTML page as a result of an XSLT transformation). They remain the same object, even if the mediating layers change. Treating object and environment separately also helps prepare us for the future promoted by Peter Robinson, where digital editors abandon the practice of providing their own interfaces and leave textual display to others, while still allowing us to version intelligibly within the integrated reading environments common today.[21]

In distinguishing object from environment, I do not mean to suggest that environment is intellectually insignificant. Environments form an integral part of the reading experience, and constructing environments for digital editions is important scholarly work. In the long term, the field must also grapple with the ways environments may be versioned, cited, and preserved. Object and environment are both conceptually and practically separable, and recognizing this separation will position us to begin versioning objects—significantly lower-hanging fruit for the field of digital editing.

Developing Versioning Protocols for the *Piers Plowman Electronic Archive*

To demonstrate some considerations involved in putting versioning into practice, I turn to a case study based on my work in creating a formal versioning policy for the *Piers Plowman Electronic Archive* (PPEA), an open-access online resource, one that aims to document the complete medieval and early modern textual tradition of the Middle English alliterative poem *Piers Plowman* through TEI-encoded documentary editions of individual witnesses and critical editions of archetypal texts. This long-running project, which began in 1987, demonstrates both the need for and the challenge of clear versioning practices.[22]

The first seven PPEA editions were published on CD-ROM, from 2000 to 2011, in separate partnerships between the Society for Early English and Norse Electronic Texts (SEENET) and the University of Michigan Press, Boydell and Brewer, and the Medieval Academy of America. The first two CD-ROMs were encoded in SGML and presented using the proprietary Multidoc Pro SGML browser; later editions were encoded in XML and published using software that ran within a web browser. In 2014, all texts were made openly available online, in a new web interface created by the Institute for Advanced Technology in the Humanities at the University of Virginia. The new online Archive saw the release of previously unpublished editions; older editions were updated to XML conforming to the P4 version of the TEI guidelines. Since 2014, intermittent changes have been made to the appearance and function of the web editions. Forthcoming updates will create additional versions of existing texts: the Archive is in the process of updating its texts to TEI P5, and the newly launched PPEA in Print series publishes print volumes derived from electronic texts.[23]

In addition to changes in medium, file format, and technical infrastructure, the PPEA, like any project of its age and scope, has had to deal with errors in its materials. The web versions of the texts were updated to correct known errors. These changes were not explicitly recognized on the pages for the text. For texts originally published on CD-ROM, the website used to provide errata lists recording corrections to the CD-ROM texts. However, these lists are no longer maintained given the age of the CD-ROMs, and errata lists were never created for texts first published online. The corrections and alterations made to files spanned a wide range of types and significances, including changes to the format of line numbers (but not the lineation), minor changes to markup unlikely to affect the output on the screen, and correction of textual errors.

As part of a CLIR (Council on Library and Information Resources) Postdoctoral Fellowship in Data Curation for Medieval Studies at the North Carolina State University Libraries, I set out to create standards for assigning version numbers to texts. My primary goals were (1) to allow users of the *Archive* to record and cite unambiguously which version of a text they consulted; (2) to permit previously published versions of texts to be archived and retrieved; (3) to make the history of a given text legible; and (4) to allow users with references to two versions of the same text to have a basic understanding of the relationship between them.

The first fundamental question my work faced was which resource was actually being versioned. First, guided by Kirschenbaum's work, I concluded that edition content and the way that content is displayed cannot be described by the same version numbers. While versioning our display software is a long-term desideratum, my goal was to version the texts themselves. Accordingly, any version numbers we provided would have to refer to the source files for an edition—in this case, the TEI-encoded XML—rather than to its rendered text. The decision to privilege the XML made sense as the XML files can be easily archived, and because it recognizes the markup of an edition as a significant intellectual product. Versioning the XML files also allows us to link them with any derivatives produced from them. For example, editions published in the PPEA in Print series carry a statement on the copyright page declaring the version of the XML files to which the print text corresponds.

Choosing XML files as the targets of versioning has additional consequences. The component files of an edition will be versioned separately. Each full edition consists of, at minimum, separate XML files for the introduction and the edited text. If the versioned objects are XML files, a change to the text does not affect the status of the introduction. Even though the PPEA conceives of each edition as a single coherent publication—and they are also peer reviewed as integral wholes—they are made up of separate data sources whose version histories must be managed independently. (This is a more practical approach than creating data packages versioned as a single unit because it allows us to include a file's version number within the file itself without having to modify files that have not otherwise changed.)

One more question concerned what resources must actually be versioned. The PPEA website contains many pages with background information and supplementary resources that are not part of individual editions—some of which, such as site credits, may change frequently. Further, editions include files such as prefaces, which are not advancing the same sort of scholarly claims as the texts and introductions. At least for the time being, I decided to version only content subject to peer review, meaning the text, apparatus, and introductions of editions.

Because one goal of creating a versioning policy was to make it possible to understand the relationship between versions of a resource, it was immediately apparent that our version numbering plan would need to capture the scope of changes between versions. Simple integers, or a pattern like Calendar Versioning emphasizing time, would not be sufficient: users of our data should be able to have a sense, simply by looking at the version numbers, of how significant a difference between two files was likely to be.

The problem this posed, of course, was defining the significance of given changes. The persuasive arguments within the software development world against ad hoc version numbering suggest that there need to be standards for what make an increase in version major or minor. Inspired in part by the careful and precise distinctions suggested by SemVer, I first attempted to theorize "breaking changes" for the digital edition, trying to identify what kinds of change would render two states of the same file "incompatible" with each other. I soon realized that identifying "breaking changes" requires committing to a particular theory of the digital edited text and the primary form of interface it provides. People using the edition mainly as a documentary text will have different concerns from those most interested in the editors' arguments; those studying dialect will prioritize different features from those examining scribal decoration and, again, from scholars interested in markup practices; readers working directly with the XML files will have a very different experience of changes from the probable majority who are reading through the mediation of a web interface. In the context of digital editing, nearly every change is potentially a breaking change for *someone* (a claim Ashkenas made about many software packages). Indeed, the concept of a "patch," a change intended only to correct an error and restore expected behavior, does not apply to an edition, because edition contents may have been used as the grounds for scholarly argument, and the change from a mistaken reading to a correct one may thus have great scholarly significance.

The nature of a new version of an object in a digital edition, then, cannot be understood as a matter of compatibility in a simple technical sense, where some changes are free of side effects while others carry consequences. So, what qualities make one set of changes more significant than another? The answer, I realized in considering the history of the PPEA and its texts, is scale. Changes that systematically affected the editorial or markup approaches to a file constitute a highest or most significant level of change. A file's markup might change completely—it might, indeed, be re-created from the ground up in a new format (for instance in HTML rather than XML)—without any differences being visible to users of the edition. However, given the intellectual significance of the way a text is marked up, these two files would be radically different from each other as data. Accordingly, I reasoned, the conversion of a file from one format to another (from SGML to XML, or between major versions of an encoding scheme, like the transition from TEI P4 to P5) would constitute a major release (at the highest level of versioning): even if the intent is to keep the textual content the same, the different affordances of different file formats and encoding schemes mean that the nature of the file has fundamentally changed.

A file modified in this way is also incompatible with previous versions in a concrete sense, because software that worked with earlier versions may not display it successfully. (Still, minor changes to the way data is stored or expressed, like a switch between minor versions of TEI or a change in character encoding from ISO-8859-1 to UTF-8, maintain the fundamental identity of the file and do not rise to the level of a major release.) Similarly, systematic editorial revisions to a file—the kind of editorial campaign that might result in publishing a new edition of a print book, for instance—would constitute a new major release because they represent a far-reaching editorial reassessment that disrupts intellectual continuity with the existing version.

On the other hand, local changes—a revised reading, a corrected typo, a new note—constitute a comparatively minor change in version. Such changes might well be significant; a single altered word could have huge scholarly ramifications. But they do not represent a major shift in the nature of the edition as an edition. A scholar aware of such a revision would want to find out what had changed in the contents, but that scholar would not need to reassess any understanding of the edition as a whole.[24]

Putting this understanding of changes to our materials into practice, the PPEA adopted a two-part system for version numbers, in the form of [major version].[minor version], where the segments have the following meanings:

- The first segment, *major version*, increases when we make a large number of changes systematically across the text that have a significant effect on its markup or on the way it is edited as a whole. Moving from P4 to P5 of the TEI protocols, which requires non-trivial changes in markup across the text, is an example of a change that would increase the number of the major version segment. (However, some types of widespread changes do not rise to the level of constituting a new major version, because they are intellectually trivial and do not involve theories of the text or its encoding. One example previously encountered by the project is changing the format in which line numbers are written without changing the numbers themselves. The significance of any program of changes must be assessed by the resource's maintainers in terms of the needs of the community that will use the resource, as the Semantic Versioning debate suggests.)
- The second segment, *minor version*, increases when we make any other change. These include corrections to readings, updates to notes or paratexts, modification of markup, or changes of any other kind as long as they do not rise to the systematic, significant status that would constitute a new major version.

Users in possession of an XML file should be able to determine the version from that file, so the policy stipulates that wherever possible, the version number should be recorded internally within the file to which it applies. In TEI documents, we record the version number using the @n attribute within the <edition> element in the <editionStmt> section of the header. We also recommend documenting the revision history of the file using <change> entities within the <revisionDesc> section of the header; the version number should be attached to each change newly introduced within a particular version using the @n attribute on the <change> entity. In this way, we can both identity particular states of files and construct a human-readable history of how the file developed. Where version numbers and change histories cannot practically be included in the file itself, we will store them in a supplementary text file to be archived and distributed with the data files.

Three Principles

The practices considered and developed by the PPEA offer a starting point for versioning digital projects, laying out standards for what needs to be versioned and how version numbers can make the status of files and their histories more intelligible. Other projects, with different needs, materials, data formats, and philosophies may need to develop different strategies in order to make their material comprehensible and usable. Development of standard practices would benefit the field of digital editing as a whole. Until a community consensus emerges, individual projects will need to develop their own approaches to versioning their data. Accordingly, instead of a set of rules, I conclude with three principles that can help to guide discussions about versions of texts.

1. Digital editions must version their underlying data and communicate those versions to users, independent of the way that data is displayed. This is not the same as tracking file history in a revision control system, nor is it the same as the bibliographical analysis scholars of future generations may want to perform. It is a declarative act in which digital editors make assertions about the state of their work. Where editorial projects offer reading interfaces, they should strongly consider versioning their software environments, due to the complicated technological interactions required to display a text. However, versioning the data itself is of paramount importance. Wherever possible, editions should provide direct access to their versioned data (for example, in the form of TEI-encoded XML files) so that users can examine the data directly apart from the environment that has been provided.
2. Versioning is social. As debates in the software community have suggested, versioning is not an abstract concept but is inherently tied to *use*. Developing versioning principles will require editorial projects to have a use-model of

their resources, one that takes into account what kinds of changes are intellectually and practically significant. This means, for instance, deciding what types of object are fundamental to the resource and at what level they should be versioned. (A single epigraph, or a corpus? Chapter or novel? Poem or volume? Given both creators and users, how should we understand the resource as transforming?)

3. Digital editions must explicitly scope the revisions, delivering version numbers that communicate with users (based on their needs) the scale and significance of the change. It should be possible to understand through version numbers not only what version of a resource is most recent but also how "compatible" they are, and how likely it is that the differences have a significant impact on their intellectual coherence or their probable uses. In both individual projects and the field of digital editing as a whole, we should develop explicit guidelines that make these versions meaningful. We should be working to make the concept of version expressive and interoperable within the domain of digital editing.

Notes

My thanks to Timothy Stinson for his feedback on this chapter and to Matthew Kirschenbaum for his comments on an earlier version of this work. I am also grateful to my many generous interlocutors at the BH and DH conference where I first presented these ideas. This research was made possible by the support of a CLIR Postdoctoral Fellowship in Data Curation for Medieval Studies at the North Carolina State University Libraries. Another version of this chapter and related research appears in Paul A. Broyles, "Digital Editions and Version Numbering," *Digital Humanities Quarterly* 14, no. 2 (2020), http://www.digitalhumanities.org/dhq/vol/14/2/000455/000455.html.

1. Elena Pierazzo, "Digital Documentary Editions and the Others," *Scholarly Editing* 35 (2014), http://scholarlyediting.org/2014/pdf/essay.pierazzo.pdf.

2. Jerome McGann, *Radiant Textuality: Literature after the World Wide Web* (New York: Palgrave, 2001), 69, 71.

3. For an overview of version tracking and numbering practices in a sample of published digital editions, see Broyles, "Digital Editions and Version Numbering," Appendix 1.

4. http://wwa-changelog.blogspot.com/. The blog also provides descriptions of additions and modifications to the *Archive* website apart from updates to the XML data, although the blog description notes that minor changes in appearance and events such as server outages are not recorded. For the Archive itself, see https://whitmanarchive.org.

5. http://www.blakearchive.org.

6. Christian Wittern, "Beyond TEI: Returning the Text to the Reader," *Journal of the Text Encoding Initiative* 4 (March 2013): ¶ 4, https://dx.doi.org/10.4000/jtei.1171.

7. Bernadette Farias Lóscio, Caroline Burle, and Newton Calegari, eds., "Data on the Web Best Practices," W3C recommendation, January 31, 2017, §8.6 and Best Practice 7, https://www.w3.org/TR/2017/REC-dwbp-20170131/.

8. Australian National Data Service, "Data Versioning," https://www.ands.org.au/working-with-data/data-management/data-versioning, accessed September 1, 2017.

9. Lars Holm Nielsen, "Zenodo Now Supports DOI Versioning!" May 30, 2017, http://blog.zenodo.org/2017/05/30/doi-versioning-launched/.

10. See Fredson Bowers, *Principles of Bibliographical Description* (New Castle, DE: Oak Knoll Press, 2005), 37–42, 406–11; G. Thomas Tanselle, "The Bibliographical Concepts of *Issue* and *State*," *Papers of the Bibliographical Society of America* 69, no. 1 (1975): 17–66.

11. Bowers, *Principles of Bibliographical Description*, 67.

12. Mahmoud Hashemi et al, "CalVer: Timely Software Versioning," May 1, 2017, http://calver.org. The CalVer proposal was released in 2016, but as the authors note, the practices they describe predate the document. Rather than trying to impose a standard format, the CalVer convention seeks to provide a common vocabulary and expose influential practices.

13. Tom Preston-Werner, "Semantic Versioning," version 2.0.0, https://semver.org/spec/v2.0.0.html, accessed July 15, 2018. Ironically, the SemVer specification has suffered from its own versioning problems; as of August 3, 2019, the version cited differed in two minor details from the version available at https://semver.org/, even though both are labeled as version 2.0.0. This disagreement has since been silently corrected, without any change to the version number listed on either page.

14. Jeremy Ashkenas, "Why Semantic Versioning Isn't," February 20, 2015, https://gist.github.com/jashkenas/cbd2b088e20279ae2c8e/39e281d9bc8f3090dd79347b5271a a9b30c2bb8b. In light of this chapter's argument, it is worth pointing out that Ashkenas posted his manifesto to GitHub's Gist service, which tracks revisions using Git. The document has been revised several times since its creation, and the hash in the URL allows me to link to a particular state of the document but does not provide a way to signal whether it is older or newer than any other state.

15. For a satiric presentation of "sentimental versioning," see Dominic Tarr, "Sentimental Versioning, Version One Dot Oh, Okay Then," http://sentimentalversioning.org, accessed July 15, 2018.

16. Niels Rosen Abildgaard, "On Versioning," February 25, 2015, http://blog.hypesystem.dk/on-versioning. Digital editions might well be consumed in both ways: read by individual human users and queried by other computer programs.

17. Jerome McDonough et al., "Twisty Little Passages Almost All Alike: Applying the FRBR Model to a Classic Computer Game," *Digital Humanities Quarterly* 4, no. 2 (2010): ¶ 18, http://www.digitalhumanities.org/dhq/vol/4/2/000089/000089.html.

18. Matthew G. Kirschenbaum, "Editing the Interface: Textual Studies and First Generation Electronic Objects," *Text* 14 (2002): 15–51, here 47.

19. Kirschenbaum, "Editing the Interface," 48.

20. https://scta.info. Witt is an associate professor of philosophy at Loyola University Maryland; the SCTA maintains a network graph connecting data from scholastic texts encoded according to common standards, as well as various applications to make that data accessible to users.

21. Peter Robinson, "What Digital Humanists Don't Know about Scholarly Editing; What Scholarly Editors Don't Know about the Digital World," 2013, https://www.academia.edu/4124828/SDSE_2013_why_digital_humanists_should_get_out_of_textual_scholarship.

22. http://piers.chass.ncsu.edu. On the history of the PPEA, see Jim Knowles and Timothy Stinson, "The Piers Plowman Electronic Archive on the Web: An Introduction," *Yearbook of Langland Studies* 28 (2014): 225–38. On its early publication practices, see Hoyt N. Duggan and Eugene W. Lyman, "A Progress Report on *The Piers Plowman Electronic Archive*," *Digital Medievalist* 1 (2005), http://doi.org/10.16995/dm.5.

23. The first volume of this series was published in 2018: John A. Burrow and Thorlac Turville-Peter, eds., *Piers Plowman: The B-Version Archetype (Bx)*, PPEA Print Series 1 (Raleigh, NC: Society for Early English and Norse Electronic Texts, 2018).

24. I investigated a further distinction: given that the core of an edition is arguably the text it provides, might we consider localized changes to readings as a distinct kind of change, more significant than changes to paratext, such as editorial notes? This proposed distinction proved unwieldy and was ultimately abandoned—not least because we sought to develop a versioning policy that could apply to all our data objects, and the reading/paratext distinction did not apply to objects like editors' introductions.

Materialisms and the Cultural Turn in Digital Humanities

Mattie Burkert

Since 2012, the Debates in the Digital Humanities series published by the University of Minnesota Press has played an important role in defining the key concepts, questions, and problems shaping the interdisciplinary field of digital humanities (DH). Even the framework of the first collection—the idea of DH as an agonistic space defined by a set of "debates"—has had a profound influence on conference programs and syllabi alike. At the same time that it is agenda-setting, the series is also responsive, recording broader shifts in the conversations taking place among digital humanities scholars, teachers, and practitioners. One such set of shifts is immediately obvious from a comparison of the essays and reprinted blog posts in the first *Debates in the Digital Humanities* volume in 2012 with those in its successors, *Debates in the Digital Humanities 2016* and *Debates in the Digital Humanities 2019*. Only four of the 49 pieces in the 2012 collection explicitly foreground issues of race, gender, and disability in their titles; tellingly, three of these entries appear in the section "Critiquing the Digital Humanities," marking a tension between the questions of identity they raise and the mainstream concerns occupying the field as a whole.[1] Alan Liu's essay "Where Is Cultural Criticism in the Digital Humanities?" closes out the 2016 volume by lamenting the failure of digital humanists to "extend their critique [of data, code, and tools] to the full register of society, economics, politics, or culture."[2] Liu argues that the apolitical disposition of much DH work circa 2012 stems from its roots in humanities computing, and he urges readers to attend to the kinds of critique happening in the other fields from which DH is descended, such as media studies and science and technology studies.

In contrast to the 2012 *Debates*, the 2016 update includes at least one essay in each of its six sections that expresses a commitment to broader cultural concerns, with particular attention to questions of race, gender, and sexuality. The editors Matthew K. Gold and Lauren F. Klein note the "markedly political bent" of the volume in their introduction, connecting scholars' renewed attention to issues of identity and justice to the emergence of high-profile social movements like Black Lives Matter.[3] The subsequent *Debates in the Digital Humanities 2019* further insists that all practitioners, regardless of whether their work engages explicitly with these topics, have an obligation to recognize "how social and cultural biases pervade our technologies, infrastructures, platforms, and devices" and how "history, culture, society, and politics overdetermine each and every one of our engagements with our work and the tools that enable it."[4] The 2019 volume marks a significant shift in the field: the recognition of the political, not as a distinct realm of content or methodology but as the terrain in which all DH scholarship is already rooted.

This chapter traces the relationship between the increased attention to issues of identity, power, and social justice in digital humanities and a set of related methodological turns—away from rhetorics of scale, objectivity, and novelty, and toward an increased focus on the material specificity and social embeddedness of digital artifacts. I identify two major research threads of current interest: first, a focus on the political dimensions of the datasets, algorithms, and visualizations that are the bread and butter of computational work in digital humanities; and second, an inquiry into the politics of the material stuff of technology—devices, storage media, computing infrastructures, e-waste, and the like. In some ways, this division maps onto the bifurcation identified by Alan Liu, a holdover from the field's dual histories in humanities computing and media studies. Still, work in these arenas is increasingly convergent and mutually informative, as the digital humanities community works together toward a fuller picture of the social and political networks in which its materials are embedded. Digital recovery and preservation efforts are uniquely positioned to bring together these two threads. The chapter concludes with a reflection on how this important and undervalued work makes visible the links between data, tools, infrastructures, and politics.

The Politics of Data

In recent years, a number of scholars have explored the ways in which data collection, curation, modeling, and analysis are not neutral activities but rather interpretive tasks embedded in larger intellectual and cultural frameworks. In their introduction to the collection *"Raw Data" Is an Oxymoron*, Lisa Gitelman and Virginia Jackson insist that "data are always already 'cooked,'" an assertion that pushes against the perception that "data are transparent, that information is self-evident." Rather than place "faith in their neutrality and autonomy, their objectivity," researchers should ask how their datasets "harbor the interpretive structures of their own imagining."[5] Johanna Drucker likewise calls for humanists to attend to the ways in which their data reflects the material and social conditions of its creation, a form of self-reflection that she contends would be best encouraged through the adoption of a new term. Instead of "data"—which comes from the Latin for "given"—Drucker proposes calling humanities information "capta," from the word "captured." Such a shift would signal a commitment to a constructivist approach more reflective of humanities epistemologies: "From this distinction, a world of differences arises. Humanistic inquiry acknowledges the situated, partial, and constitutive character of knowledge production, the recognition that knowledge is constructed, taken, not simply given as a natural representation of pre-existing fact."[6] Drucker's essay, published in 2011, and Gitelman and Jackson's collection, published in 2013, helped usher in a major push against certain ideologies of neutrality and objectivity that had dominated public discourse around computational approaches to humanities research around the turn of the century.

Drucker positioned her essay as a response to the concern that digital humanists might too easily adopting naïvely realist models of knowledge, failing to approach the apparent solidity of data visualizations from a suitably critical standpoint. Lori Emerson, in her monograph *Reading Writing Interfaces: From the Digital to the Bookbound*, calls attention to a related set of concerns about the visual interfaces through which we interact with our data. Designed according to ideals of "user-friendliness" and "invisibility," software interfaces can tempt users to take information at face value, abandoning our usual awareness of the social and cultural conditions of knowledge production.[7] Like Drucker, Emerson emphasizes the ways that humanists can intervene in broader cultural approaches to data, visualization, and computation. Against the "dream" put forth by technology companies "in which the boundary between human and information is eradicated," Emerson proposes that we create interfaces that sacrifice seamless invisibility in order to make room for "creativity, tinkering, and making."[8] Emerson's case studies, ranging from poems by Emily Dickinson to contemporary electronic literature, highlight the ways in which writers have long used craft to critique the (digital, but also analog) interfaces through which their materials are produced and consumed.

Safiya Umoja Noble's book *Algorithms of Oppression: How Search Engines Reinforce Racism* lends urgency to this critique of the ideology of neutrality: "While we often think of terms such as 'big data' and 'algorithms' as being benign, neutral, or objective, they are anything but."[9] Noble's study reveals how the seeming impartiality of search algorithms and interfaces naturalizes the racialized and gendered biases they reproduce—as, for example, when the hypersexualized images of women of color are returned for a Google search of "Black girls," reproducing the Jezebel stereotype originally used to justify the rape of enslaved women.[10] The appearance of a neutral, algorithmically generated guide to the most popular and relevant websites masks the corporate profit motive driving decisions about how users will navigate the web; in essence, Noble argues, companies like Google make money from the perpetuation of racist and sexist ideologies. Going a step further, Ruha Benjamin finds that this belief that technology is neutral not only conceals implicit biases but can even accelerate and deepen discrimination. In a nod to Michelle Alexander's influential formulation of the over-incarceration of African Americans as "the New Jim Crow," Benjamin coins the term "the New Jim Code" to encapsulate the ways that the tech industry, like the prison system, espouses a "colorblind" ideology that enables it to reproduce deeply rooted inequities under the guise of social progress.[11] The myth of neutrality is therefore central to the mechanisms by which digital technologies reinscribe racialized hierarchies.

Whereas Benjamin is a sociologist by training, Noble's background is in critical information studies. Julia Flanders and Fotis Jannadis point out that this is a particularly vibrant area for the study of "the ideological and cultural dimensions that inform all modeling activities" as well as "the issues of power and information access that determine who participates in the creation of reference models and standards, and hence determine the shape of those models and standards."[12] In *The Shape of Data in Digital Humanities: Modeling Texts and Text-Based Resources*, Flanders and Jannadis provide readers with a practical, hands-on introduction to data modeling techniques, with an "Orientation" section followed by a series of "Topics" chapters, concluding with a glossary of keywords and explanation of technical terms. Even at this introductory level, however, their collection instantiates an awareness of the ways that user interfaces may obscure data models, and they warn that the general best practice of designing data to be tool agnostic can mask the ways data models are always informed by the questions we want to ask, the disciplinary approaches we bring, and the ways we want to be able to present our findings.[13]

Andrew Piper, in his monograph *Enumerations: Data and Literary Study*, likewise advocates for a critical approach to data models that can make transparent humanities approaches to knowledge making. Rejecting discourses of "distance, bigness, or objectivity" that have tended to dominate conversations about computational reading in literary studies, Piper argues that thinking with models forces us to focus on "representativeness" and therefore mediates between "large and small, close and distant."[14] Piper deftly reverses charges that computational literary analysis is intrinsically lacking in transparency, showing instead how traditional approaches to textual criticism have often tended to black box their assumptions and the forms of expertise and subjectivity they encode. In Piper's formulation, it is literary analysis that too often obscures the critic's positionality. Ideally, the construction of quantitative models for literary study can be a more transparent approach, although that has not always been the case to date. Throughout his progressively more sophisticated experiments with large literary corpora, Piper continuously foregrounds the way that we as inquirers are "implicated in the very structures and networks through which we build our representations of those structures and networks."[15]

This awareness of the socially and culturally situated nature of data models and computational analysis techniques can enable more critical approaches to issues of identity, marginality, and representation within humanities datasets. A 2018 special issue of the *Journal of Cultural Analytics* (of which Piper currently serves as editor) on the topic of "Identity" probes, as Susan Brown and Laura Mandell put it, "the extent to which large datasets can be used to elucidate the kinds of questions that humanities scholars want to ask about historical and representational processes that structure social relations and positions," including "ethnicities, genders, class categories, and racial terminology."[16] Many of the essays in this issue are animated by the tension between the ways that data modeling, on the one hand, "necessarily engages in both abstraction and reduction," and on the other hand, the awareness that "the very act of modelling carries with it the seeds of a constructionist recognition that a phenomenon could be modelled differently"—a recognition that "can reveal the dynamic and contingent nature of identity categories."[17] In other words, this special issue attempts to mediate between the problems of temporarily stabilizing identity within datasets—with all the biases that can encode—and the potential of self-conscious data modeling to make transparent the assumptions that hide behind the shiny, user-friendly interfaces we encounter daily.

A prime example of a study that engages actively with this tension is Richard Jean So, Hoyt Long, and Yuancheng Zhu's article "Race, Writing, and Computation: Racial Difference and the US Novel, 1880–2000."[18] These authors begin by presenting the results of an experiment using sequence alignment (a technique used to analyze DNA) to discover shared strings in a corpus of texts coded by author race. They find that in terms of citationality, for example the King James Version of the Bible—as opposed to, say, popular music—"represents the major site of shared discourse between white and Black authors in the twentieth century." While this finding seems to support Northrop Frye's argument about the Bible as "the Great Code of Art," the authors point out that such an interpretation fails to account for the "complex and embattled relationship to the Bible and Christianity" many Black writers hold "due to legacies of slavery and social oppression." By coding a subset of their corpus for citation contexts and then training a model to predict whether a scene was "social" or "nonsocial," the authors found that writers identified as Black were more likely to quote the Bible in certain social contexts, which allowed for dialogism, irony, and critique. This finding essentially provides a computational metric for identifying texts that align with an existing insight from Black literary studies. Even so, the authors admit, the coding process necessary to conduct this experiment participates in the reification of racial categories. Finally, then, the authors used a "sociality" coefficient derived through their computational analysis to identify textual exemplars at the extremes of the continuum, allowing them to "read the interaction of race, writing, and religion across a set of shared formal tendencies—shared 'models of language'—and not across the categorical labels provisionally assigned to authors." Ultimately, the authors use a temporary and strategic stabilization of racial categories to conduct readings that expose assumptions at work in that very act of categorization, not only in their own study but also in literary history more broadly.

So, Long, and Zhu foreground the assumptions at work in the data modeling process, as much as the results obtained from that process, in order to lay bare the socially and culturally embedded nature of their own research data. Like all the authors featured in the *JCA*, they make their data and code open for review and for replication of their results. Yet it is not only users of sophisticated quantitative approaches who have a responsibility to practice this kind of transparency. As Jo Guldi argues elsewhere in the same special issue, all humanities scholars who interact with digital archives and databases have a responsibility to document rigorously their research processes. Guldi proposes a method called "critical search," a strategy that foregrounds how "no search is complete until all of its aspects—the choice of keywords, the algorithm, the exceptions, and the particular texts taken as exemplary evidence of the result—have been subjected to iterative examination."[19] Just as Noble calls for us to be more critical users of Google, Guldi reminds us to take a similarly rigorous approach to the scholarly databases and archives that increasingly underpin even non-computational research in the humanities. In this sense, the cultural turn in quantitative DH has the potential to help all humanities scholars recognize their own situated position within a network of datasets, interfaces, and tools that are never neutral but always politically and historically charged.

The Politics of Technologies and Infrastructures

As the previous discussion suggests, quantitative projects in the humanities have become increasingly transparent about the social and cultural dimensions of data collection, curation, analysis, and visualization. As a group, digital humanists influenced by media archaeology have begun to draw increased attention to the ways in which our material encounters with technology are situated, historicized, and politicized. Just as new work in computational cultural analysis pushes against discourses of objectivity and scale inherited from humanities computing, recent media archaeological work has complicated ideas from media studies about the novelty of new media, even as it has come to embrace cultural critique in important ways.

Attempts to push back against this discourse of novelty have often come from scholars with backgrounds in fields like bibliography and book history, and who are interested in positioning new media studies within a broader comparative and transhistorical context. For example, Matthew J. Kirschenbaum's *Mechanisms: New Media and the Forensic Imagination* (2008) is a deeply materialist study of electronic textuality. Kirschenbaum takes up artifacts like William Gibson's 1992 electronic poem *Agrippa* with minute attention to technical questions of storage media, software versions, and interactive interfaces that would seem specific to the digital condition. Here, Kirschenbaum places these concerns on a continuum with questions that have long concerned scholars interested in "the material matrix governing writing and inscriptions in all forms: erasure, variability, repeatability, and survivability."[20] In taking this approach, Kirschenbaum complicates the common perception of digital media as particularly ephemeral, marking how writing on electronic storage media, like that on vellum and paper, can be both vulnerable and surprisingly durable. Along related lines, N. Katherine Hayles and Jessica Pressman call, in their 2013 edited collection *Comparative Textual Media*, for an approach that encompasses "the scroll, the manuscript codex, the early print codex, the variations of book forms produced by changes from letterpress to offset to digital publishing machines, and born-digital forms such as electronic literature and computer games."[21] They bring together essays on topics ranging from job printing to critical code studies in order to demonstrate the continuities, rather than the ruptures, between media environments past and present.

Interventions like these are necessarily indebted to the field of media archaeology, which has long questioned commonplace notions of digital media as radically new. As Jussi Parikka explains, media archaeologists are united by a conviction that "[o]lder technical media play an important part in the histories and genealogies, the archaeological layers conditioning our present."[22] This approach is exemplified, for example, in the influential work of the twentieth-century German media theorist Friedrich Kittler. Yet, as Parikka points out, Kittler's highly technical, materialist approach stood in opposition "a wide range of politically engaged work" that examined media from the standpoints of poststructuralist theory and cultural studies, taking up "[i]ssues of gender, sex, embodiment, and affect" as well as questions of "labor, global logistics, [and] modes of production."[23] At the end of the twentieth century, then, new media studies were divided. On the one hand, poststructuralists conducted important critiques of the linguistic, social, and cultural effects of digital technology, but their disinterest in the material workings of the digital led them to make ahistorical generalizations about the novelty, ephemerality, and singularity of new media technologies. On the other hand, media archaeologists paid close attention to the material specificity and deep histories of technologies, but with little attention to the broader cultural implications of those histories.

This divide was laid bare in *New Media, Old Media: A History and Theory Reader*, Wendy Hui Kyong Chun and Thomas Keenan's 2005 anthology. In the introduction, Chun draws attention to the friction within its pages between "continental European media archaeologists, who have tended to concentrate on the logics and physics of hardware and software, and Anglo-speaking critics, who have focused on the subjective and cultural effects of media, or on the transformative possibilities of interfaces."[24] Importantly, Chun insists, the collection brings both camps together side by side, without attempting to reconcile their differences. It does, however, suggest a Foucauldian way forward, one that takes seriously the particular material conditions shaping new media technologies *in order to* tackle broader political questions.

In the seventeen years since *New Media, Old Media*'s publication, Chun and a growing number of scholars have attempted to bridge this gap, bringing together questions of technology's materiality with its social, political, and cultural meanings. For example, Chun's *Updating to Remain the Same: Habitual New Media* investigates the habits inculcated in users through their interactions with devices and networks developed by large technology companies. Chun exposes the changing sense of temporality inaugurated by our experiences with technology—for example, the ways that we have become habituated to crisis through the cycles of hacks exposing software vulnerabilities, which require urgent patching in order to allow us to return to our patterns of browsing. While this approach may seem, at first, invested in the subjective experience of the individual, Chun insists that a "focus on habit moves us . . . toward questions of infrastructure and justice." She gives the example of studying an Ebola outbreak: in place of "a narrative that manages and diagnoses communicable disease by concentrating on identifying an emerging infection and the global networks through which it travels and is contained," Chun calls for "understanding the conditions that made this spread possible: from crumbling medical infrastructures to new patterns of mobility brought about by globalization to the lingering impacts of colonialism and civil wars."[25] In sum, Chun's study attempts to move between the affective and cultural dimensions of our interactions with new media, the specific technological conditions of those interactions, and the infrastructures that underpin and make possible those technological developments, with attention to the social problems raised at all points in this system.

Like Chun's, Parikka's work yokes media-specific approaches to political concerns, taking infrastructure as a key object of inquiry. His trilogy—*Digital Contagions: A Media Archaeology of Computer Viruses* (Peter Lang, 2007); *Insect Media: An Archaeology of Animals and Technology* (University of Minnesota Press, 2010); and *A Geology of Media* (University of Minnesota Press, 2015)—concerns itself with questions of media ecology. *A Geology of Media*, in particular, takes up ethical questions surrounding the environmental impacts of the infrastructures underpinning twenty-first-century technologies. As Parikka puts it, this book "is interested in the connections of media technologies, their materiality, hardware, and energy, with the geophysical nature," or in other words, the ways "nature affords and bears the weight of media culture, from metals and minerals to its waste load."[26] While drawing explicitly on the intellectual tradition of media archaeology, Parikka frames his own brand of ecocritical materialism as one that rejects earlier technodeterministic approaches, investing instead in environmental concerns that are profoundly social and political.

Nanna Bonde Thylstrup likewise considers problems of infrastructure in *The Politics of Mass Digitization*, coining the term "infrapolitics" to refer to "the building and living of infrastructures, both as spaces of contestation and processes of naturalization."[27] The particular infrastructures that interest Thylstrup are those that have sprung up around the large-scale digitization of cultural objects, especially books. Thylstrup's study examines how endeavors like Project Gutenberg, Gallica, the Internet Archive, Google Books, and the Digital Public Library of America (DPLA) have required the development of new legal and technical interfaces between academic and cultural heritage institutions, large corporations, and sovereign states. Thylstrup remains interested in the social and cultural implications of these developments; she shows how institutions of cultural memory are changing under these pressures, moving from a "traditional symbolic politics of scarcity, sovereignty, and cultural capital" to an "infrapolitics of standardization and subversion." She also examines how individual users are increasingly interacting with cultural artifacts in terms shaped by "digital capitalism with its ethos of access, speed, and participation."[28] Although she takes a poststructuralist interest in questions of signification and meaning, Thylstrup acknowledges but brackets political questions of identity. She notes that "mass digitization suffers from the combined gendered and racialized reality of cultural institutions, tech corporations, and infrastructural projects," but she does not make these concerns a focus of her study, calling instead for more work to be done both to analyze and to redress this reality.[29]

By contrast, Elizabeth Losh and Jacqueline Wernimont foreground questions of race and gender in their 2018 edited collection *Bodies of Information: Intersectional Feminism and Digital Humanities*. In response to "an ongoing denigration of feminist and antiracist theory and practice in the digital humanities," Wernimont and Losh insist on the historical and ongoing centrality of intersectional feminism—defined, following Kimberle Crenshaw, as an approach that "acknowledges the interactions of multiple power structures (including race, sexuality, class, and ability)"—to the field of DH.[30] Losh and Wernimont explicitly reject the language of earlier poststructuralist approaches to media theory and insist that a materialist approach is better suited to investigating the political concerns that motivate their featured authors: "By emphasizing the material, situated, contingent, tacit, embodied, affective, labor-intensive, and political characteristics of digital archives and their supporting infrastructures and practices rather than friction-free visions of pure Cartesian 'virtual reality' or 'cyberspace,' feminist theorists are also expressing their concerns about present-day power relations and signifying interest in collective and communal consciousness-raising efforts."[31] The essays in their book tackle topics ranging from the gender dynamics of DH funding models, to the role of race on the social media sites where DH discourse circulates, to the interactions between DH projects and historically marginalized communities. These essays draw attention to the strong links between the political concerns that are front and center in this collection, and the methodological commitment to understanding digital culture in highly specific, material, embodied terms rather than in abstract or generalized ones.

Bodies of Information's coeditor Wernimont expresses similar commitments in her 2018 monograph *Numbered Lives: Life and Death in Quantum Media*. Drawing on "deep time" methods from media archaeology, Wernimont investigates technologies for quantifying bodies from the early modern period to the present, showing how "critical family resemblances exist between the Fitbit and seventeenth-century life writing as well as between Anglo-American demography and plantation ledgers."[32] Here again, a media archaeological investigation of the materiality of particular technologies is not opposed to but rather placed in service to an investigation of cultural and political concerns. Wernimont pays particular attention to the ways that such "quantum media," from death counts to fitness trackers, have served as "racializing, gendering, and colonizing technologies."[33] In fact, Wernimont's book was published as part of MIT Press's new Media Origins series, and as such, participates in that series' broader project. As the foreword states, this series aims to advance media archaeological narratives that call into question discourses of novelty around digital technologies using "feminist, postcolonial, queer, or antiracist theory." Far from viewing a tension between these two aims, the series editors Elizabeth Losh and Celia Pearce insist that skepticism of novelty actually enables the recovery of voices and histories under erasure. As they put it, the "alarming ahistoricism" of many new media narratives tends to reinforce the "inventor myth" of a "lone auteur," which "usually comes at the expense of often-marginalized groups and participants that were instrumental at inception or adoption."[34] This series, then, represents a strong answer to the challenge identified by Chun in 2005: more than simply reconciling materialist and poststructuralist approaches to new media, the editors position media archaeological work as a uniquely important site for exploring issues of identity, power, and social justice that have long concerned cultural critics and that are increasingly central to digital humanities conversations today.

The Politics of Recovery and Preservation

In 2005, Chun marked the tension between politically attuned cultural critics of new media and their more technodeterminist colleagues in media studies. In 2012, Liu lamented the apoliticism of most quantitative DH work, so much at odds with broader trends in humanities disciplines. In the years since, both data-driven and media archaeological approaches have increasingly taken up the political and cultural questions they initially bracketed, paying greater attention to issues of identity and power at work in data structures, algorithms, visualizations, devices, and infrastructures that have a growing influence not only on humanities scholarship but on our twenty-first-century world. The value thus placed on technical detail and specificity in media archaeological approaches has helped to temper dangerous tendencies toward abstraction and generalization, both in the poststructuralist new media studies of the 1990s (with their emphasis on novelty, ephemerality, and disembodiment) and in the cultural analytics work of the early 2000s (with its recourse to rhetorics of scale, objectivity, and distance). Taken together, these trends have led to the development of a significant new body of digital humanities work, one that leverages materialist approaches in order to better interrogate the politics of digital culture. I conclude by arguing that scholars working in this vein should recognize digital recovery and preservation as particularly rich and important sites for continuing this work.

Kirschenbaum alludes briefly to the critical dimension of preservation in the introduction to *Mechanisms*, noting that "the practical concerns of digital preservation can function as a vehicle for critical inquiry into the nature of new media and electronic textuality."[35] In particular, this inquiry has the potential to open up social, cultural, and political critiques because digital preservation challenges "while massively technical to be sure, are also ultimately—and profoundly—social."[36] Protecting digital resources against the constant and accelerating threat of technological obsolescence is not merely a question of managing data formats, storage media, and interfaces for access. It also involves navigating the shifting priorities, values, and biases of funding agencies, academic and cultural heritage institutions, and both nonprofit and for-profit technology companies. As such, it opens up new opportunities for interrogating the infrastructures—technical, institutional, and ideological—that have historically enabled and limited digital humanities work, and that continue to do so today.

A few notable DH scholars have been using the recovery of past projects to engage in cultural critique. Julianne Nyhan is at the forefront of chronicling the early history of humanities computing; with Andrew Flinn, she published *Computation and the Humanities: Towards an Oral History of Digital Humanities* (Springer, 2016), and her recent work is interested in uncovering the lesser-known contributors to this history. One project, which she and Melissa Terras describe in *Debates in the Digital Humanities 2016*, focuses on the female punch card operatives who entered the data for Father Roberto Busa's computerized concordance *Index Thomisticus*, frequently cited as one of the first humanities computing projects. Semi-structured interviews with the previously unidentified women who worked on the project in the 1950s uncovered "a number of insights into the social, cultural, and organizational conditions that they worked under and how they, as women, were treated in what was a male-dominated environment."[37] When they recovered these histories, Terras and Nyhan gained new insights into the technical workflows and organizational hierarchies of Busa's operation, and they unearthed documents that now have been archived for the first time. This is one of several projects contributing to our growing understanding of the importance (and erasure) of women's labor within the early history of computing. The work of women of color is particularly vulnerable to exploitation, both symbolic and material, as Lisa Nakamura has shown in her examination of the role of Navajo women in the early days of Silicon Valley.[38]

Within the same collection as Terras and Nyhan, Molly O'Hagan Hardy reports on her work to understand the racialized assumptions underpinning the information architecture of the "Printers' File" held in the Reading Room of the American Antiquarian Society (AAS).[39] In the process of digitizing this card catalog of pre-1820 participants in the book trades, Hardy discovered the history of four unusual cards labeled "Black Printers" containing names elsewhere absent from the catalog. Her essay reflects on the ways in which the history of exclusion marked by these cards is necessarily lost in the AAS's new relational data structure, but how that structure also enables previously impossible searches by race and gender—an impossibility that motivated the creation of these four cards. In meditating on the confluence and simultaneous incommensurability of Printers' Files past and present, Hardy shows how a recovery project can lead to new insights about the power dynamics at work in present-day data structures.

Finally, Amy Earhart has done significant work charting the more recent but equally endangered history of digital humanities projects from the past 25 years. Her book, *Traces of the Old, Uses of the New: The Emergence of Digital Literary Studies* (University of Michigan Press, 2015) focuses on the ways that intradisciplinary histories and debates have shaped digital humanities as an interdisciplinary field; her companion blog *The Diverse History of Digital Humanities* (2015–16) catalogs activist digital projects from the 1990s and 2000s.[40] Her screenshots and descriptions of sites like the *Lesbian Herstory Archives*, *NativeWeb*, and *Africabib.org* do the work of memorializing and making visible important contributions to DH at the risk of disappearance due to technological obsolescence, server migration, personnel changes, and the like. Earhart documents and at least partially preserves sites that are, in turn, devoted to recovering and preserving the cultural and intellectual outputs of marginalized communities.

As principal investigator for the *London Stage Database* (LSDB), I lead a media archaeological recovery of an early humanities computing artifact and the invisible labor that went into its creation.[41] The *London Stage Information Bank*, a theater history database developed in the 1970s and subsequently lost, contained information about thousands of eighteenth-century stage performances. Restoring and revitalizing this project has led me to the story of the Hong Kong–based women who generated the underlying data by transcribing 8,000 pages of printed reference books. These typists were hired because their labor was significantly less expensive than US-based alternatives, and they were also imagined in highly gendered, racialized terms. As Ben R. Schneider, the project director, stated in his memoir *Travels in Computerland*, he was intrigued not only by the price point but also by the sight of "a beautiful pair of Oriental eyes gazing over the top of an IBM card" in an advertisement for China Data's key-punching services.[42] Schneider treated these women's labor as largely mechanical and documented none of their names, but working closely with the data reveals that they interpreted his transcription instructions in individualized ways with important implications for the database itself. Even where we are unable to preserve all of the variations in the way this information was transcribed and encoded, my team and I make the original data visible alongside the changes we have made, preserving as much detail as possible about the history of the data's creation, transmission, and transformation.

This commitment to transparency is influenced by Catherine D'Ignazio and Lauren Klein, who point out in *Data Feminism* (2020) that much of the work underpinning data science remains invisible and uncredited. The act of making a dataset's history visible helps to surface that labor. As D'Ignazio and Klein put it: "When designing data products from a feminist perspective, we must similarly aspire to show the work involved in the entire lifecycle of the project. This remains true even as it can be difficult to name each individual involved or when the work may be collective in nature and not able to be attributed to a single source."[43] Media archaeological recovery projects offer a unique opportunity to open up the lost and forgotten stories of digital humanities, as well as to unpack the cultural and political forces that shaped them and that continue to shape DH work today. By practicing transparency and acknowledging our situated, partial perspectives, we can foster an alternative ethos around data that resists broader cultural fantasies about its objectivity, neutrality, and freedom from context.[44] This work brings together all of the threads I have traced here, from the materialist approaches increasingly informing quantitative humanities to the growing awareness that media archaeology need not be the apolitical antagonist of poststructuralist critique. In this sense, the work of recovery and preservation represents one of the most important new frontiers in the digital humanities' cultural turn.

Notes

1. Matthew K. Gold, ed., *Debates in the Digital Humanities* (Minneapolis: University of Minnesota Press, 2012), https://doi.org/10.5749/9781452963754. In this initial volume, see Tara McPherson's "Why Are the Digital Humanities So White? or Thinking the Histories of Race and Computation," George H. Williams's "Disability, Universal Design, and the Digital Humanities," and Bethany Nowviskie's "What Do Girls Dig?" all appear in Part III, "Critiquing the Digital Humanities." Amy E. Earhart's "Can Information Be Unfettered? Race and the New Digital Humanities Canon" appears in Part IV, "Practicing the Digital Humanities."

2. Alan Liu, "Where Is Cultural Criticism in the Digital Humanities?" in *Debates in the Digital Humanities 2016*, ed. Matthew K. Gold and Lauren F. Klein (Minneapolis: University of Minnesota Press, 2016), 491.

3. Lauren F. Klein and Matthew K. Gold, "Digital Humanities: The Expanded Field," in Gold and Klein, *Debates in the Digital Humanities 2016*, https://doi.org/10.5749/9781452963761, xiii–xiv.

4. Gold and Klein, "Introduction: A DH That Matters," in Gold and Klein, *Debates in the Digital Humanities 2019*, https://doi.org/10.5749/9781452963785, xi–xii.

5. Lisa Gitelman and Virginia Jackson, "Introduction" to *"Raw Data" Is an Oxymoron*, ed. Lisa Gitelman (Cambridge, MA: MIT Press, 2013), 2–3.

6. Johanna Drucker, "Humanities Approaches to Graphical Display," *Digital Humanities Quarterly* 5, no. 1 (2011), http://www.digitalhumanities.org/dhq/vol/5/1/000091/000091.html.

7. Lori Emerson, *Reading Writing Interfaces: From the Digital to the Bookbound* (Minneapolis: University of Minnesota Press, 2014), x–xi, xi. See also Alexander R. Galloway, *The Interface Effect* (Cambridge, UK: Polity Press, 2012).

8. Emerson, *Reading Writing Interfaces*.

9. Safiya Umoja Noble, *Algorithms of Oppression: How Search Engines Reinforce Racism* (New York: NYU Press, 2018), 1.

10. Noble, *Algorithms of Oppression*, 96–98.

11. Ruha Benjamin, *Race after Technology: Abolitionist Tools for the New Jim Code* (Cambridge, UK: Polity Press, 2019); Michelle Alexander, *The New Jim Crow: Mass Incarceration in the Age of Colorblindness* (New York: New Press, 2010).

12. Julia Flanders and Fotis Jannadis, "Data Modeling in a Digital Humanities Context: An Introduction," in *The Shape of Data in Digital Humanities: Modeling Texts and Text-Based Resources*, ed. Julia Flanders and Fotis Jannadis (Abingdon, UK: Routledge, 2019), 23.

13. Flanders and Jannadis, "Data Modeling," 14–15.

14. Andrew Piper, *Enumerations: Data and Literary Study* (Chicago: University of Chicago Press, 2018), ix–x, 9.

15. Piper, *Enumerations*, 19.

16. Susan Brown and Laura Mandell, "The Identity Issue," *JCA* 1, no. 1 (2018): 1, https://doi.org/10.22148/16.020.

17. Brown and Mandell, "Identity Issue," 17.

18. Richard Jean So, Hoyt Long, and Yuancheng Zhu, "Race, Writing, and Computation: Racial Difference and the US Novel, 1880–2000," *JCA* 1, no. 1 (2018): 19, https://doi.org/10.22148/16.031.

19. Jo Guldi, "Critical Search: A Procedure for Guided Reading in Large-Scale Textual Corpora," *JCA* 1, no. 2 (2018): 6, https://doi.org/10.22148/16.030.

20. Matthew J. Kirschenbaum, *Mechanisms: New Media and the Forensic Imagination* (Cambridge, MA: MIT Press, 2008), xii–xiii.

21. N. Katherine Hayles and Jessica Pressman, "Introduction, Making, Critique: A Media Framework," in *Comparative Textual Media: Transforming the Humanities in the Postprint Era*, ed. N. Katherine Hayles and Jessica Pressman (Minneapolis: University of Minnesota Press, 2013), vii. See also N. Katherine Hayles, "Narrative and Database: Natural Symbionts," *PMLA: Publications of The Modern Language Association of America* 122, no. 5 (October 2007): 1603–8.

22. Jussi Parikka, *A Geology of Media* (Minneapolis: University of Minnesota Press, 2015), 2–3.

23. Parikka, *Geology of Media*, 3.

24. Wendy Hui Kyong Chun, "Introduction: Did Somebody Say New Media?" in *New Media, Old Media: A History and Theory Reader*, ed. Wendy Hui Kyong Chun and Thomas Keenan (New York: Routledge, 2005), 4.

25. Wendy Hui Kyong Chun, *Updating to Remain the Same* (Cambridge, MA: MIT Press, 2016), 15.

26. Parikka, *Geology of Media*, viii.

27. Nanna Bonde Thylstrup, *The Politics of Mass Digitization* (Cambridge, MA: MIT Press, 2018), 25.

28. Thylstrup, *Politics of Mass Digitization*, 5, 6.

29. Thylstrup, *Politics of Mass Digitization*, 7.

30. Elizabeth Losh and Jacqueline Wernimont, introduction to *Bodies of Information: Intersectional Feminism and Digital Humanities*, ed. Elizabeth Losh and Jacqueline Wernimont (Minneapolis: University of Minnesota Press, 2018), xi, https://doi.org/10.5749/9781452963792. See also Kimberle Crenshaw, "Mapping the Margins: Intersectionality, Identity Politics, and Violence against Women of Color," *Stanford Law Review* 43, no. 6 (1991): 1241–99.

31. Losh and Wernimont, introduction, xiii.

32. Jacqueline Wernimont, *Numbered Lives: Life and Death in Quantum Media* (Cambridge, MA: MIT Press, 2018), 6.

33. Wernimont, *Numbered Lives*, 3.

34. Wernimont, *Numbered Lives*, series foreword.

35. Kirschenbaum, *Mechanisms*, 18.

36. Kirschenbaum, *Mechanisms*, 21.

37. Melissa Terras and Julianne Nyhan, "Father Busa's Female Punch Card Operatives," in Gold and Klein, *Debates in the Digital Humanities 2016*, 62.

38. Lisa Nakamura, "Indigenous Circuits: Navajo Women and the Racialization of Early Electronic Manufacture," *American Quarterly* 66, no. 4 (2014): 919–41.

39. Molly O'Hagan Hardy, "'Black Printers' on White Cards: Information Architecture in the Data Structures of the Early American Book Trades," in Gold and Klein, *Debates in the Digital Humanities 2016*, 377–83.

40. Amy E. Earhart, *The Diverse History of Digital Humanities*, http://dhhistory .blogspot.com.

41. The *London Stage Database* (https://londonstagedatabase.uoregon.edu) is made possible in part by an Advancement Grant from the Office of Digital Humanities at the National Endowment for the Humanities, along with support from the Office of Research, the College of Humanities and Social Sciences, and the Department of English at Utah State University, and the College of Arts and Sciences at the University of Oregon. Any views, findings, conclusions, or recommendations expressed here do not necessarily represent those of the National Endowment for the Humanities.

42. Ben Ross Schneider Jr., *Travels in Computerland; or, Incompatibilities and Interfaces. A Full and True Account of the Implementation of the London Stage Information Bank* (Reading, MA: Addison-Wesley, 1974), 98.

43. Catherine D'Ignazio and Lauren Klein, *Data Feminism* (Cambridge, MA: MIT Press, 2020), 189, https://doi.org/10.7551/mitpress/11805.001.0001.

44. D'Ignazio and Klein, *Data Feminism*, 83; Donna Haraway, "Situated Knowledges: The Science Question in Feminism and the Privilege of Partial Perspective," *Feminist Studies* 14, no. 3 (1988): 581.

Contributors

Alexandra Alvis is a book historian and a rare book cataloguer at Washington, DC–based antiquarian book dealer Type Punch Matrix. They have worked in special collections libraries in the United States and the United Kingdom, and they have written on topics such as the history of bookshelf organization and the conservation work of bookbinder Douglas Cockerell and Son.

Paul A. Broyles is a lecturer in English at North Carolina State University, where he previously held a CLIR Postdoctoral Fellowship in Data Curation for Medieval Studies. He serves as technical director of the Society for Early English and Norse Electronic Texts (SEENET) and technical editor of the *Piers Plowman Electronic Archive*. His technical work includes programming and data management for digital humanities projects; other research areas include medieval romance, geographic thought, and textual transmission.

Mattie Burkert is an assistant professor of digital humanities in the English Department at the University of Oregon, which is situated on the traditional indigenous homeland of the Kalapuya people. She is the author of *Speculative Enterprise: Public Theaters and Financial Markets in London, 1688–1763* (2021) and the principal investigator and project director of the London Stage Database (https://londonstagedatabase.uoregon.edu).

Matthew Kirschenbaum is a professor of English and digital studies at the University of Maryland, where he cofounded and codirects BookLab, a makerspace for the book arts. He is the author most recently of *Bitstreams: The Future of Digital Literary Heritage* (2021).

Mary Learner is a PhD candidate in English and comparative literature at the University of North Carolina at Chapel Hill, completing a dissertation entitled "Material Sampling and Patterns of Thought in Early Modern England" on methods of "sampling" in women's writing and seventeenth-century scientific print. Her work has appeared in *Nuncius* and is forthcoming in the essay collection *Early Modern Criticism*.

Joseph L. Locke is an associate professor of history at the University of Houston–Victoria. He is the author of *Making the Bible Belt: Texas Prohibitionists and the Politicization of Southern Religion* (2017) and coeditor of *The American Yawp: A Massively Collaborative Open U.S. History Textbook* (2019).

Clayton P. Michaud is an economist with the USDA's Economic Research Service (ERS), where he works on issues related to diversity, equity, and inclusion. He received his PhD in environmental and natural resource economics from the University of Rhode Island.

Christy L. Pottroff is an assistant professor of English at Boston College, where she specializes in nineteenth-century media studies, book history, and digital humanities. Her monograph-in-progress investigates the intended and unintended effects of postal infrastructure on nineteenth-century American literature and culture. Her work has appeared in *American Literature*, *Early American Literature*, *Early American Studies*, and *Common-place*.

Mark Vareschi is an associate professor in the Department of English at the University of Wisconsin–Madison. Vareschi is a specialist in eighteenth-century British literature and digital studies and is the author of *Everywhere and Nowhere: Anonymity and Mediation in Eighteenth-Century Britain* (2018).

Heather Wacha is a former postdoctoral fellow and associate coordinator for the Center for the History of Print and Digital Culture at the University of Wisconsin–Madison. She is coauthor with Yvonne Seale of *The Cartulary of the Abbey of Prémontré: A Joint Print/Digital Edition* (2022).

Catherine A. Winters is an independent scholar who received her PhD in English from the University of Rhode Island.

Ben Wright is an associate professor of history at the University of Texas at Dallas. He is the author of *Bonds of Salvation: How Christianity Inspired and Limited American Abolitionism* (2020), coeditor of *The American Yawp: A Massively Collabora-*

tive Open U.S. History Textbook (2019), and coeditor with Zachary W. Dresser of *Apocalypse and the Millennium in the American Civil War Era* (2013).

Jayme Yahr is an associate curator at the Crocker Art Museum in Sacramento, California, where she curates the photography, American works on paper, and Native American art collections. She is the author of "Human Nature: The Body/Environment Relationship in Photographs of Twinka Thiebaud" in the exhibition catalogue *Twinka Thiebaud and the Art of the Pose* (2022) and "The Rise and Fall of the *Century Illustrated Monthly Magazine* (1881–1930)" in *Re-reading the Age of Innovation: Victorians, Moderns, and Literary Newness* (2022).

Index

Abildgaard, Niels Roesen, 155
Adams, Thomas R., 5
Adelman, Joseph, 21
Africabib.org, 179
Against a Sharp White Background (Fielder and Senchyne), 3
Agrippa (Gibson), 173
Alexander, Michelle, 170
Algorithms of Oppression: How Search Engines Reinforce Racism (Noble), 170
Allen, Cliff, 95
Alliance of Digital Humanities Organizations (ADHO), ix
Alvis, Alexandra, 12, 109–19, 185
American Antiquarian Society (AAS), 179
American Community Survey, 52
American Historical Association, 97
American Philosophical Society Library, 32, 38n15, 39n18
American Revolution, 22, 31, 34
American Studies Association, 8
American Yawp (Locke and Wright), 11–12, 96, 98, 101, 107, 186
Anderson, Benedict, 20, 31
Andrew W. Mellon Foundation, 41

Anna Karenina.viz project, 42, 50–54
Apess, William, 130
APIs (Applications Programming Interfaces), 154
Apocalypse and the Millennium in the American Civil War Era (Wright and Dresser), 187
"Apology for Raymond Sebond" (de Montaigne), 78
Aristotle, 65
Armitage, David, 92, 100
Ashkenas, Jeremy, 154–55
Association for Computers and the Humanities (ACH/ALLC), ix
Association of American University Presses, 100
Australian National Data Service, 150
"Authoring Tools and an Educational Object Economy" (NSF), 91
authors: collaboration and, 97–99; cultural turn and, 171, 176; MERLOT and, 91; museum studies and, 46, 51–54; new models of, 97–99; online text collections and, 123–39; open access and, 12–13, 88–91, 97–99, 103
Avery, Marguerite, 91

Bacon, Francis, 66–67
Bailey, Moya, 8
Baraniuk, Richard, 92
Barker, Nicolas, 5
Baur, Dominikus, 52
Best, Stephen, 62
"BH & DH: Book History and Digital Humanities" conference, 9–10
Bible, 171–72
bibliography: Broyles on, 13; cultural turn and, 173; libraries and, 111, 141n28; McKenzie on, 6–7; museum studies and, 45–46; New Bibliography, 7–8; reinterpretation of, 61; Savage and, 69, 72; textual criticism and, 148; versioning and, 13, 148–53, 156–57, 163n1
Bibliothèque nationale de France, 63
big data, xi, 170
Bitstreams: The Future of Digital Literary Heritage (Kirschenbaum), 185
Black Lives Matter, 168
Black Printers, 179
Blair, Ann, 20, 85n53
Bodies of Information: Intersectional Feminism and Digital Humanities (Losh and Wernimont), 176–77
Bonds of Salvation: How Christianity Inspired and Limited American Abolitionism (Wright), 186
Booke of Flowers Fruicts Beastes Birds and Flies, A (Gessner), 76
BookLab, 185
Books of Hours, 49, 12, 109–17, 118n14
Booth, Alison, 8–9
Boston College, 186
botany: collaboration and, 76, 79–80; engravings and, 64–66, 69, 73, 75–77, 82n12, 85n47, 85n49; florilegia, 11, 63–66, 69–73, 76–77, 81, 82n12, 84n44; Gerard and, 65, 85n49; herbals, 11, 63–66, 69, 76; Internet Archive and, 70; Linnaean system and, 65, 77; metadata and, 61, 64, 78, 81; needlework and, 11, 61, 63–64, 66–70, 76–81, 83n26, 84n33, 85n47, 87n69; pattern books and, 67–68, 77, 79, 82n14, 87n69; sampling and, 67–68, 72, 76, 79, 81; scientific art and, 65; surface reading and, 11, 61–63; symptomatic reading and, 61–62; taxonomies and, 63, 65; van de Passe on, 66, 69–73, 76–77, 82n15
Boundless Learning, 95–96
Boundless U.S. History, 95
Bowers, Fredson, 152
Boyle, Robert, 67
Bradford, Andrew, 21
brand accounts, 111
Brayman, Heidi, 68
Brennan, Sheila A., 44, 56n18
British Colonial Mail, 29, 31, 34
British Library, 74, 76
Brown, Robert, 91
Brown, Susan, 171
Broyles, Paul A., 13, 147–66, 185
Budapest Open Access Initiative, 91–92
Building the American Republic (University of Chicago Press), 101
Bureau of Labor Statistics, 93
Burkert, Mattie, 13–14, 167–83, 185
Busa, Roberto, 7, 178–79
Butler, Ruth Lapham, 30

Cabot, Nancy Graves, 68–69
Calendar Versioning (CalVer), 153, 160, 165n12
California Institute for Telecommunication, 50
California State University, 91
Cal Tech, 93
Cambridge University, 74, 100
Carnegie Mellon, 91

Index

Cartulary of the Abbey of Prémontré: A Joint Print/Digital Edition (Wacha and Seale), 186
Case, Kristen, 20
Cavendish, Margaret, 80–81
CD-ROMs, 156–57, 159
Center for Open Education, 99–100
Center for the History of Print and Digital Culture (CHPDC), 3, 9, 186
Century Illustrated Monthly Magazine, The, 46–48, 187
Chartier, Roger, 6, 62
Chow, Jay, 52
Christensen, Neil B., 99
Christianity, 118n14, 172, 186
Chun, Wendy Hui Kyong, 174–75
circulation studies, 5; Franklin and, 10, 20–22, 26, 29, 31–37; libraries and, 12; life cycles of books and, 62
City University of New York, 50
"Classics in the Million Book Library," 124
CLIR (Council on Library and Information Resources), 159, 164, 185
Clusius, Carolus, 65, 69
Cohen, Matt, 34
collaboration: authors and, 97–99; botany and, 76, 79–80; museum studies and, 44, 47, 49, 52–53, 56n13; online text collections and, 125; open access and, 88–90, 96–99, 102–3
Collabra (University of California Press), 99
College Board, 93
Columbia University, 130
CommentPress, 102
communication: Alvis on, 12; Darnton on, 5, 7; Franklin and, 21–22, 24, 26, 29–35, 38n14; libraries and, 110, 117; McKenzie on, 5, 7; museum studies and, 50; ScienceAF and, 110
communications circuit, 5

Comparative Textual Media (Hayles and Pressman), 173
"Computational Case against Computational Literary Studies, The" (Da), 5
Computation and the Humanities: Towards an Oral History of Digital Humanities (Nyhan and Flinn), 178
Cong-Huyen, Anne, 8
Congnoscite Lilia (van de Passe the Elder), 73
Congressional Hearing on Libraries and Their Role in the Information Infrastructure, 138–39
Connexions, 92, 102
continuous publishing, 157–58
copyright: digital editions and, 160; Google Books and, 126, 141n18; online text collections and, 127–28, 139n2, 141n18, 142n30; open access and, 92, 98–101; PPEA in Print and, 160; public domain and, 45, 92, 123, 126–29, 139n2, 142n30; versioning and, 160
Cornell University, 41–42, 45, 54
COVE (Collaborative Organization for Virtual Education), 97
Covid-19, 96
Crane, Gregory, x, 124
Creative Commons, 98, 101
Crenshaw, Kimberle, 176
Crocker Art Museum, 187
CSS (Cascading Style Sheets), 156
Cultural Analytics Lab (CAL), 42, 50–55
cultural turn: authors and, 171, 176; bibliography and, 173; encoding and, 171, 180; gender and, 167–71, 174–80; Google and, 170, 172, 175; Google Books and, 175; identity and, 167–68, 171, 176–78; Internet Archive and, 175; Liu and, 9, 167–68, 177; machines and, 173; media

cultural turn (*continued*)
   studies and, 168, 173–74, 177–78; politics of data and, 168–73; politics of recovery and preservation and, 177–80; politics of technologies and infrastructures, 173–77; Project Gutenberg and, 175; race and, 167–72, 176, 179; social media and, 176
Curator of Early Modern Books and Manuscripts, 111
curators, 187; libraries and, 111; metadata and, 57n21; museum studies and, 10–11, 43–44, 49–54, 56n13, 57n21
curiosity cabinets, 42–43

Da, Nan, 5
Darnton, Robert, 5, 7
Data Feminism (D'Ignazo and Klein), 180
"Data on the Web Best Practices" (W3C), 150
Debates in the Digital Humanities (University of Minnesota Press), 8, 100, 102, 167, 178
Defoe, Daniel, 19
De Hamel, Christopher, 115
democracy, 89, 103
Den Blom-hof (van de Passe), 66
De Vorsey, Louis, 35
Dickinson, Emily, 169
Digital Contagions: A Media Archaeology of Computer Viruses (Parikka), 175
digital editions: continuous publishing and, 157–58; copyright and, 160; describing, 156–58; encoding and, 148, 156, 158–63, 166n20; hashes and, 149; hypertext and, 147; practicality of, xi; Text Encoding Initiative (TEI), x, 148, 158–63; textual multiplicity and, 147; versioning and, 147–64; XML files and, 148, 156, 158–63, 164n4

Digital History (Mintz and McNeil), 94, 101–2
Digital Humanities (DH) conference, ix–xi
Digital Humanities (Burdick et al.), 88
Digital Object Identifiers (DOIs), 150
Digital Public Library of American (DPLA), 175–76
D'Ignazio, Catherine, 180
Dioscorides, 65
Directions for Deputy Postmasters (Franklin and Hunter), 27
Diverse History of Digital Humanities, The (Earhart), 179
diversity: identity and, 9, 140n10, 144n144; Michaud and, 186; online text collections and, 12, 130, 133, 140n10, 144n44
DIY History, 42, 49–50, 53–54, 55n5
Dodoens, Rembert, 65
Douglas Cockerell and Son, 185
Dresser, Zachary W., 187
Drucker, Johanna, 169

Earhart, Amy, 7, 90–91, 179
Early English Books Online (EEBO), 63, 73–74, 75
eBooks, 101, 125–27, 141n22
"Economic and Social Conjuncture" (Darnton), 5
"Editing the Interface" (Kirschenbaum), 156
Education Fund, 93
Edwards, Caroline, 100
Edwards, Charlie, 44, 56n15
edX, 95–96
electronic objects, 13, 157
Emerson, Lori, 169
encoding: bias and, 171; cultural turn and, 171, 180; digital editions and, 148, 156, 158–63, 166n20; intellectual identity and, 13; Text Encoding Initiative (TEI), x, 148, 158–63

Index

engravings: botanical, 64–66, 69, 73, 75–77, 82n12, 85n47, 85n49; copper, 64, 76–77; Merian and, 77; scientific art and, 65; van de Passe the Elder and, 69, 73, 82n15

Enumerations: Data and Literary Study (Piper), 170–71

equity, 12, 111, 125, 186

Essays (de Montaigne), 78

Eve, Martin Paul, 92, 98, 100, 105n20

Everywhere and Nowhere: Anonymity and Mediation in Eighteenth-Century Britain (Vareschi), 186

feedback, 4, 96

Felluga, Dino Franco, 97

Fielder, Brigitte, 3

Fiormonte, Domenico, 46–47

Flanders, Julia, 51, 170

Flat World Knowledge, 95

Flickr, 42, 50

Flinn, Andrew, 178

FLORA Flowers Fruicts Beastes Birds and Flies exacly drawne (Payne), 73–74

florilegia: botany and, 11, 63–66, 69–73, 76–77, 81, 82n12, 84n44; decorative vs. substantive, 64; division of from herbals, 64–65; engravings and, 64–66, 69, 73, 76–77, 82n12; later taxonomies and, 63–64; medieval texts on, 66; needlework and, 11, 63–64, 66–70, 76–81, 83n26, 84n33, 85n47, 87n69; pattern books and, 67–68, 77, 79, 82n14, 87n69; sampling and, 67–68, 72, 76, 79, 81; scientific art and, 65; taxonomies and, 63, 65; van de Passe on, 66, 69–73, 76–77, 82n15

Florilegium Renovatum (Merian), 77

Florio, John, 78–79, 87n70

Folger, Timothy, 35

Folger Shakespeare Library, 63, 72–76

Forbes magazine, 88

Forum on the Impact of Open Courseware for Higher Education in Developing Countries, 92

Foursquare, 52

Foxcroft, John, 29

Franklin, Benjamin: *Autiobiography* of, 19; big data and, xi; bookish inclination of, 19; circulation studies and, 10, 20–22, 26, 29, 31–37; communication and, 21–22, 24, 26, 29–35, 38n14; databases of, 19–20, 31, 33–37; as Deputy Postmaster General, 20, 30; Foxcroft and, 29; Gulf Stream and, 35–37, 40n36; Hunter and, 10, 27, 29–30, 34; as Joint Deputy Postmaster General, 26–27, 33; moral account book of, 19–20; narratives in records of, 33–37; Philadelphia Post Office and, 21–22, 24, 27, 33, 38n9; postal account books of, 20–37, 38nn16–17; as Postmaster General, 27, 32; "Post Office Instructions and Directions," 32, 34; as printer, 19, 21, 26, 37n2

Free Software Foundation, 90

Frye, Northrop, 172

Fuchs, Leonhart, 69

Gallica, 63, 70, 175–76

Gaskell, Philip, 6

gender: binary code and, 9; cultural turn and, 167–71, 174–80; divided literacies and, 63; needlework and, 63, 67, 79–80; online text collections and, 12–13, 124–25, 128–34, 138, 140n10, 144n44; race and, 6–13, 103, 124–25, 128–38, 140n10, 144n44, 145nn56–57, 167–68, 170, 176, 179; #transformDH and, 8; Women Writers Project (WWP), 125, 138

Geology of Media, A (Parikka), 175

Gerard, John, 65, 85n49
Gessner, Conrad, 65, 69, 76, 85n53
Gibson, William, 173
Gitelman, Lisa, 169
Git repository, 148–49
GNU Project, 90
Goddemeyer, Daniel, 52
Gold, Matthew, 102, 168
Goodreads, 143n35
Google, 88, 144n47, 170, 172
Google Books, x; copyright and, 127, 141n18; cultural turn and, 175; online text collections and, 12, 123–28, 141n18, 141n28; university contracts and, 141n28
Google Image Search, 115–16
Google Street View, 52–53
Graduate Center, The, 50
Grafton, Anthony, 97
Grandjean, Katherine, 34
Grazia, Margreta de, 62
Green, Cable, 98, 106n43
Green, Jim, 37n2
Greg, W. W., 6
Guillory, John, 5
Guldi, Jo, 92, 100, 172
Gulf Stream, 35–37, 40n36

Hain, Ludwig, 6
Hardy, Molly O'Hagan, 179
Harnad, Stevan, 98
Harper's New Monthly Magazine, 48
Harvard University, 47, 111–12
hashes, 149
hashtags, 8, 111, 117
HathiTrust, 42, 45–50, 54
Hawthorne, Nathaniel, 133
Hayles, N. Katherine, 4, 33, 173
Heider, Cynthia, 32
herball on Generall histories of plantes, The (Gerard), 65
herbals, 11, 63–66, 69, 76

Hewlett Foundation, 99
Historia plantarum (Gessner), 76
@HistoryInPics, 115
History Manifesto, The (Armitage and Guldi), 92, 100
Holzman, Alex, 91
Hooke, Robert, 67
Hortus Floridus (van de Passe the Younger), 66, 69–73, 76–77, 82n15
Houghton Library, 111–13
Howells, William Dean, 130
Huber, William, 52
"Human Nature: The Body/Environment Relationship in Photographs of Twinka Thiebaud" (Yahr), 187
Hunter, William, 10, 27, 29–30, 34
Hypothes.is, 102

IBM, 7, 90, 180
identity: cultural turn and, 167–68, 171, 176–78; diversity and, 9, 140n10, 144n144; intellectual, 13, 152, 158; marginalization and, 14; online text collections and, 123, 135, 140n10, 144n44; open access and, 90; organizational, 123; versioning and, 152, 158, 162–63
Incidents in the Life of a Slave Girl (Jacobs), 129–30, 133
inclusion, 12, 124–25, 128, 139, 141n28, 144n44, 186
Indaco, Agustin, 52
Index Thomisticus (Busa), 7, 178
Indiana University, 47
inequality, 88–90, 93, 114–16
Insect Media: An Archaeology of Animals and Technology (Parikka), 175
Instagram, 52–53, 111
Institute for the Future of the Book, 102
Instructions to Deputy Postmasters (Franklin and Hunter), 27

Index

Interacting with Print (collection), 62
intermediation, 4–9, 14
Internet Archive: botany and, 70; cultural turn and, 175; museum studies and, 48; online text collections and, 48, 63, 70, 124, 127–28, 141n22, 142n29, 175
Ithaka, 102

Jackson, Virginia, 169
Jacobs, Harriet, 129–30, 133
James, Henry, 133
Jannadis, Fotis, 170
Johnson, Thomas, 65–66
Journal of American History, 94
Journal of Cultural Analytics, 171–72

Kahle, Brewster, 127
Keenan, Thomas, 174–75
King James Version of the Bible, 171
Kinukawa, Tomomi, 67
Kirschenbaum, Matthew, ix–xii; *Bitstreams: The Future of Digital Literary Heritage*, 185; Broyles and, 13; cataloging and, 10; "Editing the Interface," 156; intermediate horizons and, 3–4; *Mechanisms: New Media and the Forensic Imagination*, 173, 178; objects and, 157; versioning and, 157, 160
Kittler, Friedrich, 174
Klein, Lauren F., 9, 168, 180
Knight, Jeffrey Todd, 68, 73
Koh, Adeline, 94
Koontz, Rex, 54
Koszary, Adam, 114
Kusukawa, Sachiko, 76

Laroche, Rebecca, 66
Learner, Mary, xi, 11, 61–87, 186
Learning and Teaching Support Network (LTSN), 95, 105n34
Leaves of Grass (Whitman), 129–30

Lee, Maurice S., 131, 133
Lesbian Herstory Archives, 179
libertarianism, 140n10
libraries: access issues and, 114–16; bibliography and, 111, 141n18; Books of Hours and, 112–17, 118n14; circulation studies and, 12; CLIR and, 159, 164, 185; communication and, 110, 117; Congressional Hearing on Libraries and Their Role in the Information Infrastructure, 138–39; curators and, 111; diversification and, 109–10; equity and, 111; hashtags, 111, 117; HathiTrust and, 46–47, 49, 54; rare book protection and, 109; social media and, 12, 109–17, 118n20; special collections and, 12, 109–17, 185; statistics on, 112, 116; video and, 114, 116, 118n19
Library of Alexandria, 127
#LibraryTwitter, 111, 117
licenses, 12, 92, 100–101, 126, 142n30
Lindauer, Margaret, 58n32
Linnaeus, Carl, 65, 77
Liu, Alan, 9, 167–68, 177
Locke, Joseph L., xi–xii, 11–12, 88–108, 186
London Stage Database (LSDB), 179–80, 183n41
London Stage Information Bank, 180
Long, Hoyt, 171–72
Losh, Elizabeth, 15n9, 176–77
Lothian, Alexis, 8
Loughran, Trish, 31
Love, Heather, 20
Lovings, Lauren, 54
Luminos, 99
LUNA database, 63, 72–73

machines: concordances and, 7; cultural turn and, 173; feedback loops and, 4; IBM, 7, 90, 180; learning by, 50;

machines (*continued*)
    online text collections and, 127, 138; open access and, 90; recursivity and, 5; versioning and, 155; Wayback Machine and, 127
Making of America Collection (MOA): Anna Karenina.viz, 42, 50–54; case study of, 42, 45–49; *The Century* and, 46–48; collection of, 41–42; Cultural Analytics Lab and, 42; DIY History and, 42, 49–50, 53–54, 55n5; Fiormonte and, 46–47; *Harper's Magazine* and, 48; HathiTrust and, 42, 45–50, 54; museum studies and, 41–42, 45–54, 57n22; On Broadway and, 42, 50, 52–53; optical character recognition (OCR), 41, 45–46, 49; recent digital solutions and, 49–53; *Science* and *Popular Science* and, 42, 50–52; search choices and, 46; "Towards a Cultural Critique of the Digital Humanities" and, 46; visual/spatial juxtapositions and, 54
Making the Bible Belt: Prohibitionists and the Politicization of Southern Religion (Locke), 186
Mandell, Laura, 171
Manovich, Lev, 51–52
Marcus, Sharon, 62
Marrel, Jacob, 77
Marxism, 61
Massively Open Online Classes (MOOCs), 95–96
"Material Sampling and Patterns of Thought in Early Modern England" (Learner), 186
Mather, 19
Mattiolo, Pietro, 65
McAfee, R. Preston, 93
McDonough, Jerome, 156
McGann, Jerome, ix, 147
McGill, Meredith, 20

McKenzie, D. F., 5–7, 62
McLuhan, Marshall, 5–6
McNeil, Sara, 94
McPherson, Tara, 15n20
Mechanisms: New Media and the Forensic Imagination (Kirschenbaum), 173, 178
Media Origins, 177
media studies, 8, 186; cultural turn and, 168, 173–74, 177–78; museum studies and, 41
@MedievalReacts, 115
Meisterlin, Leah, 52
Mellon Foundation, 100–101
Melville, Herman, 130–31
Merian, Maria Sibylla, 77–78
Merian, Matthäus, 77
MERLOT (Multimedia Education Resource for Learning and Online Teaching), 91
metadata: botany and, 61, 64, 78, 81; copy-specific, 61; as curatorial process, 57n21; museum studies and, 46, 52–53, 57n21; needlework and, 78; online text collections and, 141n28; transparent practices and, 64; versioning and, 148, 155–56
Michaud, Clayton P., xi, 12–13, 123–46, 186
Michigan State University, 47
Microsoft, 153
Middle Ages, 114–15
Midsummer Night's Dream, A (Shakespeare), 79–80
Miller, Bayard, 32
Miller, Daniel, 110
Mintz, Steven, 94, 101–2
MIT OpenCourseWare, 91–92
MIT Press, 100, 177
Montaigne, Michel de, 78–79, 86n64
Morales, Michelle, 52
Moss, Emanuel, 52
Multidoc Pro SGML, 159

Index

museum studies: Anna Karenina.viz, 42, 50–54; authors and, 46, 51–54; bibliography and, 45–46; cabinets of curiosity and, 42–43; *The Century* and, 46–48; collaboration and, 44, 47, 49, 52–53, 56n13; communication and, 50; Cultural Analytics Lab and, 42; curators and, 10–11, 43–44, 49–54, 56n13, 57n21; digital objects and, 41; DIY History and, 42, 49–50, 53–54, 55n5; framework of, 42–45; Internet Archive and, 48; media studies and, 41; metadata and, 46, 52–53, 57n21; On Broadway and, 42, 50, 52–53; optical character recognition (OCR), 41, 45–46, 49; Peale and, 43; public domain and, 45; recent digital solutions and, 49–53; *Science* and *Popular Science*, 42, 50–52; search choices and, 46; social media and, 44, 46, 50, 53; special collections and, 49; wonder rooms and, 42–43, 49

Nakamura, Lisa, 179
National Science Foundation, 91
NativeWeb, 179
natural logs, 134, 145n52
needlework: Bacon on, 66–67; botany and, 11, 61, 67–70, 78–81; embroidery, 11, 63–64, 66–69, 76–80, 83n26, 84n33, 85n47, 87n69; florilegia and, 11, 69–70, 81; gender and, 63, 67, 80; metadata and, 78; pattern books and, 67–68, 77, 79, 82n14, 87n69; pouncing and, 68, 72–74, 78, 81, 84n33, 85n47; sampling and, 67–68, 72, 76, 79, 81; Shakespeare on, 79–81
Neri, Janice, 67
Nevinson, J. L., 68–69
New Atlantis (Bacon), 66–67

New Bibliography, 7–8
New Jim Crow, 170
New Left, 89
New Media, Old Media: A History and Theory Reader (Chun and Keenan), 174–75
"New Model for the Study of the Book, A" (Adams and Barker), 5
newspapers, 19, 21, 31, 38n9, 39n27, 48
New York Times, 91, 93
Noble, Safiya Umoja, 170, 172
North Carolina State University, 159, 185
Northwestern University, 47
NYC Taxi and Limousine Commission, 52
Nyhan, Julianne, 178–79

Obama, Barack, 88
"Of the Caniballes" (Florio), 78–79
Ogilvie, Brian, 64–65
Ohio State University, 47
On Broadway project, 42, 50, 52–53
online text collections: authors and, 123–39; collaboration and, 125; Congressional Hearing on Libraries and Their Role in the Information Infrastructure, 138–39; controlling for demand and, 129–30; copyright and, 127–28, 139n2, 141n18, 142n30; diversity and, 12, 130, 133, 140n10, 144n44; *Early English Books Online* (EEBO), 63, 73–74, 75; equity and, 12, 125, 186; gender and, 12–13, 124–25, 128–34, 138, 140n10, 144n44; Google Books and, 12, 123–28, 141n18, 141n28; identity and, 123, 135, 140n10, 144n44; inclusion and, 12, 124–25, 128, 139, 141n28, 144n44, 186; Internet Archive, 48, 63, 70, 124, 127–28, 141n22, 142n29, 175; machines and, 127, 138; metadata and, 141n28; Open Library, 123, 125–27; Project Gutenberg, 12, 123,

online text collections (*continued*) 125–28, 140n15, 141n22, 141n25; public domain and, 123, 126–29, 139n2, 142n30; race and, 123–25, 128–39, 140n10, 144n44, 145n54, 145nn56–58, 146n60; statistics on, 124–25, 128–38, 140n6, 143n42, 143n39, 145nn54–56; supply of digital, 125–28; Wikisource, 123–28; Women Writers Project (WWP), 125, 138

open access: *American Yawp* and, 11–12, 96, 98, 101, 107, 186; authors and, 12–13; authorship and, 88–91, 97–99, 103; case study of, 94–97; collaboration and, 88–90, 96–99, 102–3; copyright and, 92, 98–101; cost and, 89–90, 93–95, 98, 100–103; Creative Commons, 98, 101; democracy and, 89, 103; Free Software Foundation, 90; future issues, 101–3; GNU Project, 90; Hewlett Foundation and, 91; identity and, 90; ideological origins of, 90–93; inequality and, 88–90, 93, 114; MERLOT and, 91; MIT OpenCourseWare, 91–92; MOOCs, 95–96; Open Educational Resources (OER), 11–12, 89–96, 99–103; public domain and, 92; quality control and, 99–101; SHARE Operating System, 90; Stallman and, 90; technophobia and, 89; textbooks and, 4, 11, 89–103; utopianism and, 11, 88–94, 103; Wilinsky on, 88–89

Open Educational Quality Initiative, 100

Open Educational Resources (OER): *American Yawp* and, 11–12, 96, 98, 101, 107, 186; open access and, 11–12, 89–96, 99–103

Open Learning Initiative (OLI), 91

Open Learning Support, 91

Open Library, 123, 125–27

Open Library of Humanities (OLH), 100

open licensing, 12, 92, 100–101

Open Science, 150

OpenStax, 101

Open Textbook Library (OTL), 100

Open Textbook Network (OTN), 99–100

Open Textbook Toolkit, 100

optical character recognition (OCR), 41, 45–46, 49, 126

Ordinary Least Squares (OLS), 134, 145n53

Oregon State University, 101

Orlando Project, The (Cambridge University Press), 100

Overholt, John, 111, 113

Panzer, G. W., 6

Parikka, Jussi, 174–75

pattern books, 67–68, 77, 79, 82n14, 87n69

Payne, John, 73–74

Peale, Charles Wilson, 43

Pearce, Celia, 177

Peer 2 Peer University (P2PU), 95

Pendergrass, Rachel, 110, 114

Pennsylvania Hospital, 32

personal accounts, 111–15

Philadelphia Gazette, 29

Philadelphia Post Office, 21–22, 24, 27, 33, 38n9

Phillips, Amanda, 8

Piers Plowman Electronic Archive (PPEA), 13, 158–63

Pilgrim's Progress (Bunyan), 19

Piper, Andrew, 170–71

PLOS (Public Library of Science), 92

PMLA journal, 8

Poe, Edgar Allan, 133

Poems, and Fancies (Cavendish), 80–81

Politics of Mass Digitalization, The (Thylstrup), 175–76

Popular Science magazine, 42, 50–52

Posner, Miriam, 8–9

Index

"Post Office Instructions and Directions" (Franklin and Hunter), 32, 34
Post-Office Leidger No. 1, 22–24
Pottroff, Christy L., xi, 10, 19–40, 186
pouncing, 68, 72–74, 78, 81, 84n33, 85n47
Pressman, Jessica, 173
Preston-Werner, Tom, 154, 165n13
Price, Daniel, 54
Printers' Files, 179
Project Gutenberg: cultural turn and, 175; Distributed Proofreaders, 126; hierarchical system of, 128; online text collections and, 12, 123, 125–28, 140n15, 141n22, 141n25
psychoanalysis, 61
public domain: museum studies and, 45; online text collections and, 123, 126–29, 139n2, 142n30; open access and, 92

quality, 99–101

race: Black Lives Matter, 168; Congressional Hearing on Libraries and Their Role in the Information Infrastructure, 138–39; cultural turn and, 167–72, 176, 179; distant reading and, 9; gender and, 6–13, 103, 124–25, 128–38, 140n10, 144n44, 145nn56–57, 167–68, 170, 176, 179; New Jim Crow and, 170; Noble on, 170; online text collections and, 123–25, 128–39, 140n10, 144n44, 145n54, 145nn56–58, 146n60; #transformDH and, 8; slavery and, 97, 129, 133, 170, 172
"Race, Writing, and Computation: Racial Difference and the US Novel, 1880–2000" (So, Long, and Zhu), 171–72
Ramos, Maria, 138–39
Ramsay, Stephen, 20, 42
rare books, 61, 63, 109, 185
"Rationale of Hypertext, The" (McGann), 147

"Raw Data" Is an Oxymoron (Gitelman and Jackson), 169
Reading Writing Interfaces: From the Digital to the Bookbound (Emerson), 169
recursivity, 4–5, 9
regression analysis, 12, 124–25, 134, 136, 140n6, 145n53
Renaissance, 62, 79
Renouard, A. A., 6
Rhaptos, 102
Rice University, 92
"Rise and Fall of the *Century Illustrated Monthly Magazine*, The" (Yahr), 187
Rise of Silas Lapham, The (Howells), 130
Roland, Edwin, 9
Romantic Versioning, 155
Ruskin, John, 115
Russian Messenger, The (periodical), 51

Sam Houston State University, 130
sampling, 67–68, 72, 76, 79, 81, 129–30
Savage, Spencer, 69–72, 75–77
Schneider, Ben R., 180
Scholastic Commentary and Text Archive, 158
Schrader, Stephanie, 77
ScienceAF, 110
Science and *Popular Science* project, 42, 50–52
Seale, Yvonne, 186
Semantic Versioning (SemVer), 153–56, 161, 165n13
Senchyne, Jonathan, 3
Sentimental Versioning, 155
SGML, 159, 161
SHA-1 algorithm, 149
Shakespeare, William, 79–81
Shape of Data in Digital Humanities, The: Modeling Texts and Text-Based Resources (Flanders and Jannadis), 170
SHARE Operating System, 90
Shepherd, Brynn, 52
Silicon Valley, 88–89, 95, 179

Slauter, Eric, 20
slavery, 97, 129, 133, 170, 172
Smith, Megan, 88
Smith, Pamela, 64–65, 67
Smith, Steven Escar, 113–14
Smithsonian Libraries, 111–12
So, Richard Jean, 9, 171–72
social media: access issues and, 114–16; Books of Hours and, 112–17, 118n14; brand accounts, 111; content decisions and, 110; cultural turn and, 176; hashtags, 8, 111, 117; Instagram, 52–53, 111; libraries and, 12, 109–17, 118n20; museum studies and, 44, 46, 50, 53; personal accounts, 111–15; Tumblr, 111; Twitter, 12, 52, 110–11, 115–17
Society for Early English and Norse Electronic Texts (SEENET), 159, 185
Software Studies Initiative, 52
Soll, Jacob, 21–22, 38n14
Son of the Forest, A (Apess), 130
special collections, 61; libraries and, 12, 109–17, 118n20, 185; museum studies and, 49
Species Plantarum (Linnaeus), 77
Stallman, Richard, 90
Stallybrass, Peter, 37n2, 62
Standard General Markup Language (SGML), x
Stanford University, 101
statistics: Bureau of Labor Statistics and, 93; data collection, 130–31; libraries and, 112, 116; natural logs and, 134, 145n52; online text collections and, 12, 124–25, 128–38, 140n6, 143n39, 143n42, 145nn54–56; Ordinary Least Squares (OLS), 134, 145n53; practicality of digital editions, xi; regression analysis, 12, 124–25, 134, 136, 140n6, 145n53; sampling, 129–30, 143n42; summary, 131–33
Stefaner, Moritz, 52

Striphas, Ted, 4
surface reading, 11, 61–63
Svensson, Patrik, 41
Swain, Margaret, 68
symptomatic reading, 61–62
Systema Naturae (Linnaeus), 77

Taxi Statistics, 53
taxonomies, 63, 65
Terras, Melissa, 178–79
textbooks: authorship and, 88–91, 97–99, 103; cost and, 89–90, 93–95, 98, 100–103; inequality and, 88–90, 93, 114; MERLOT and, 91; open access, 4, 11, 89–103; Open Textbook Network (OTN), 99–100
Text Encoding Initiative (TEI), x, 148, 158–63
textuality, ix, 5, 155, 173, 178
Theisen, Colleen, 109–10, 112, 114, 116
Thiel, Peter, 95
Thylstrup, Nanna Bonde, 175–76
Tifentale, Alise, 52
Tolstoy, Leo, 51
Traces of the Old, Uses of the New: The Emergence of Digital Literary Studies (Earhart), 179
Traister, Daniel, 109
#transformDH, 8
Travels in Computerland (Schneider), 180
Trettien, Whitney, 68
Tumblr, 111
Turner, Nancy, 77
Twain, Mark, 133
Twitter, 8, 12, 52, 110–11, 115–17
Type Punch Matrix, 185

Understanding Media (McLuhan), 5–6
United Nations Educational, Scientific and Cultural Organization (UNESCO), 92
University of California, 47, 99, 130

University of Chicago, 101
University of Houston, 186
University of Iowa, 49–50, 54
University of Maryland, 185
University of Michigan, 47, 100, 102
University of Minnesota, 47, 99–100, 102, 167
University of New Mexico, 130
University of North Carolina, 186
University of Oregon, 185
University of Pennsylvania, 130
University of Rhode Island, 186
University of Tennessee, 130
University of Texas, 186
University of Virginia, 97, 100
University of Wisconsin, 186
"University Publishing in a Digital Age" (Ithaka), 102
University System of Georgia, 100–101
US Census Bureau, 52
user design exits (UX), 44, 56n18
US Post Office Department, 31
Utah State University, 91, 92
utopianism: Bacon on, 66–67; open access and, 11, 88–94, 103

van de Passe, Crispijn the Elder, 69, 73, 82n15
van de Passe, Crispijn the Younger, 66, 69–73, 76–77, 85n47
van Praet, J. B. B., 6
Varela, Miguel Escobar, 48
Vareschi, Mark, 3–16, 186
"Varieties of Digital Humanities" (Booth and Posner), 8–9
Veldman, Ilia, 66
Vershbow, Ben, 102
versioning: Ashkenas on, 154–55; bibliography and, 13, 148–53, 156–57, 163; Calendar (CalVer), 153, 160, 165n12; concept of, 148–50, 152; continuous publishing and, 157–58; copy and, 157; copyright and, 160; developing protocols for, 158–64; digital editions and, 147–64; electronic objects and, 13, 157; hashes and, 149; identity and, 152, 158, 162–63; instance and, 157; lack of clear practices for, 147–48; machines and, 155; metadata and, 148, 155–56; Piers Plowman Electronic Archive (PPEA) and, 13, 158–63; Preston-Werner on, 154, 165n13; protocols for, 149–50; Romantic, 155; segmenting, 151–52; Semantic (SemVer), 153–56, 161, 165n13; Sentimental, 155; *Whitman Archive* and, 148–49; *William Blake Archive* and, 149; XML files and, 148, 156, 158–63, 164n4
Vest, Charles, 91, 96
video, 6, 114, 116, 118n19
Vinciolo, Frederico de, 79, 87n69
von Humboldt, Wilhelm, 97

Wacha, Heather, 3–16, 186
Wall, Wendy, 66
Warner, Michael, 20, 31
Warner, William Beatty, 21, 29, 38n14
Wayback Machine, 127
Weller, Martin, 92
Werner, Sarah, 10, 63
Wernimont, Jacqueline, 15n9, 176–77
Wexler, Laura, 15n9
"What Is the History of Books?" (Darnton), 5
"Where Is Cultural Criticism in the Digital Humanities?" (Liu), 167–68
Whitman, Walt, 96–97, 129–30, 148–49
Wiegand, Wayne, 3
Wikimedia Commons, 128
Wikipedia, 95
Wikisource, 123–28
Wiles, Kate, 116

Wiley, David, 92
William and Flora Hewlett Foundation, 91
William Blake Archive, 149
Willinsky, John, 88–89, 98
Winters, Catherine A., xi, 12–13, 123–46, 186
WIRED magazine, xi
Witt, Jeffrey, 158, 166n20
Wittern, Christian, 149
Wolfe, John, 87n70
Women Writers Project (WWP), 125, 138
wonder rooms, 42–43, 49
Word Press, 102
World Wide Web Consortium (W3C), 150
Wright, Ben, xi–xii, 11–12, 88–108, 186–87

Writing History in the Digital Age (University of Michigan Press), 100, 102
Wu, Hong-An, 15n9
Wunderkammer (wonder rooms), 42–43, 49

XML files, 148, 156, 158–63, 164n4
XSLT (Extensible Stylesheet Language Transformations), 156, 158

Yahr, Jayme, 10–11, 41–58, 187
Yazdani, Mehrdad, 52
Yocco, Nancy, 77

Zenodo, 150
Zepel, Tara, 52
Zhu, Yuancheng, 171–72

The History of Print and Digital Culture

James P. Danky and **Adam R. Nelson**
Series Editors

Science in Print: Essays on the History of Science and the Culture of Print
Edited by Rima D. Apple, Gregory J. Downey, and
Stephen L. Vaughn

Libraries as Agencies of Culture
Edited by Thomas Augst and Wayne Wiegand

Protest on the Page: Essays on Print and the Culture of Dissent since 1865
Edited by James L. Baughman, Jennifer Ratner-Rosenhagen, and
James P. Danky

Purity in Print: Book Censorship in America from the Gilded Age to the Computer Age,
Second Edition
Paul S. Boyer

Religion and the Culture of Print in Modern America
Edited by Charles L. Cohen and Paul S. Boyer

*Women in Print: Essays on the Print Culture of American Women from the Nineteenth
and Twentieth Centuries*
Edited by James P. Danky and Wayne A. Wiegand

Bookwomen: Creating an Empire in Children's Book Publishing, 1919–1939
Jacalyn Eddy

Against a Sharp White Background: Infrastructures of African American Print
Edited by Brigitte Fielder and Jonathan Senchyne

Apostles of Culture: The Public Librarian and American Society, 1876–1920
Lora Dee Garrison

Education and the Culture of Print in Modern America
Edited by Adam R. Nelson and John L. Rudolph

Libraries and the Reading Public in Twentieth-Century America
Edited by Christine Pawley and Louise S. Robbins

Intermediate Horizons: Book History and Digital Humanities
Edited by Mark Vareschi and Heather Wacha